EDWARD BOND

Plays: One

Saved
Early Morning
The Pope's Wedding

With an Author's Note: 'On Violence'

Methuen Drama

METHUEN WORLD CLASSICS

This collection first published in 1977 by Eyre Methuen Ltd

1 3 5 7 9 10 8 6 4 2

This edition published 1997

Random House UK Limited
20 Vauxhall Bridge Road, London SW1V 2SA

Random House Australia (Pty) Limited
20 Alfred Street, Milsons Point, Sydney, New South Wales 2061, Australia

Random House New Zealand Limited
18 Poland Road, Glenfield, Auckland 10, New Zealand

Random House South Africa (Pty) Limited
Endulini, 5a Jubilee Road, Parktown 2193, South Africa

Random House UK Limited Reg. No. 954009

A CIP catalogue record for this book is available from the British Library

Papers used by Random House UK Limited
are natural, recyclable products made from wood grown in sustainable
forests. The manufacturing processes conform to the environmental
regulations of the country of origin

The front cover shows a detail from Pink and Green Sleepers *by Henry
Moore (Wash and crayon, 1941). It is reproduced by kind permission of the
Henry Moore Foundation and of the Tate Gallery, London*

Printed and bound in Great Britain by Cox & Wyman Ltd, Reading, Berks

ISBN 0 413 45410 X

CAUTION

CONTENTS

Edward Bond
A Chronology

PLAY	*First performance*
The Pope's Wedding	9.12.1962
Saved	3.11.1965
A Chaste Maid in Cheapside (*adaptation*)	13.1.1966
The Three Sisters (*translation*)	18.4.1967
Early Morning	31.3.1968
Narrow Road to the Deep North	24.6.1968
Black Mass (*part of* Sharpeville Sequence)	22.3.1970
Passion	11.4.1971
Lear	29.9.1971
The Sea	22.5.1973
Bingo: Scenes of money and death	14.11.1973
Spring Awakening (*translation*)	28.5.1974
The Fool: Scenes of bread and love	18.11.1975
Stone	8.6.1976
We Come to the River	12.7.1976
The White Devil (*adaptation*)	12.7.1976
Grandma Faust (*part one of* A-A-America!)	25.10.1976
The Swing (*part two of* A-A-America!)	22.11.1976
The Bundle: New Narrow Road to the Deep North	13.1.1978
The Woman	10.8.1978
The Worlds	8.3.1979
Restoration	21.7.1981
Summer	27.1.1982
Derek	18.10.1982
After the Assassinations	1.3.1983
The Cat (*performed as* The English Cat)	2.6.1983
Human Cannon	(published 14.3.1985)
The War Plays	
Part I: Red Black and Ignorant	29.5.1985
Part II: The Tin Can People	29.5.1985
Part III: Great Peace	17.7.1985
Jackets	24.1.1989
September	16.9.1989

Saved

Author's Note
On Violence

Violence is a biological mechanism which evolved before human beings evolved, and which has been inherited by them. It first occurred in animals lower than human beings in the order of biological organisation. When these animals are threatened, and have no alternative, they may violently attack whatever is threatening them. It is a last defence, used in a crisis, and its value for primitive animals is clear: it helps to ensure the continuation of their species. But for human beings the opposite is true. Violence threatens the continuation of our species, at least in a civilised form. How has this happened and what must we do about it?

Hunting sometimes resembles violence in appearance. They may both have the same speed, intensity and energy. But searching for food can't be connected with hating it. Hunting is violence only when the prey becomes a threat. Nor, I should add, do cannibals hunt and eat each other because they are hungry; they wage war on each other for social reasons. So we must distinguish violence from hunting.

The distinction is vital. We do not need to be violent. We need food and warmth, but we have only a capacity for violence. A dog has a capacity to swim the first time it goes into water, but it has no need to swim because it has no need to go into water. Human beings are violent animals only in the way that dogs are swimming animals. We need to eat; but only when we're starving does there have to be the possibility that we will use our capacity for violence to satisfy our need for food. Violence is a means not an end. If it were an end, a need, it would probably be a very serious biological weakness.

9

One wonders if an animal with such a need could long survive. To satisfy its need it would have to seek out violent situations, so that animals in which the need was stronger would be at greater risk than those in which it was weaker, and they would therefore tend to die out. The survival of the fittest would aid the survival of animals in which the need was weaker, not – as is usually supposed – animals in which it was stronger. This argument would apply not only to aggression outside a group but also to aggression within a group, where it helps in sorting out the order of rank, except that in the animals in these groups built-in restraints on aggression are as strong as built-in aggression. Human beings, however, are said to be the only animals living in groups of which this isn't true.

The idea that human beings are necessarily violent is a political device, the modern equivalent of the doctrine of original sin. For a long time this doctrine helped to enforce acceptance of the existing social order. For reasons the church could not explain everyone was born to eternal pain after death unless the church saved them. It carefully monopolised all the sacraments which were the only means to salvation. To be saved a man had to accept the church's teaching on the way secular society should be organised; if that society ever needed restraining or reforming, the only ways of doing this that the church permitted were admonishment and excommunication. Leaders of church and state often came from the same families; and before a poor man was elevated to any rank in the church he had to accept its teaching on secular society. Those who wouldn't, whether clerical or lay, were handed over to the state to be tortured and burned. This vividly demonstrated to everyone else the eternal hell in which all dissent would be punished. God is a secular mechanism, a device of class-rule.

But because the idea of god is incompatible with modern science, science has been mis-used to formulate the doctrine of necessary human violence. This is a political invention, not a scientific discovery. The man who cries wolf must constantly shout louder, and, in an analogous way, capitalism has had to drag its hell up out of the ground and set it in our midst. If men are necessarily violent they will always endanger one another, so there must be a strong authority that will use violence to control violence. This authority is the ruling class. It maintains its existence by using violence and being able to organise it politically. The rest doesn't necessarily follow, but in practice it always does: as the ruling class best understands the human condition, its members are the best and most intelligent of human beings, and they are therefore acting only for the common good when they control and monopolise for themselves education, information, art, money, living space, medicine and everything else desirable.

Plato wanted his rulers to knowingly lie. The members of our ruling class are not liars but – worse – fools who believe their own mythology. In ignorance they teach an intellectual corruption, and it is accepted in naïvety. The consequences are heard in bar room chatter, 'We throw babies against the wall because we're animals at heart', and seen in the conservative MP who, some time about 1970, wanted young offenders publicly exhibited in cages.

The ruling mythology has a spurious plausibility. As evidence there are the mountains of bodies from twentieth-century wars, the world-litter of H-bombs, and the increasing aggression of affluent society (which is seen as a very special proof of the incorrigibility of the *need* to be violent). No one could deny that human beings can be violent. But the argument is about why they are violent. Human violence is contingent not necessary, and occurs in situations that can be identified and prevented. These are situations in which people are at such physical and emotional risk that their life is neither natural nor free. I don't want to try to describe these situations in detail here, but as freedom and natural living are so often misunderstood I must point out a few things to make my view clear. Firstly, it is as natural to live in a city as in the country;

whether one is wise to live in a particular city or village depends on what sort of city or village it is. Secondly, mutually sharing common social obligations and restraints is not a repression of our natural egotism; on the contrary, at their best these social bonds are not just the condition of human freedom, they are the essence of it. Thirdly, we create our subjective selves through our objective social relations, and our self-consciousness is not primarily the fruit of private introspection but of social interaction. Fourthly, I am not substituting one absurdity for another by claiming that although people are not innately evil they *are* innately good. Human nature is not fixed at birth, it is created through our relation to the culture of our society. It could be said that every child is born an orphan and must be adopted by its society. The only innate part of our nature can be seen as the capacity for this social, cultural adoption; it is our natural biological expectation of society. As human nature is created by society in this way, it is possible for us to bring up people to be, within reasonable limits, good. All that is necessary is a culture which is sufficiently rational. Abolishing violence would not in itself create this society; the truth is that violence can only be abolished as part of the creation of this society. However, I don't want to go further into these points now. I only want to make clear that the cause and solution of the problem of human violence lie not in our instincts but in our social relationships. Violence is not an instinct we must forever repress because it threatens civilised social relationships; we are violent because we have not yet made those relationships civilised.

Clearly two people punching one another in the street could give rise to misunderstandings about this. But I can't see how the extraordinarily complicated organisation, research, dedication and skill, as well as the long periods of excitement, tedium, discipline and indifference needed to invent, make and deploy hydrogen weapons can be put down to the individual need to be violent, when they are so obviously the products of a social organisation. There is some excuse for saying that, if I punch my neighbour's nose, I did it because of my violent instinct; but to blame the creation of H-bombs on the human instinct for violence is close to intellectual charlatanism. Yet that is the received idea of an age of science!

Because human beings are very adaptable we have to put anything into its social context before we can say it has caused violence. For example, a woman may enjoy living in a high-rise flat with a good view; but if she has young children she may worry about the height and may smack them if they run on the balcony. Routine, elementary work may make people trapped by it aggressive; but if it takes a woman out of an isolated flat so that she can talk and laugh with some friends, then it may be enjoyable. A couple who share a small, dark room with other people might for a few weeks think they were in paradise if they got a small, dark room of their own. Sport releases energy through skill – that is, creatively – and this makes it enjoyable; but it may cause frustration and aggression in people who pass most of their life as spectators not only of sport but of almost everything else, people whose political role is being a ball and not a player. There is a popular idea that mass-spectator sports are a safe means of getting rid of necessary aggression. This piece of potted wisdom must have amused a real joker like Hitler.

Fortunately the causes of human violence can be easily summed up. It occurs in situations of injustice. It is caused not only by physical threats, but even more significantly by threats to human dignity. That is why, in spite of all the physical benefits of affluence, violence flourishes under capitalism. There will always be minor human aggressions; even in Utopia people will fall in love with the wrong person, forget proper gratitude, lose their temper; but whenever there is serious and constant violence, that is a sign of the presence of some major social injustice. Violence can't be contained by an equal or even greater force of counter-violence; it can't be sublimated in games; it can't be controlled by a drug in the water supply (because this would also remove the creative tensions necessary to any society); it will only stop when we live in a just society in which all people are equal in all significant respects. Human beings are much more likely to be violent than many other animals, but in a curious way this is a necessary part of their ethical development: no human society can be a lasting or stable home for injustice. Class society must be violent, but it must also create the frustration, stimulation, aggression and – if necessary – physical violence that are the means by which it can change into a classless society. The only alternatives to this – which in the last few years technology has made possible – are the destruction of our species or, perhaps even worse, its dehumanisation.

Violence is getting cheaper nowadays – cheaper, because it is usually punished lightly. (Political violence is sometimes an exception, for obvious reasons.) By keeping it cheap capitalism shows its self-serving wisdom. If it punished it severely it would provoke even greater unrest and violence. This would show that the scapegoat device no longer contains violence (not least because we are no longer a sacramental society) and this is the real reason why Tory governments don't after all put offenders in public cages. But more important, in an effort to free itself from the increasing barbarism that severer punishments would provoke, capitalism would have to look again at the causes of violence. Capitalism can't do this because its political ethos is competitiveness, and it cannot afford to admit that under the pressure of economic struggle this leads not only to commercial aggression between firms but also to commercial aggression by firms against the public. This is seen in the way that commerce often misuses technology and industry so that they exacerbate social problems, instead of solving them and helping to create a humane society. Of course, I don't mean that our class-society should punish criminals more severely; on the contrary, it is a mark of its decadence that it no longer has the moral right, and probably not even the political authority, to deal with violence – with hooliganism, vandalism and crime – any more than it has the intellectual vitality to understand it. It's easy to see that capitalism has made its ethos of violence very readily available on TV, but sometimes it's not noticed that it sells it at very reduced prices in its courts. Capitalism has made violence a cheap consumer commodity.

There are four features that can be used to classify violence. One, it is used either to maintain injustice or, two, to react to injustice; and three, its users are either conscious of its cause and significance or, four, unconscious of them. Probably the cause of an act of violence is often a mixture of these things, and this could be true for both sides of a confrontation. These four features work in this way: the ruling class has a conscious, though false, rationale for its violence; it calls this the maintenance of law and order. At the same time, it unconsciously fears its victims and so tends to be violent anyway. On the other side, the victims of unjust social relations may act violently to make these relations more just. Their degree of consciousness can range from workers protecting their jobs by smashing machines to a revolutionary party fighting to take over a whole country. Or, finally, they may merely react violently because of an unconscious motive, an unidentified discontent. When this happens their victims may be innocent – indeed they may be chosen for them by the ruling class, as sometimes happens in racialism. In some respects the young murderers in *Saved* belong to this group. Some of their cries while they murder the baby are ruling-class slogans. This is the way in which working-class anger and aggression can be used to strengthen the unjust social relations that cause its anger and aggression, and the ruling class can recreate, in an increasingly inhumane form, the social conditions which it claims as the justification for its power. This persecution of victims by victims results from a culture which must surely be one of the most abject intellectual conditions the human mind could achieve; its most pitiable manifestation is working-class support of fascism.

All four forms of violence may occur together, and that is one reason why there is so much confusion about the cause of violence and why so many mistakes are made in dealing with it. The only rational way to respond to violence is to change the conditions that give rise to it; and the only way that that can be done, or even the first steps towards it can be taken, is by decreasing the gap between reason and social organisation. Obviously it would be better if everyone understood the origin and significance of violence, but equally obviously the victims of social injustice don't have their education in their own hands. At school they learn the mythology of their own natural nihilism, the absurdity of life and the futility of altruism, glossed over with a few Bible stories. Working and living in a very complex, capitalist technocracy forces them to behave in ways from which it is easy for them to draw the same conclusion, so that the mythology seems to be constantly affirmed by experience. Perhaps the increasing barbarism of modern civilisation will force people to look more closely at the nature of man and society, and then society might be reformed by becoming increasingly more rational. But it is unlikely that change will be so easy. Capitalism is inimical to reason.

I believe in solving political and social problems in rational ways whenever possible. The dangers of violence, even in a just cause, are too obvious for me to think otherwise. Violence has no romantic attraction for me. Sartre's notion of finding oneself through violence seems to be absurd and unreal. But many people don't have the chance to ask whether they should be violent. The question does not even occur to them. If it did the only alternative open to them would be a fruitless martyrdom. To ask the question means you are already in a privileged position. If you decide never to use violence you have still done nothing to make the world less violent. That can only be done by making it more just. I am not a pacifist, we have to say what things are and not what we would like them to be. Reason is not yet always effective, and we are still at a stage when to create a rational society we may sometimes have to use irrational means. Right-wing political violence cannot be justified because it always serves irrationality; but left-wing political violence is justified when it helps to create a more rational society, and when that help cannot be given in a pacific form.

We have to understand that not only is capitalism destructive in war *and* peace, but that it is *as* destructive in peace as in war. Its peacetime destructiveness is caused not so much by naked force as by its false culture. This false culture is hidden by its interpretation of culture – they come to the same thing – but its destructiveness can be clearly seen in its waste of life, resources and human energy. Worse, it is an intellectual attack on mankind. Culture is the way we live, and when it is nihilistic, cynical or despairing, then there are waste and violence at all the stages of our life and in all our relationships. Nehru said it cost a lot of money to keep Gandhi poor; we can add that it takes a lot of violence to keep a capitalist peace, and that under capitalism war can never lead to peace. Using violence to create socialism out of capitalism would not mean introducing violence into the peaceful politics of a world of law and order; whenever you walk quietly down the orderly street of a capitalist society you are surrounded by the hidden debris of waste and destruction and are already involved in a prolonged act of communal violence. Violence is not a function of human nature but of human societies.

SAVED was first presented by the English Stage Society at the Royal Court Theatre, London, on 3 November 1965 with the following cast:

LEN, twenty-one. Tall, slim, firm, bony. Big hands. High, sharp cheekbones. Pleasant pale complexion – not ashen. Blue eyes, thick fair hair a bit oily, brushed sideways from a parting. Prominent feet.

John Castle

FRED, twenty-one. Blond, very curly hair. Medium height. Well-shaped, steady, powerful body. Light tenor voice.

Tony Selby

HARRY, sixty-eight. Tall. Long thin arms. Long hands. Heavy, bony head with large eye-sockets and small eyes. Loose chin. Grey.

Richard Butler

PETE, twenty-five. Tallish. Well-built, red-faced. Makes very few gestures. Soft hair that tends to stick up lightly.

Ronald Pickup

COLIN, shortish. A bit thin. Loose (but not big) mouth. Shiny ears, curved featureless face. A few spots. Shouts to make himself heard. Eighteen.

Dennis Waterman

MIKE, tall. Well-built. Strong, easy, emphatic movements. Pleasant. Dark hair. Twenty.

John Bull

BARRY, twenty. A little below medium height. Fat.

William Stewart

PAM, twenty-three. Thin, sharp-busted. Heavy, nodal hips. Dark hair. Long narrow face. Pale eyes. Small mouth. Looks tall from a distance, but is shorter than she looks.

Barbara Ferris

MARY, fifty-three. Shortish. Round heavy shoulders. Big buttocks. Bulky breasts, lifeless but still high. Big thighs and little ankles. Curled grey hair that looks as if it is in a hair-net. Homely.

Gwen Nelson

LIZ, exactly as she sounds.

Alison Frazer

Directed by William Gaskill
Assistant to Director Jane Howell
Designed by John Gunter
Stage Manager Juliet Alliston
Assistant to Stage Manager Allison Rockley

Scene one	Living-room	Scene eight	Living-room
Scene two	Park	Scene nine	Living-room
Scene three	Park	Scene ten	Café
Scene four	Living-room	Scene eleven	Living-room
Scene five	Bedroom	Scene twelve	Bedroom
Scene six	Park	Scene thirteen	Living-room
Scene seven	Cell		

The area of the play is South London

The stage is as bare as possible – sometimes completely bare.

There should be an interval after Scene Seven.

SCENE ONE

The living-room. The front and the two side walls make a triangle that slopes to a door back centre.

Furniture: table down right, sofa left, TV set left front, armchair up right centre, two chairs close to the table.

Empty.

The door opens. Len comes in. He goes straight out again.

PAM (*off*). In there.

LEN *comes in. He goes down to the sofa. He stares at it.*

All right?

Pause. PAM *comes in.*

LEN. This ain' the bedroom.

PAM. Bed ain' made.

LEN. Oo's bothered?

PAM. It's awful. 'Ere's nice.

LEN. Suit yourself. Yer don't mind if I take me shoes off? (*He kicks them off.*) No one 'ome?

PAM. No.

LEN. Live on yer tod?

PAM. No.

LEN. O.

Pause. He sits back on the couch.

Yer all right? Come over 'ere.

PAM. In a minit.

LEN. Wass yer name?

PAM. Yer ain' arf nosey.

LEN. Somethin' up?

PAM. Can't I blow me nose?

She puts her hanky back in her bag and puts it on the table.
    Better.

She sits on the couch.

LEN. Wass yer name?

PAM. Wass yourn?

LEN. Len.

PAM. Pam.

LEN. O. (*He feels the couch behind with his hand.*) This big
    enough?

PAM. What yer want? Bligh!

LEN. Don't wan' a push yer off. Shove that cushion up.

PAM. 'Ang on.

LEN. 'Ow often yer done this?

PAM. Don't be nosey.

LEN. Take yer shoes off.

PAM. In a minit.

LEN. Can yer move yer – thass better.

PAM. Yer d'narf fidget.

LEN. I'm okay now.

PAM. Ow!

LEN. D'yer 'ave the light on?

PAM. Suit yerself.

LEN. I ain' fussy.

PAM. Ow!

LEN. Can yer shut them curtains?

PAM *goes left to the curtains.*

    Yer got a fair ol'arse.

PAM. Like your mug.

LEN. Know somethin'? – I ain' touched a tart for weeks.

PAM. Don't know what yer missin'.

LEN. Don't I?

PAM *sits on the couch, on the edge.* LEN *pulls her closer and takes off her shoes.*

Lucky.

PAM. What?

LEN. Bumpin' in t'you.

PAM. Yeh.

LEN. Yer don't mind me?

PAM. No.

LEN. Sure?

PAM. Yer wan'a get on with it.

LEN. Give us a shout if I do somethin' yer don't reckon.

PAM. Bligh! Yer ain' better 'ave.

LEN. I could go for you. Know that?

Pause.

This is the life.

PAM. Ow!

LEN. Sh! Keep quiet now.

PAM. Oi!

LEN. Sh!

PAM. Yer told me t'shout!

The door opens. HARRY *comes in. He goes straight out again.*

LEN (*lifts his head*). 'Ere!

PAM. What?

LEN. Oo's that?

PAM. Ol' man.

LEN (*sits*). Whass 'e want?

PAM. That cushion's stickin' in me back.

LEN. I thought yer reckon yer was on yer tod?

PAM. 'E's late for work.

LEN. O. Why?

PAM. Why?

LEN. Yeh.

PAM. I don't know.

LEN. Reckon 'e saw?

PAM. Shouldn't be surprised.

LEN. Will 'e be long?

PAM. Don't arst me.

LEN. O. Well.

They lie down again. Slight pause. LEN *lifts his head.*

'Ear that?

PAM. No.

LEN. I 'eard somethin'.

He goes to the door. He listens. He goes back to the couch and sits on the end.

PAM. Well?

LEN. Better 'ang on.

PAM. Why?

LEN. Better 'ad.

PAM. Think yer'll last?

LEN. Not if yer lie around like that.

PAM. Like what?

LEN. Sit up.

PAM. I juss got right.

LEN. More'n I 'ave. Chriss. (*He feels in his pocket.*) You smoke?

PAM. In me bag.

LEN. Where's yer bag?

PAM *nods at the table. He goes to the bag and takes out a cigarette. He lights it. He starts putting the cigarettes back.*

Oh, sorry.

He holds the packet out to her.

PAM. No thanks.

LEN (*he puts the cigarettes away. He sits on the edge of the*

couch. Pause. He taps his foot three or four times). Wass
  'is caper?

PAM. Wan'a cup 'a tea?

LEN. After.

PAM. 'E won't be long.

LEN. 'Adn't better. 'Ave a puff?

PAM. No.

LEN. Do yer dress up.

PAM. Sorry.

LEN. Yer never know 'oo's poppin' in.

He goes to the door and opens it.

PAM. You off?

LEN. I could'a swore I 'eard 'eavy breathin'.

PAM. Thass you.

LEN. 'Oo else yer got knockin' about? Yer ain't stuffed yer
  grannie under the sofa?

PAM. She's dead.

LEN. 'Ard luck. – Wass 'is caper?

He sits on a chair.

  My blinkin' luck.

He stands and walks.

  'E'll be late, won't 'e! I 'ope they dock 'is bloody packet.

He listens by the door.

  Not a twitter.

PAM. 'E ain' bin out the back yet.

LEN. The ol' twit.

PAM *laughs.*

  Wass the joke?

PAM. You.

LEN (*amused*). Yeh. Me. Ha! 'E's a right ol' twit, ain' 'e!
'Ere, can I stay the night?

PAM. Ain' yer got nowhere?

LEN. Yeh! – Well?

PAM. No.

LEN. Yer're the loser. – Sure's 'e's goin'? – Why can't I?

PAM. Bligh! I only juss met yer.

LEN. Suppose 'e's stoppin' 'ome? Got a cold or somethin'.
I'd do me nut! – Yer'd enjoy it.

PAM. Big 'ead.

LEN. 'Ow many blokes yer 'ad this week?

PAM. We ain't finished Monday yet!

LEN. We'll take that into consideration.

PAM. Saucy bugger!

They laugh.

'Ow many times yer 'ad it this week?

LEN. I told yer once! 'Ow many blokes yer 'ad all told?

They laugh.

PAM. What about you an' girls?

LEN. Can't count over sixty.

They laugh.

PAM. Sh!

LEN. 'E'll 'ear. – Oi, tell us!

PAM. 'Ow many times yer done it in one night?

They laugh.

LEN. Why did the woman with three tits shoot 'erself?

PAM. Eh?

LEN. She only 'ad two nipples.

They laugh.

PAM. I don't get it. (*She laughs.*) What did the midwife say to the nun?

LEN. Don' know.

She whispers in his ear. They laugh.

You're great! What about the woman with three tits 'oo 'ad quads?

PAM. Eh?
LEN. That'll teach 'er t'sleep with siamese twins!

They laugh. He whispers in her ear.

PAM. Yer ought a be locked up!
LEN. That's a feedin' problem!
PAM. Sh – thass the back door. 'E's bin out the lav.
LEN. Less give 'im a thrill.

He jumps noisily on the couch.

Cor – blimey!
PAM. You're terrible!

He takes some sweets from her bag.

They're my sweets.
LEN. Less 'ave a choose. (*Loudly.*) 'Ow's that for size?
PAM. What yer shoutin?
LEN (*he puts a sweet in her mouth*). Go easy! Yer wanna make it last!

She laughs. He bites a sweet in half and looks at it.

Oo, yer got a lovely little soft centre.
(*Aside to* PAM). First time I seen choclit round it!

He jumps on the sofa.

PAM (*shrill*). Yer awful!
LEN. That still 'ard?

PAM (*laughs*). Leave off!

LEN. Come on, there's plenty more where that come from.

He puts a sweet in her mouth.

PAM (*splutters*). Can't take no more!

LEN. Yeh – open it. Yer can do a bit more!

PAM. Ow!

LEN. Oorr lovely!

He tickles her. She chokes.

This'll put 'airs on yer chest!

They try to laugh quietly. The door opens. HARRY *puts his head in. He goes out. He shuts the door.* LEN *calls:*

'Ave a toffee!

PAM. Oo-oo 'ave a toffee!

LEN. Tried that mint with the 'ole in it?

PAM. 'Ave a toffee!

LEN. What about the ol' dolly mixture? – Will 'e give yer a ruckin'?

PAM. Ain' got the nerve.

LEN (*calls*). Nosey ol' gander!

They laugh.

See 'is tongue 'angin' out?

PAM. 'E's fetchin' 'is dinner-box out the kitchen.

LEN (*calls*). Don't work too 'ard, mate!

PAM. Lay off, or 'e'll stay in out a spite.

LEN (*calls*). Take a toffee for tea break, Dad! – I'd like'a sleep round 'ere. Yer'd be lovely an' warm in the mornin'.

PAM. Yer're juss greedy!

LEN. I give yer 'alf the sweets!

PAM. I paid. Anyway, Mum'll be back.

LEN. O. That the front door?

PAM. Yeh.

She goes to the curtains.

'E's off.

LEN. Didn't take long.

PAM. I tol' yer.

LEN. Better be worth waitin' for.

PAM. Up to you, ain' it!

LEN. Thass all right then.

She comes to the sofa and starts to undo his belt.

This is the life.

SCENE TWO

Park.

PAM *and* LEN *in a rowing boat. Otherwise stage bare.*

LEN. Cold?

PAM. No.

LEN. Still pecky?

PAM. Yeh.

LEN. There's a bit'a choclit left. 'Ere.

PAM. No.

LEN. Go on.

PAM. Ta.

LEN. Thass yer lot.

PAM. Why?

LEN. No more.

Silence.

I still ain' paid me rent this week.

PAM. Me mum won't reckon that.

LEN. Ain' got round to it.

PAM. Surprised she ain' said.

Slight pause.

LEN. She ever let on?

PAM. 'Bout us?

LEN. Yeh.

PAM. No.

LEN. She don't mind?

PAM. Don't 'ave to. Your money comes in 'andy.

Silence.

LEN. She reckon me, yer reckon?

PAM. Never arst.

LEN. Thought she might'a said.

PAM. Never listen.

LEN. O.

PAM. Yer ain't spent it?

LEN. 'Er rent?

PAM. Yeh.

LEN. Nah!

PAM. Juss wondered.

LEN. Don' yer truss me?

PAM. I'm goin' a knit yer a jumper.

LEN. For me?

PAM. I ain' very quick.

LEN. Can't say I noticed.

PAM. Yer'll 'ave t'buy the wool.

LEN. Knew there'd be a catch.

PAM. I got a smashin' pattern.

LEN. You worried about that rent?

PAM. I 'ad it give us.

LEN. Yer 'adn't better be one of them naggers.

PAM. What colour's best?

LEN. Thass about one thing your ol' girl *don't* do.

PAM. What?

LEN. Nag 'er ol' man.

PAM. What's yer best colour?

LEN. They all suit me.
PAM. I like a red. Or a blue.
LEN. Anythin' bright.

Slight pause.

PAM. I 'ave t' 'ave an easy pattern.
LEN. Will it be ready for the 'oneymoon?
PAM. We ain' 'avin' 'oneymoon.
LEN. 'Oo's payin'?
PAM. You.
LEN. I can see I'll 'ave t' watch out.

Pause.

PAM. Whass the time?
LEN. Don't know.
PAM. Gettin' on.
LEN. Shouldn't wonder.
PAM. Where's the choclit?
LEN. Yer 'ad it all.
PAM. O.
LEN. Sorry.
PAM. There weren't much.
LEN. I'll get some when we go in.
PAM. I 'ad a blinkin' great dinner.
LEN. I reckon yer got a kid on the way.
PAM. I ain'.
LEN. Never know yer luck.
PAM. Yer'll 'ave t' get up early in the mornin' t' catch me.
LEN. Done me best.
PAM. Yer got a dirty mind.

Slight pause.

LEN. I'm 'andy with me 'ands. Yer know, fix up the ol'
    decoratin' lark and knock up a few things. Yeh. We'll 'ave
    a fair little place. I ain' livin' in no blinkin' sty.

PAM. Sounds all right.

LEN. Easy t' kep swep' out an' that. Yer'll be all right.

PAM. I'd better.

He puts his head in her lap. There is a slight pause.

LEN. 'S great 'ere.

Pause.

   Pam.

PAM. What?

LEN. Why did yer pick me up like that?

PAM. Why?

LEN. Yeh.

PAM. Sorry then?

LEN. Tell us.

PAM. 'Ow many girls you 'ad?

LEN. No, I tol' yer my life.

PAM. 'Old on.

LEN. What?

PAM. Yer got a spot.

LEN. Where?

PAM. 'Old still.

LEN. Is it big?

PAM. 'Old still.

LEN. Go easy!

PAM. Got it!

LEN. Ow!

She bursts a spot on his neck.

PAM. Give us yer 'anky.

LEN. Yer got it?

PAM. Yeh.

LEN. Ow! It d'narf 'urt.

He gives her his handkerchief. She dips her hand in the water and dries it on the handkerchief. She gives it back to him.

PAM. Yer wan'a wash sometimes.

LEN. Cheeky cow. (*Slight pause. They are both lying down.*)
   Yer wouldn't go back with any ol' sod?

PAM. You are rotten.

LEN. I'm sorry. Pam?

PAM. You're 'urtin' me leg.

LEN. I'm sorry.

PAM. No.

LEN. When yer goin' a start me jumper?

PAM (*still annoyed*). Why d'yer 'ave t' say that?

LEN. Tell us about me jumper.

PAM. Ain' got no wool.

LEN. I'll get it t'morra. An' we'll start lookin' for a place
   t'morra.

PAM. No places round 'ere.

LEN. Move out a bit. It's better out.

PAM. Yer'll be lucky.

LEN. Bin lucky with you. (*His head is in her lap. He twists so
   that he can put his arms round her.*) Ain' I bin lucky with you?

PAM. Yer don't deserve it.

LEN. I said I'm sorry – I won't arst no more. It's me good
   looks done it.

PAM. It *was* you. It weren't no one else.

LEN. Less go t'bed early t'night.

PAM. If yer go t' bed much earlier it won't be worth gettin' up.

LEN. Lovely. 'Ow about a sing-song.

PAM. No.

LEN (*sings*).
   Be kind to'yer four-footed friends
   That duck may be somebody's brother
   Yer may think that this is the end
   Well it is.

Slight pause.

   They must a' forgot us. We bin 'ere 'ours.

PAM. Do the rest.

LEN. Some mothers!

Pause.

Livin' like that must 'a got yer down.

PAM. Used to it.

LEN. They ought to be shot.

PAM. Why?

LEN. Don't it every worry yer?

PAM. 'Ow?

LEN. Supposed you turned out like that?

PAM. No.

LEN. 'Ow'd it start?

PAM. Never arst.

LEN. No one said?

PAM. Never listen. It's their life.

LEN. But –

PAM. Yer can't do nothin', yer know. No one'll thank yer.

LEN. 'Ow long's it bin goin' on?

PAM. Longer'n I know.

Pause. He sits and leans towards her.

LEN. Must a' bin bloody rotten when yer was a kid.

PAM. Never know'd no difference. They 'ad a boy in the war.

LEN. Theirs?

PAM. Yeh.

LEN. I ain't seen 'im.

PAM. Dead.

LEN. O.

PAM. A bomb in a park.

LEN. That what made 'em go funny?

PAM. No. I come after.

LEN. What a life.

PAM. I 'ad me moments.

LEN. I won't turn out like that. I wouldn't arst yer if I didn't know better 'n that. That sort of carry-on ain' fair.

PAM. I know.

LEN. We'll get on all right. I wonder it never sent yer off
yer nut.

PAM. Yer don't notice.

LEN. It won't be long now. Why don't yer blow up an' knock
their 'eads t'gether?

PAM (*shrugs*). I 'ope I never see 'em again. Thass all.

Slight pause. LEN *looks round.*

LEN. I ain' got a decent jumper.

Pause.

'Ow'd they manage?

PAM. When?

LEN. They writes notes or somethin'?

PAM. No.

LEN. 'Ow's that?

PAM. No need.

LEN. They must.

PAM. No.

LEN. Why?

PAM. Nothin' t' say. 'E puts 'er money over the fire every
Friday, an' thass all there is. Talk about somethin' else.

LEN. Whass she say about 'im?

PAM. Nothin'.

LEN. But –

PAM. She never mentions 'im an' 'e never mentions 'er. I
don' wanna talk about it.

LEN. They never mention each other?

PAM. I never 'eard 'em.

LEN. Not once?

PAM. *No!*

LEN. It's wet down 'ere.

Pause.

I ain' livin' with me in-laws, thass a fact.

FRED (*off*). Four!

LEN. I never got yer placed till I saw yer ol' people.

PAM. I never chose 'em!

LEN. I never meant that! –

PAM. Don't know why yer wan'a keep on about 'em!

LEN. – I never try an' get at yer!

FRED *comes on down right. His back to the audience.*

FRED. Number-four-bang-on-the-door!

PAM. Thass us.

FRED. Less 'ave yer!

LEN. Less stay out!

PAM. Why?

FRED. Oi!

PAM (*to* LEN). Come on.

LEN. We're a pirate ship.

FRED (*taking the micky*). You devil!

PAM. Yer'll 'ave t' pay.

LEN. Come an' get us!

FRED. Wass up darlin'? 'As 'e got 'is rudder stuck?

PAM (*to* LEN). I'm 'ungry.

LEN. Why didn't yer say?

LEN *starts to pull in.* FRED *moves towards them as the boat comes in.*

FRED. Lovely. 'Elp 'im darlin'. Thass lovely. She 'andles that like a duchess 'andles a navvy's pick.

LEN. All right?

FRED. Lovely.

He leans out and jerks the boat in. PAM *stands awkwardly.*

LEN. Steady.

FRED. 'Old tight, darlin'.

He lifts her out.

Yer wanna watch Captain Blood there. Very nice.

LEN. Okay?

PAM. Ta.

FRED. Very 'ow's yer father.

LEN (*stepping out*). Muddy.

PAM (*to* LEN). I enjoyed that.

FRED. Same 'ere.

LEN. We'll do it again.

FRED. Any time.

PAM (*to* LEN). Got everythin'?

FRED (*to* PAM). You 'ave.

LEN (*clowning*). Watch it!

FRED. 'Oo's bin' 'aving a bash on me duckboards?

PAM (*to* LEN). Less 'ave me bag.

FRED. Bashin's extra.

PAM. Yer wanna get yerself a job.

FRED. I got one.

PAM. 'Irin' out boats!

FRED. I'd rather 'ire you out, darlin'.

LEN (*joking*). Watch it!

PAM (*to* LEN). Ready?

LEN. Yeh.

LEN *and* PAM *start to go right.*

FRED. Why, you got a job for us? I wouldn't mind a bit a grind for you.

PAM. Yer'll 'ave t' join the union.

FRED. I'm in, love. Paid up.

LEN (*joking*). Yer'll be in the splash in a minute.

LEN *and* PAM *go out left.*

FRED (*to himself*). Right up. Like you, darlin'.

SCENE THREE

Park. Bare stage.

PETE, BARRY, MIKE, COLIN. PETE *wears a brown suit and suede shoes. The jacket is short in the seat and tight on the shoulders. His tie is black. The others wear jeans and shirts.*

MIKE. What time they bury the bugger?

PETE. Couldn't tell yer.

COLIN. Don' yer wan'a go?

PETE. Leave off! 'Oo's goin' a make me time up?

COLIN. Why yer goin' then?

PETE. The ol' lady'll ruck if I don't.

MIKE. Yeh, they reckon anythin' like this.

COLIN. Blinkin' morbid.

MIKE. Looks lovely in a black tie don' 'e!

They laugh.

PETE. What a carry on! 'E come runnin' round be'ind the bus. Only a nipper. Like a flash I thought right yer nasty bastard. Only ten or twelve. I jumps right down on me revver an' bang I got 'im on me off-side an' 'e shoots right out under this lorry comin' straight on.

MIKE. Crunch.

COLIN. Blood all over the shop.

MIKE. The Fall a the Roman Empire.

PETE. This lorry was doin' a ton in a built-up street.

BARRY. Garn! Yer never seen 'im.

PETE. No?

BARRY. 'It 'im before yer knew 'e was comin'.

PETE (*lighting his pipe*). Think I can't drive?

COLIN. What a giggle, though.

MIKE. Accidents is legal.

COLIN. Can't touch yer.

PETE. This coroner-twit says 'e's sorry for troublin' me.

MIKE. The law thanks 'im for 'is 'elp.

PETE. They paid me for comin'.

MIKE. An' the nip's mother reckons 'e ain' got a blame 'isself.

COLIN. She'll turn up at the funeral.

PETE. Rraammmmmmmmm!

COLIN. Bad for the body work.

MIKE. Can't yer claim insurance?

PETE. No.

MIKE. Choked!

COLIN. Ruined 'is paint work.

BARRY. 'E's 'avin' yer on!

MIKE. Yer creep.

COLIN. Yer big creep.

PETE. Let 'im alone. 'E don't know no better.

COLIN. 'E don't know nothin'.

MIKE. Big stingy creep.

COLIN. Yer wouldn't 'ave the guts.

BARRY. No guts?

MIKE. Yeh.

BARRY. Me?

COLIN. Not yer grannie.

BARRY. I done blokes in.

MIKE. 'Ere we go.

BARRY. More'n you 'ad 'ot dinners. In the jungle. Shootin'
up the yeller-niggers. An' cut 'em up after with the ol'
pig-sticker. Yeh.

MIKE (*hoots*).

COLIN. Do leave off!

BARRY. You lot wouldn't know a stiff if it sat up and shook
'ands with yer!

MIKE. Aa! Shootin' up the yeller-nigs!

COLIN. Sounds like brothers a your'n.

BARRY. Get stuffed!

PETE (*to them all*). Chuck it, eh?

COLIN. Yeller-niggers! My life! What yer scratchin'?

MIKE. 'E's got a dose.

PETE. Ain' surprisin'.

COLIN. Ain' it dropped off yet?

MIKE. Tied on with a ol' johnny.

COLIN. It's 'is girl.

MIKE. 'Is what?

PETE. Gunged-up ol' boot.

COLIN. 'E knocked it off in the back a 'is car last night –

MIKE. 'Is what?

PETE. Pile a ol' scrap.

MIKE. Ought a be put off the road.

COLIN. 'E was knockin' it off in the back an' –

MIKE. I 'eard.

PETE. What?

MIKE. The back-bumper fell off.

PETE. Yeh?

COLIN. I's a fact!

PETE. My life!

MIKE. An' what she say?

COLIN. Yer juss drop somethin'.

BARRY. Bollocks!

He laughs at himself.

MIKE. Yeh!

COLIN. 'Aving trouble with yer 'orn?

BARRY. It weren't no bumper! Me fog lamp come off.

MIKE. 'Is fog lamp!

They roar with laughter.

COLIN. I knew somethin' come off!

MIKE. Flippin' fog lamp!

PETE. Thass what she calls it!

COLIN. Wonder it weren't 'is engine come out.

BARRY. Better'n nothin'.

MIKE. Yer couldn't knock someone down with that!

PETE. It'd come t' a stop.

MIKE. Shootin' up the yeller-niggers!

BARRY. Yeh, yer ain' lived!

LEN *comes on down right.*

PETE. Me mum's got a dirty great wreath.

MIKE. Yeh!

COLIN. Give somethin' for it?

PETE. I ain' a 'ippocrit.

COLIN. Oi – whass-yer-name!

LEN. Eh?

COLIN. It's – Lenny, ain' it?

LEN. Yeh. – O! 'Ow's it goin', admiral?

COLIN. 'Ow's yerself?

LEN. Not so dodgy. Long time.

COLIN. Me and 'im was t'school t'gether.

MIKE. Yeh?

COLIN. What yer bin doin'?

BARRY. Reform school?

MIKE. Don't 'e show yer up!

COLIN. Take no notice. Creep! – Workin'?

LEN. Worse luck.

COLIN. I couldn't place yer for a minute. (*Slight pause.*) Yeh.

LEN. Yer ain' changed much.

BARRY. What yer doin' now?

LEN. Waitin'.

MIKE. I – I!

COLIN. It was in the park, yer 'onour!

MIKE. This girl come up t'me.

COLIN. An' drags me in the bushes.

BARRY. Yer 'onour.

He laughs.

COLIN. I knew she was thirteen.

MIKE. But she twisted me arm.

COLIN. An' 'er ol' dad 'd bin bashin' it off for years.

BARRY. Yer 'onour.

He laughs.

COLIN. Twisted yer what?

MIKE. Never know yer luck!

COLIN. Married?

LEN. Gettin' ready.

BARRY. 'Oo with?

LEN. We're waitin' –

COLIN. Pull the other one!

MIKE. What for?

PETE. Till she drops 'er nipper.

COLIN. Else it looks bad goin' up the aisle.

MIKE. She can 'ide it be'ind 'er flowers.

BARRY. Is that what they carry 'em for?

COLIN. We live an' learn.

MIKE. Takes all sorts.

MARY *comes on up right.*

LEN. Thass us.

COLIN. *That?*

LEN *goes to* MARY.

PETE. One man's meat.

MIKE. More like scrag-end.

BARRY. Bit past it, ain' she?

PETE. She's still got the regulation 'oles.

MIKE. Experience 'elps. Yer get a surprise sometimes.

LEN (*to* MARY). Less give yer a 'and.

MARY. Whew! Ta.

She gives him the shopping bags.

LEN. Okay?

MARY. I was juss goin' ter drop 'em.

MIKE. 'Ear that.

BARRY. Goin' a drop 'em!

COLIN. In the park?

MIKE. At 'alf-past twelve?

PETE (*laughing*). The dirty ol' scrubber.

LEN *and* MARY *start to cross left.*

BARRY (*to* COLIN). That what they taught yer at school?

COLIN *whistles*.

LEN (*amused*). Put a sock in it.

BARRY. What yer got at the top a your legs? What time 's breakfast?

MARY. That your mates?

LEN. They're juss 'avin' a laugh.

MARY. You all right with them bags?

LEN. Yeh.

COLIN. Roger the lodger 'ad a bad cough.

MIKE. 'E sneezed so 'ard.

COLIN. 'Is door knob fell off.

BARRY. 'Is landlady said we'll soon 'ave yer well.

COLIN. So she pulled off 'er drawers.

MIKE. An' polished 'is bell!

MARY. Lot a roughs.

LEN *and* MARY *go out left*.

PETE. Makes yer think.

COLIN. What?

PETE. Never know what yer missin'.

MIKE. True.

PETE. I knew a bloke once reckoned 'e knocked off 'is grannie.

COLIN. Yeh?

PETE. All a mistake.

COLIN. 'Ow's that?

PETE. There was a power cut at the time an' –

BARRY. – 'E thought it was 'is sister.

PETE. Ain' yer clever!

MIKE. Trust the unions!

COLIN. Makes yer think, though.

BARRY *blows a raspberry*.

PETE (*smoking his pipe*). Never know 'alf what goes on.

MIKE. That age she must be 'angin' out for it.

PETE. Stuffin' it all in before it's too late.

COLIN. Yeh.

There is a slight pause.

PETE. Ooorrr! I'll 'ave t' fix up a little bird t'night. 'Ere, wass the time?

COLIN. Time we're back t' work.

They groan.

MIKE (*to* PETE). Time yer're round the church they'll 'ave 'im down the 'ole or up the chimney or wherever 'e's goin'.

PETE. I reckon they wanna put 'im down the 'ole an' pull the chain.

SCENE FOUR

The living room. Dark.

The door opens. MARY *comes in. She puts on the light.* HARRY *is sitting in the armchair. He is partly asleep.* MARY *puts sauce, salt and pepper on the table and goes out.* HARRY *gets up. He goes to the door and puts the light out. He goes back to the armchair. Pause.*

The door opens. MARY *comes in. She puts on the light. She takes knife, fork, spoon and table napkin to the table. She lays the napkin as a small table cloth. The door opens.* PAM *comes in. She wears a slip and carries a hair brush and cosmetics. She switches on the TV set.* MARY *goes out. Without waiting to adjust the set* PAM *goes to the couch and sits. She makes up her face. The door opens.* MARY *comes in with a plate of food.*

MARY (*calls*). It's on the table.

She walks towards the table. To PAM.

I told you not to walk round like that.

MARY puts the food on the table and goes out. PAM goes to the TV set and adjusts it. She goes back to the couch and sits. She makes up her face. MARY comes in.

(*At the door*). It's on the table! That's the second time!

She goes to the TV set.

I don't know 'ow they 'ave the nerve to put it on.

She switches to another channel. She steps back to look at the picture. She steps forward to adjust it. She steps back.

Hm.

She steps forward and adjusts it again.

If yer put it in the oven it goes 'ard as nails.

She steps back and looks at the set. She goes to the couch, sits and watches TV. Pause.

PAM. More like one a them daft mirrors at a circus.
MARY. The man'll 'ave to come an' fix it.

She goes to the set and adjusts it.

You don't know 'ow to switch it on. It goes all right when I do it.

LEN comes in.

LEN. Smells great.
MARY. You've let it ruin.
LEN. Nah.
MARY. Cold as Christmas.
LEN. Do me.

He sits at the table and eats.

MARY (*goes to the set and re-adjusts it*). I don't know. – Did yer put the light out in the scullery?
LEN. Yeh.

MARY. We need a new one. That's what's wrong with it.

She goes back to the couch and sits. She watches silently. Pause.

PAM. Looks like one a them black an' white minstrels.
MARY. Well you do it, an' don't sit there pokin' 'oles.
PAM. I ain' watchin'.
MARY. Sounds like it.

LEN *eats.* MARY *watches.* PAM *makes up.* HARRY *is still. The TV is fairly loud. A very long pause.*
   Slowly a baby starts to cry. It goes on crying without a break until the end of the scene. Nothing happens until it has cried a long while. Then MARY *speaks.*

   Can yer see?
LEN. Yeh.
MARY. Move yer seat.
LEN. I can see.

Pause.

   Yer a fair ol' cook.
MARY. It's ruined. Yer get no encouragement t' try.

Pause. The baby screams with rage. After a while MARY *lifts her head in the direction of the screams.*

   Pam-laa!

Slight pause. PAM *stands and puts her cosmetics in a little bag. She goes to the TV set. She turns up the volume. She goes back to the couch and sits.*

   There's plenty of left-overs.
LEN. Full up.
MARY. An' there's rhubarb and custard.
LEN: O.

Pause. The baby chokes.

PAM. Too lazy t' get up an' fetch it.

MARY. Don't start. Let's 'ave a bit a peace for one night.

Pause.

PAM. 'Is last servant died a over-work.

LEN. I ain' finished this, nosey.

MARY. Why don't yer shut that kid up.

PAM. I can't.

MARY. Yer don't try.

PAM. Juss cries louder when I go near it.

MARY (*watching TV*). I ain' goin' up for yer. (*Still watching TV.*) High time it 'ad a father. (*To* LEN). There's plenty a tea in the pot.

LEN (*watching TV*). Yeh.

MARY (*watching TV*). That's what it needs. No wonder it cries. (*Pause. To* LEN.) Busy?

LEN. Murder.

MARY (*watching TV*). Weather don't 'elp.

LEN (*still watching TV*). Eh? (*The baby whimpers pitifully. Pause. Still watching TV.*) Ha!

Pause. PAM *picks up her things and goes out.*

MARY. About time.

LEN. Wan'a cup?

MARY. No. There's milk in that custard. It'll only get thrown out.

LEN (*stands*). I'll bust.

He goes out.

MARY (*calls*). On the top shelf.

LEN (*off*). What?

MARY. It's on the top shelf!

Pause. LEN *comes in. He carries a plate to the table.*

Did yer get it?

LEN. Yeh.

He sits.

MARY. Shut that door, Len. Me 'ead's playin' me up again.
LEN. Take some a yer anadins.
MARY. I've 'ad too many t'day. Thass what makes it worse.

LEN *goes back to the door and shuts it. He goes to the table and eats.*

   Did yer put the oven out?
LEN. An' the light.
MARY. I ain' made a money, y'know.

Suddenly the baby cries much louder.

   Put some sugar on it.

LEN *sprinkles the sugar from a teaspoon.*

   People'll send the police round 'ere next.
LEN. It'll cry itself t'sleep.

PAM *comes in. She wears a dress.*

MARY. It's still cryin'.
PAM. I thought the cat was stuck up the chimney.

She sits on the couch and pulls up her stockings.

   'Ad a good look? – I'm tired a 'im watchin' me all the time.
MARY. I told yer t' get dressed in the scullery like anybody else.
PAM. I can dress where I like in me own 'ome.
LEN (*to himself*). O no.
PAM. You say somethin'?
LEN (*calmly*). Yeh – shut up.
PAM. I suppose that's your idea a good manners.

Pause.

When yer leavin' us? I'm sick an' tired a arstin'.

MARY. I don't wanna 'ear all this again t'night.

PAM. 'E gets on me nerves.

LEN. I ain' leavin' that kid.

PAM. Why?

LEN. With you?

PAM. It ain' your kid.

LEN. No?

PAM. Yer'll 'ave t' take my word for it.

LEN. Yer don't even know when you're lyin'.

Pause. The baby cries.

PAM. I don't understan' yer. Yer ain' got no self respect.

LEN. You 'ave like.

PAM. No one with any self respect wouldn't wanna stay.

LEN *pours tea for himself.*

Yer'll 'ave t'go sometime. Yer can't juss 'ang on till yer rot.

MARY. Pack it up! No wonder that kid cries!

PAM. Why don't you tell 'im t' go? It's your job. 'E's gettin' on me nerves every night. If it goes on much longer I'll be ill.

MARY. That'll teach yer t'bring fellas back.

PAM (*to* HARRY). Why don't you tell im? It's your 'ouse. There's bin nothin' but rows an' arguments ever since 'e got 'ere. I've 'ad all I can stand! (*Slight pause.*) Dad!

HARRY. I ain' gettin' involved. Bound t'be wrong.

PAM (*to* LEN). I don't understan' yer. Yer can't enjoy stayin' 'ere.

LEN *drinks his tea.*

It's bad enough bein' stuck with a kid without 'avin' you 'anging roun' me neck. The 'ole street's laughin' be'ind yer back.

LEN. I ain' leavin' that kid.

PAM. Take it.

LEN. With me?

PAM. 'Ow else?

MARY. 'Ow can 'e?

PAM. Thass 'is worry.

MARY. 'E can't look after a kid.

PAM. Put it on the council.

MARY (*shrugs*). They wouldn't 'ave it if they've got any sense.

The baby cries.

PAM. Well?

LEN. Kids need proper 'omes.

PAM. Yer see!

LEN (*looks in the teapot*). Out a' water.

He goes out.

MARY. Wouldn't yer miss it?

PAM. That racket?

The baby whimpers. There is a ring. PAM *goes out.* MARY *quickly tidies the couch.* LEN *comes back with the teapot.*

MARY. Did the door go?

LEN (*nods*). Juss then.

FRED (*off*). All right, all right. I said I'm sorry, ain' I?

PAM *is heard indistinctly.*

  Well let's say 'allo first!

FRED *comes in.*

  'Evenin'. 'Evenin', ma.

MARY. We're just watchin' telly.

FRED. Anythin' interestin'?

MARY. Come in.

FRED. 'Lo, Len. 'Ow's life?

LEN. Usual. 'Ow's the job?

FRED. Don't talk about it.

PAM *comes in.*

PAM. I still don't see 'ow that makes yer all this late.

FRED. Give it a rest, Pam.

PAM. The same last time.

MARY. Take yer coat off.

PAM. Yer oughta let me know if yer're goin'a be late.

FRED. 'Ow could I? Sorry love. We'll juss 'ave t' make it later in future.

PAM (*to* MARY). Can I put the kid in your room?

MARY. No wonder it can't sleep. Pushed around like some ol' door mat.

PAM. Can I or can't I? I ain' sittin' there with that row goin' on.

MARY. Do what yer like.

FRED (*to* PAM). Got plenty a fags?

MARY. Yer will anyway.

PAM (*to* FRED). Ready?

FRED. See yer, Lenny boy.

LEN. Yeh.

PAM. It's all the same if I was meetin' yer outside in the street. I'd be left standin' in the cold.

FRED (*following* PAM *to the door*). Got any fags? I left mine be'ind.

PAM *and* FRED *go out.* LEN *stacks the things on the table and takes some of them out. The baby's crying suddenly gets louder.* LEN *comes in again. He picks up the sauce and the table napkin and goes out.* MARY *turns off the TV set and goes out.* HARRY *goes to the table and pours himself tea.* LEN *comes back.*

LEN. O.

HARRY. Finished.

LEN. Ta.

Pause.

Wish t'God I could take that kid out a this.

HARRY (*drinks*). Better.

LEN. No life growin' up 'ere.

HARRY (*wipes his mouth on the back of his hand*). Ah.

LEN. Wish t' God I 'ad some place.

HARRY. Yer wan'a keep yer door shut.

LEN. What?

HARRY. T'night.

LEN. Me door?

HARRY. Yer always keep yer door open when 'e's sleepin' with 'er.

LEN. I listen out for the kid. They ain' bothered.

MARY (*off*). Night, Len.

LEN (*calls*). Night. (*To* HARRY.) More?

HARRY. No.

LEN. Plenty in the pot.

HARRY (*wipes his mouth on the back of his hand*). Yer'll catch cold with it open.

LEN (*holding the teapot*). Night, then.

He goes to the door.

HARRY (*sitting in the armchair*). Put that light out.

LEN *puts the light out and goes. The crying sobs away to silence.*

SCENE FIVE

LEN's *bedroom. It is shaped like the living-room. Furniture: a single bed up right, a wooden chair close to it.* PAM *is in bed.* LEN *stands centre, away from her.*

LEN. Did yer take yer medicine?

Pause.

Feelin' better?

PAM. I'm movin' down t' me own room t'morra. Yer'll 'ave t' move back up 'ere.

LEN. Quieter up 'ere.

PAM. Like a blinkin' grave.

LEN. Why don't yer 'ave the telly up?

PAM. No.

LEN. Easy fix a plug.

PAM. Did yer see Fred?

LEN. Yer never took yer medicine. (*He pours her medicine and gives it to her.*) 'Ere. (PAM *takes it.*) Say ta. (*She drinks it and gives a small genuine* 'Ugh!') Read yer magazines?

PAM. Did Fred say anythin'?

MARY (*off*). Pam-laa! She gettin' up, Len?

PAM (*to herself*). O God.

MARY (*off*). The doctor says there's nothin' t' stop yer gettin' up. Yer're as well as I am.

LEN *closes the door but the voice is still heard.*

Pam-laa! The dinner's on the table.

LEN. Yer better off up 'ere out a 'er way.

PAM. The cow.

LEN *straightens the bed.*

Leave that.

LEN. You're comin' undone.

PAM. Leave it.

LEN. It's all –

PAM. I said leave it!

LEN (*continuing*). Someone's got a give yer a 'and.

PAM. I won't 'ave yer pullin' me about.

LEN (*walking away*). Why don't yer sit in a chair for 'alf 'our?

PAM. Mind yer own business.

LEN. Yer ain't doin' yerself no good lyin' there.

MARY (*off*). She gettin' up?

LEN. I'm only tryin' a 'elp.

PAM. Don't want yer 'elp.

LEN. Yer got bugger all idea 'ow to look after yerself.

PAM. Go away.

LEN. Some one –

PAM. For Chrissake!

LEN. Someone's got a stick up for yer. (*Slight pause.*) Yer treated me like dirt. But I ain't goin' a carry on like that.

MARY (*off*). Pamm-laa!

PAM (*calls*). Shut up! I'm sick a' the lot of yer! (*Slight pause.*) Shut up!

LEN *goes out.*

PAM. Thank Chriss for that.

MARY (*off*). She up yet?

LEN *answers indistinctly. Pause.* PAM *pulls out the blankets that* LEN *tucked in.* LEN *comes back with the baby.*

LEN (*to baby*). 'Ello then! 'Ello then!

PAM. O no.

LEN. Look-ee that. 'Oo that mummy-there?

PAM. She's got the grub out on the table.

LEN. It'll keep.

PAM. She ain' better row me out for it.

LEN. Take it.

PAM. Put it back.

LEN. Yer ought a take it.

PAM. Don't keep tellin' me what I ought a do.

LEN. Yer ain' even looked at it for weeks.

PAM. Ain' going to.

LEN. Yer'd feel better.

Pause.

   'Ello then.

PAM. Did yer give 'im what I wrote?

LEN. 'E's busy, 'e reckons. It's 'is busy time.

PAM. Ha!

LEN. 'Avin' yourn on a tray?

PAM. If yer like.

LEN. It knows yer voice.

PAM. Put it away before it starts.

LEN. Good for its lungs.

PAM. Yer d'narf annoy me, Len.

LEN. I know.

PAM. Yer're always pesterin' me.

LEN. Someone's got a look after yer.

PAM. There yer are! Thass another annoyin' thing t' say. (*She sits.*) This dump gives me the 'ump. Put that away.

LEN. Yer can't let it lie on its back all day. Someone's got a pick it up.

PAM (*sitting back*). Why should I worry? Its father don't give a damn. I could be dyin' an' 'e can't find ten minutes.

LEN. I'm blowed if I'm goin' a put meself out if yer can't co-operate.

He tries to put the baby in her arms.

PAM. I tol' yer take it back! Get off a me! Yer bloody lunatic! Bleedin' cheek! (*Calls.*) Mum!

LEN. You 'ave it for a change!

He puts the baby on the bed.

PAM. Yer goin' mad! It's fallin'. Catch it!

LEN *puts the baby so that it is safe.*

LEN. I ain' your paid nurse!

PAM (*calls*). Mum! – I know why Fred ain' come – yer bin tearin' up me letters.

LEN. 'E did!

PAM. Yer little liar! (*She turns away from the baby.*) I ain' touchin' it.

LEN. It'll stay there all night!

PAM. Thass what yer call 'elpin' me.

A long silence. LEN *picks up the baby.*

See!

LEN. Can't give it a cold juss because we're rowin'.

He goes towards the door. He stops.

'E said 'e'd look in.

PAM (*she turns round*). When? (*She turns back to the wall.*)
What did 'e say?

LEN. I said yer wanted to see 'im. 'E goes 'e's up to 'is eyes
in it. So I said I got a couple of tickets for Crystal Palace.
'E's knockin' off early.

PAM. Saturday?

LEN. T'night.

PAM (*turns*). Yer got 'im downstairs!

LEN. No.

PAM (*calls*). Mum – is Fred there? Fred? – 'E might be early.

LEN. There's a good 'alf 'our yet.

PAM (*excited*). I 'ope 'is lot wins.

LEN. 'E might be late.

PAM. Not for football. Yer can say she's upstairs if yer wan'
a go. Put it like that.

LEN (*looks at child*). 'E's well away.

PAM. I ain' cut me nails all the time I bin in bed.

MARY (*off*). Lennie!

LEN. Shall I get the scissors?

PAM. She won't shut up till yer go down. I got me own.

MARY (*off*). Leonard! I keep callin' yer. (*Outside the door.*)
'Ow many more times. (*She comes in.*) I bin callin' the last
'alf 'our. Dinner won't be fit t'eat.

LEN. Juss puttin' the nipper back.

MARY. That's the last time I cook a 'ot meal in this 'ouse.
I mean it this time. (*To* PAM.) Yer can make yer own bed

t'morra, you. (*To* LEN.) I ain' sweatin' over a 'ot stove.
No one offers t'buy me a new one. (*To* PAM.) I can't afford
t' keep yer on yer national 'ealth no longer. I'm the one 'oo
ought to be in bed.

MARY *goes out.*

PAM. I got all patches under me eyes.
LEN. No.
PAM. I feel awful.
LEN. Yer look nice.
PAM. I'll 'ave t' 'ave a wash.
LEN. Yeh.

SCENE SIX

The Park. A bare stage. FRED *holds a fishing-rod out over the
stalls. He wears jeans and an old dull leather jacket.* LEN *sits
beside him on a small tin box. On the ground there are a bait
box, odds and ends box, float box, milk bottle, sugar bottle, flask
and net.*

LEN. Round our place t'night?
FRED. No.
LEN. It's Saturday.
FRED. O yeh.
LEN. She won't like it.
FRED. No.

Pause.

Yer wan' a get yerself a good rod.
LEN. Can't afford it.

FRED. Suit yerself.

LEN. Lend us yourn.

FRED. Get knotted.

Slight pause.

LEN. I in yer way then?

FRED. Eh?

LEN. Sittin' 'ere.

FRED. Free country.

LEN. Yer'd never think it.

FRED. Nippy.

LEN. Lend us yer jacket.

FRED. Jump in.

LEN. 'Ow much yer give for that?

FRED. Yer get 'em on h.p.

LEN. Fair bit a work.

FRED (*runs his hand along the rod*). Comes in 'andy.

Pause.

LEN. She said yer was comin' round for the telly.

FRED. News t' me.

LEN. Don't know whass on.

FRED. Don't care.

LEN. Never looked. (*Slight pause.*) Never bothers me. Easy find out from the paper if yer –

FRED. Don't keep on about it.

LEN. Eh?

FRED. Don't bloody well keep on about it.

LEN. Suits me. (*Slight pause.*) I was agreein' with yer. I thought like –

FRED. Oi – Len, I come out for the fishin'. I don't wanna 'ear all your ol' crap.

Slight pause. LEN *turns his head right and stares at the river.*

'Onest, Len – yer d'narf go on.

LEN. I only said I was agreein' with yer. Blimey, if yer can't ...

He stops. Pause.

FRED. Sod!
LEN. Whass up?
FRED. Bait's gone.
LEN. Gone? They've 'ad it away.
FRED. Never.
LEN. Must 'ave.
FRED. More like wriggled off.
LEN. I mounted it 'ow yer said.
FRED (*winds in*). Come 'ere. Look.

He takes a worm from the worm box.

Right, yer take yer worm. Yer roll it in yer 'and t' knock it
out. Thass first. Then yer break a bit off. Cop 'old o' that.

He gives part of the worm to LEN.

LEN. Ta.
FRED. Now yer thread yer 'ook through this bit. Push it up
on yer gut. Leave it. – Give us that bit. Ta. Yer thread
yer other bit on the 'ook, but yer leave a fair bit 'angin'
off like that, why, t'wriggle in the water. Then yer push
yer top bit down off the gut and camer-flarge yer shank.
Got it?
LEN. Thass 'ow I done it.
FRED. Yeh. Main thing, keep it neat.

He casts. The line hums.

Lovely.

A long silence.

The life.

Silence.

LEN. Down the labour Monday.

FRED *grunts*.

   Start somethin'.

Silence.

   No life, broke.

FRED. True.

Silence. LEN *pokes in the worm box with a stick.*

   Feed 'em on milk.

LEN. Fact?

Silence.

   I'll tell 'er yer ain' comin'.

FRED. Len!

LEN. Well yer got a let 'er know.

FRED. 'Oo says?

LEN. Yer can't juss –

FRED. Well?

LEN. Shut up a minute.

FRED. Listen, mate, shut yer trap an' give us a snout.

LEN. No.

FRED. Yer're loaded.

LEN. Scroungin' git! Smoke yer own. – She'll be up 'alf the
   night. That'll be great. – I reckon yer got a bloody nerve
   takin' my fags, yer know I'm broke. – Yer believe in keepin'
   em waitin' for it.

Slight pause.

FRED. Yer used to knock 'er off, that right?

LEN. Once.

FRED. There yer are then.

LEN. What?

FRED. It's all yourn.

LEN. She don't wan'a know.

FRED. 'Ow's that?

LEN. Since you 'ad 'er.

FRED. What d'yer expect? No – they're like that. Once they go off, they go right off.

LEN. Don't even get a feel.

FRED. 'Appens all the time. Give us a snout.

LEN. No.

FRED. Tight arse.

Slight pause.

LEN. Skip?

FRED. Yeh?

LEN. What yer reckon on 'er?

FRED. For a lay?

LEN. Yeh.

FRED. Fair. Depends on the bloke.

LEN. Well?

FRED. No – get that any time.

Silence.

LEN. Gettin' dark.

Silence.

FRED. Call it a day.

LEN. In a minute.

FRED. Never know why yer stick that dump.

LEN. Seen worse.

FRED. I ain'.

Slight pause.

LEN. Skip?

FRED. Whass up now?

LEN. Why's she go for you?

FRED. They all do mate.

LEN. No, why's she – ill over it?

FRED. Come off it, she 'ad a drop a the ol' flu.

LEN. Yeh. But why's she like that?

FRED. It ain' me money.

LEN. They all want the same thing, I reckon. So you must 'ave more a it.

FRED. Thass true! Oi!

LEN. What?

FRED. Still.

Pause.

Thought I 'ad a touch.

Pause.

Nah.

They ease off. FRED *looks up at the sky.*

Jack it in.

LEN. Anyway, thass what they reckon.

FRED. Eh?

LEN. They all want the same thing.

FRED. O.

LEN. I reckon yer're 'avin' me on.

FRED. Me?

LEN. Like the fish that got away.

FRED. I ain' with yer.

He shakes his head.

LEN. That big! (*He holds his hands eighteen inches apart.*)

FRED (*laughs*). More like that! (*He holds his hands three feet apart.*)

LEN. Ha! Thass why she's sick.

FRED. Now give us a fag.

LEN. No.

FRED (*spits*). 'Ave t' light one a me own.

He takes one of his own cigarettes from a packet in his breast pocket. He does not take the packet from the pocket.

LEN. Mind the moths.

FRED. Yer ever 'ad worms up yer nose, in yer ears, an' down yer throat?

LEN. Not lately.

FRED. Yer will in a minute.

LEN. Well give us a snout then.

FRED. Slimey ponce!

He gives LEN *a cigarette.* LEN *gives* FRED *a light.*

LEN. I used a 'ear, know that?

FRED. 'Ear what? – 'E's like a flippin' riddle.

LEN. You an' 'er.

FRED. Me an' 'oo?

LEN. On the bash.

FRED. Do what?

LEN. Straight up.

FRED. Chriss.

LEN. Yeh.

FRED. Yer kiddin'.

LEN. On my life. Kep me up 'alf the night. Yer must a bin trying for the cup.

FRED (*draws his cigarette*). Why didn't yer let on?

LEN. No, it's all a giggle, ain't it?

FRED (*shrugs*). Yeh? Makes yer feel a right charlie.

He drops his cigarette on the floor and treads on it.

Chriss. Thass one good reason for jackin' 'er in.

LEN. Don't start blamin' me.

FRED. An' you was listenin'?

LEN. Couldn't 'elp it.

FRED. O.

He lays his rod on the ground and crouches to pack his things.

Yer didn't mind me goin' round 'er's.

LEN. Same if I did.

FRED. I didn't know like.

LEN. Yer never ruddy thought. Any'ow, I don't mind.

FRED. I thought she was goin' spare.

LEN. Wan'a 'and?

FRED. No. Give us that tin.

He packs in silence.

I reckon it was up t' you t' say. Yer got a tongue in yer 'ead.

Silence. MIKE *comes in. He has a haversack slung from one shoulder and carries a rod. He wears a small, flashy hat.*

FRED. No luck?

MIKE. Wouldn't feed a cat.

LEN. Waste a time.

MIKE. Same 'ere.

FRED. Got a breeze up.

MIKE. What yer doin'?

FRED. Now?

MIKE. Yeh, t'night.

FRED. Reckon anythin'?

MIKE. Bit a fun.

FRED. Suits me.

MIKE. You're on.

FRED. Up the other end?

MIKE. 'Ow's the cash?

FRED. Broke. You?

MIKE. I'll touch up the ol' lady.

FRED. Get a couple for me.

LEN. That'll pay the fares.

MIKE. Pick yer up roun' your place.

FRED. Not too early. 'Ave a bath first.

MIKE. Never know 'oo yer'll be sleepin' with.

FRED. After eight.

MIKE. I feel juss right for it.

LEN. What?

MIKE. Out on the 'unt.

FRED (*imitates a bullet*). Tschewwwwww!

MIKE. 'E picks 'em up at a 'undred yards.

FRED. It's me magnetic cobblers.

PAM *comes in. She pushes the pram. The hood is up. A long blue sausage balloon floats from a corner of the hood.*

PAM. 'Ello.

FRED. Whass up?

PAM. Out for a walk.

MIKE (*nods at pram*). Bit late for that, ain' it?

PAM (*to* FRED). What yer got?

FRED. Nothin'.

PAM (*tries to look*). Less 'ave a look.

FRED. Nothin' for you!

PAM. Keep yer shirt on.

MIKE. Yer nearly missed us.

PAM (*to* FRED). Don't get so 'airy-ated.

MIKE. We was juss off.

FRED. What yer cartin' that about for?

PAM. Felt like a walk.

FRED. Bit late.

PAM. Why?

FRED. That ought a be in bed.

PAM. Fresh air won't kill it.

FRED. Should a done it earlier.

PAM. Never 'ad time. Why didn't you?

FRED. You know best.

PAM. When yer comin' round?

FRED. I'll look in.

PAM. When?

FRED. I don't know.

PAM. When about?

FRED. Later on.

PAM. Shall I get somethin' to eat?

FRED. No.

PAM. No bother.

FRED. The ol' lady'll 'ave it all set up.

PAM. I got two nice chops.

FRED. Shame.

PAM. Well see 'ow yer feel. There's no one in now. I got rid
a 'em.

FRED. Pity yer didn't say.

PAM. What time then?

FRED. I'll be there.

PAM. Sure?

FRED. Yeh.

PAM. Say so if yer ain'.

FRED. I'll be there.

PAM. That means yer won't.

FRED. Up t'you.

PAM. Why don't yer say so?

FRED (*picks up his gear. To* MIKE). Thass the lot.

PAM. It ain' no fun waitin' in all night for nothin'.

MIKE. Ready?

FRED (*takes a look round*). Yeh.

PAM. Why can't yer tell the truth for once?

FRED. Fair enough. I ain' comin'.

LEN. Pam –

PAM. Yer 'ad no intention a comin'.

LEN. Yer left the brake off again.

MIKE (*to* FRED). Okay?

PAM (*to* LEN). Put it on, clever.

FRED (*to* MIKE). Yeh.

PAM (*to* FRED). I knew all along.

FRED. Come on, Pam. Go 'ome.

PAM. Fred.

FRED. I know.

PAM. I didn't mean t' go off. I was goin' a be nice, I still ain' better.

FRED. Go 'ome an' get in the warm. It's late.

LEN (*putting on the brake*). Yer wan' a be more careful.

PAM (*to* FRED). It's my fault. I never stop t'think.

FRED. Yer wan' a stop thinkin' about yerself, I know that.

PAM. It's them pills they give me.

MIKE (*to* FRED). You comin' or ain' yer.

FRED. Yeh.

PAM. No.

FRED. I'll come round one night next week.

PAM. No.

FRED. Monday night. Ow's that?

PAM. Yer'll change yer mind.

FRED. Straight from work.

PAM. Yer said that before.

FRED. It's the best I can offer.

PAM. I can't go back there now.

FRED. Yer'll be okay.

PAM. If I sit on me own in that room another night I'll go round the bend.

FRED. Yer got the kid.

PAM. Juss t'night. I couldn't stand it on me own no more. I 'ad a come out. I don't know what I'm doin'. That kid ought a be in bed. Less take it 'ome, Fred. It's 'ad new-moanier once.

FRED. You take it 'ome.

PAM. Juss this last time? I won't arst no more. I'll get mum t' stay in with me.

FRED. It's no use.

PAM. Yer ain' seen it in a long time, 'ave yer?

She turns the pram round.

It's puttin' on weight.

FRED. Eh?

PAM. It don't cry like it used to. Not all the time.

MIKE. Past carin'.

PAM. Doo-dee-doo-dee. Say da-daa.

FRED. Yeh, lovely.

He looks away.

LEN (*looking at the baby*). Blind.

PAM (*to* LEN). Like a top.

FRED. What yer give it?

PAM. Asprins.

FRED. That all right?

PAM. Won't wake up till t'morra. It won't disturb yer. What time'll I see yer?

FRED. I'll look in. I ain' sayin' definite.

PAM. I don't mind. Long as I know yer're comin'.

FRED. All right.

PAM. Pity t' waste the chops. I think I'll do 'em in case –

FRED. Yeh, right. It's all accordin'.

PAM. I'll wait up.

FRED. It'll be late, see.

PAM. Thass all right.

FRED. Pam.

PAM. I'll treat meself t' box a choclits.

FRED. There's plenty a blokes knockin' about. Why don't yer pick on someone else.

PAM. No.

MIKE. Yer can 'ave me, darlin'. But yer'll 'ave t' learn a bit more respect.

PAM. 'Ow can I get out with that 'angin' round me neck? 'Oo's goin' a look at me?

FRED. Yer ol' girl'll take it off yer 'ands.

MIKE. Drop 'er a few bob.

FRED. Yer don't try.

PAM. I can't!

FRED. Yer'll 'ave to.

PAM. I can't! I ain' goin' to!

FRED. I ain' goin' a see yer no more.

PAM. No.

FRED. We got a sort this out some time.

PAM. Yer promised!

FRED. It's a waste a time!

PAM. *They* 'eard!

FRED. No.

MIKE. Come on, mate.

FRED. It's finished.

MIKE. Thank Chriss. Less shift!

PAM. Juss t'night. I don't care if yer bin with yer girls. Come 'ome after. Juss once. I won't bother yer. I'll let yer sleep. Please.

FRED. Chriss.

PAM. O what d'you care? I was flat on me back three bloody weeks! 'Oo lifted a finger? I could a bin dyin'! No one!

She starts pushing the pram.

MIKE. Good riddance!

PAM (*stops*). You're that kid's father! Yeh! Yer ain't wrigglin' out a that!

FRED. Prove it.

PAM. I *know*!

FRED. You *know*?

MIKE. Chriss.

FRED. 'Alf the bloody manor's bin through you.

PAM. Rotten liar!

FRED. Yeh?

To MIKE. Ain' you 'ad 'er?

MIKE. Not yet.

FRED. Yer'll be next.

Points to LEN.

What about 'im?

To LEN. Eh?

To MIKE. Your's must be the only stiff outside the church-
yard she ain' knocked off.

PAM. I 'ate you!

FRED. Now we're gettin' somewhere.

PAM. Pig!

FRED. Thass better. Now piss off!

PAM. I will.

MIKE. Ta-ta!

PAM. An' yer can take yer bloody bastard round yer tart's!
Tell 'er it's a present from me!

PAM *goes out. She leaves the pram.*

MIKE. Lovely start t' the evenin's entertainment.

FRED (*calls*). I ain' takin' it! It'll bloody stay 'ere!

MIKE. What yer wan'a let 'er get away with –

FRED. Don't you start! I 'ad enough with 'er!

LEN. I'd better go after 'er.

FRED. Send 'er back.

LEN. See 'ow she is.

LEN *goes out after* PAM.

FRED (*calls*). Don't leave 'er kid. Take it with yer.

MIKE *whistles after her.* FRED *throws his gear down.*
Lumbered!

MIKE. 'E'll send 'er back.

FRED. 'E ain' got the gumption. We'll drop it in on the way
back.

MIKE. Leave it 'ere. Won't be worth goin' time we're ready.

FRED. Give it five minutes.

MIKE. Yer won't see 'er again.

FRED. That won't be the worst thing in me life.

MIKE. Can't yer arst your Liz t' look after it?

FRED. She'd tear me eyes out.

Pause. They sit.

MIKE. They opened that new church on the corner.

FRED. What?

MIKE. They got a club.

FRED. O yeh.

MIKE. We'll 'ave a quick little case round.

FRED. T'night?

MIKE. Yeh.

FRED. Get stuffed.

MIKE. Straight up.

FRED. Pull the other one.

MIKE. Best place out for'n easy pick up.

FRED. Since when?

MIKE. I done it before. There's little pieces all over the shop, nothin' a do.

FRED. Fact?

MIKE. The ol' bleeder shuts 'is eyes for prayers an' they're touchin' 'em up all over the place. Then the law raided this one an' they 'ad it shut down.

FRED. Do leave off.

PETE *and* COLIN *come in right.*

PETE. 'Ow's it then?

MIKE. Buggered up.

COLIN. Like your arse.

MIKE. Like your flippin' ear in a minute.

PETE. I – I!

COLIN. Wass on t'night?

MIKE. Laugh.

BARRY *comes in after* PETE *and* COLIN.

BARRY. Fishin'?

FRED. 'Angin' the Chrissmas decorations.

BARRY. 'Oo's bin chuckin' big dog ends?

MIKE. Where?

BARRY. 'Ardly bin lit.

PETE. 'E's juss waitin' for us t'shift an' 'e'll be on it.

FRED (*holds it out*). On the 'ouse.

MIKE. 'As 'e got a little tin?

COLIN. Like'n ol' tramp?

BARRY. O yeh – 'oo's mindin' the baby?

COLIN (*seeing pram*). Wass that for?

MIKE. Pushin' the spuds in.

FRED (*flicks the dog end to* BARRY). Catch!

COLIN. 'Oo left it 'ere?

BARRY. 'E's takin' it for a walk.

PETE. Nice.

FRED. Piss off.

BARRY. We don't wan' the little nipper t'ear that! Oi, come 'ere.

COLIN *and* PETE *go to the pram*.

Oo's 'e look like?

They laugh.

MIKE. Don't stick your ugly mug in its face!

PETE. It'll crap itself t' death.

BARRY. Dad'll change its nappies.

COLIN (*amused*). Bloody nutter!

FRED. You wake it up an' yer can put it t'sleep.

COLIN *and* PETE *laugh*.

BARRY. Put it t'sleep?

COLIN. 'E'll put it t'sleep for good.

PETE. With a brick.

MIKE. 'E don't care if it's awake all night.

BARRY. 'Oo don't? I'm like a bloody uncle t' the kids round our way. (*He pushes the pram.*) Doo-dee-doo-dee-doo-dee.

MIKE (*to* FRED). Jack it in eh?

FRED. Give 'er another minute.

MIKE. We should a made Len stay with it.

FRED. Slipped up. 'E dodged off bloody sharpish.

MIKE. Sly bleeder.

FRED. I don't know – bloody women!

MIKE. Know a better way?

FRED *and* MIKE *are sitting down left.* PETE *and* COLIN *are right.* BARRY *pushes the pram.*

BARRY.

> Rock a bye baby on a tree top
> When the wind blows the cradle will rock
> When the bough breaks the cradle will fall
> And down will come baby and cradle and tree
>> an' bash its little brains out an' dad'll scoop
> 'em up and use 'em for bait.

They laugh.

FRED. Save money.

BARRY *takes the balloon. He poses with it.*

COLIN. Thought they was pink now.

BARRY (*pokes at* COLIN'S *head*). Come t' the pictures t'night darlin'? (*He bends it.*) It's got a bend in it.

MIKE. Don't take after its dad.

BARRY (*blows it up*). Ow's that then?

COLIN. Go easy.

BARRY (*blows again*). Thass more like it. (*Blows again.*)

COLIN. Do leave off.

MIKE. That reminds me I said I'd meet the girl t'night.

BARRY *blows. The balloon bursts.*

COLIN. Got me!

He falls dead. BARRY *pushes the pram over him.*

Get off! I'll 'ave a new suit out a you.

BARRY (*pushing the pram round*). Off the same barrer?

PETE. Ain' seen you 'ere before, darlin'.

BARRY. 'Op it!

PETE. 'Ow about poppin' in the bushes?

COLIN. Two's up.

BARRY. What about the nipper?

PETE. Too young for me.

He 'touches' BARRY.

BARRY. 'Ere! Dirty bastard!

He projects the pram viciously after COLIN. It hits PETE.

PETE. Bastard!

PETE *and* BARRY *look at each other.* PETE *gets ready to push the pram back – but plays at keeping* BARRY *guessing.* MIKE *and* FRED *are heard talking in their corner.*

MIKE. If there's nothin' in the church, know what?

FRED. No.

MIKE. Do the all-night laundries.

FRED. Yer got a 'and it to yer for tryin'.

MIKE. Yer get all them little 'ousewives there.

FRED. Bit past it though.

MIKE. Yeh, but all right.

PETE *pushes the pram violently at* BARRY. *He catches it straight on the flat of his boot and sends it back with the utmost ferocity.* PETE *sidesteps.* COLIN *stops it.*

PETE. Stupid git!

COLIN. Wass up with 'im?

BARRY. Keep yer dirty 'ands off me!

PETE. 'E'll 'ave the little perisher out!

BARRY. O yeh? An' 'oo reckoned they run a kid down?

PETE. Thass different.

BARRY. Yeh – no one t' see yer.

PETE *pulls the pram from* COLIN, *spins it round and pushes it violently at* BARRY. BARRY *sidesteps and catches it by the handle as it goes past.*

BARRY. Oi – oi!

He looks in the pram.

COLIN. Wass up?

COLIN *and* PETE *come over.*

It can't open its eyes.
BARRY. Yer woke it.
PETE. Look at its fists.
COLIN. Yeh.
PETE. It's tryin' a clout 'im.
COLIN. Don't blame it.
PETE. Goin' a be a boxer.
BARRY. Is it a girl?
PETE. Yer wouldn't know the difference.
BARRY. 'Ow d'yer get 'em t'sleep?
PETE. Pull their 'air.
COLIN. Eh?
PETE. Like that.

He pulls its hair.

COLIN. That 'urt.

They laugh.

MIKE. Wass 'e doin'?
COLIN. Pullin' its 'air.
FRED. 'E'll 'ave its ol' woman after 'im.
MIKE. Poor sod.
BARRY. 'E's showin' off.
COLIN. 'E wants the coroner's medal.
MIKE (*comes to the pram*). Less see yer do it.

PETE *pulls its hair.*

O yeh.
BARRY. It don't say nothin'.
COLIN. Little bleeder's 'alf dead a fright.

MIKE. Still awake.

PETE. Ain' co-operatin'.

BARRY. Try a pinch.

MIKE. That ought a work.

BARRY. Like this.

He pinches the baby.

COLIN. Look at that mouth.

BARRY. Flippin' yawn.

PETE. Least it's tryin'.

MIKE. Pull its drawers off.

COLIN. Yeh!

MIKE. Less case its ol' crutch.

PETE. Ha!

BARRY. Yeh!

He throws the nappy in the air.

   Yippee!

COLIN. Look at that!

They laugh.

MIKE. Look at its little legs goin'.

COLIN. Ain' they ugly!

BARRY. Ugh!

MIKE. Can't keep 'em still!

PETE. 'Avin' a fit.

BARRY. It's dirty.

They groan.

COLIN. 'Old its nose.

MIKE. Thass for 'iccups.

BARRY. Gob its crutch.

He spits.

MIKE. Yeh!

COLIN. Ha!

He spits.

MIKE. Got it!

PETE. Give it a punch.

MIKE. Yeh less!

COLIN. There's no one about!

PETE *punches it.*

Ugh! Mind yer don't 'urt it.

MIKE. Yer can't.

BARRY. Not at that age.

MIKE. Course yer can't, no feelin's.

PETE. Like animals.

MIKE. 'It it again.

COLIN. I can't see!

BARRY. 'Arder.

PETE. Yeh.

BARRY. Like that!

He hits it.

COLIN. An' that!

He also hits it.

MIKE. What a giggle!

PETE. Cloutin's good for 'em. I read it.

BARRY (*to* FRED). Why don't you clout it?

FRED. It ain' mine.

PETE. Sherker. Yer got a do yer duty.

FRED. Ain' my worry. Serves 'er right.

BARRY. 'Ere, can I piss on it?

COLIN. Gungy bastard!

MIKE. Got any matches?

They laugh.

PETE. Couldn't yer break them little fingers easy though?

COLIN. Snap!

PETE. Know what they used a do?

MIKE. Yeh.

PETE. Smother 'em.

BARRY. Yeh. That'd be somethin'.

COLIN. Looks like a yeller-nigger.

BARRY. 'Onk like a yid.

FRED. Leave it alone.

PETE. Why?

FRED. Yer don't wan' a row.

PETE. What row?

MIKE. What kid?

COLIN. I ain' seen no kid.

BARRY. Not me!

PETE. Yer wouldn't grass on yer muckers?

FRED. Grow up.

BARRY. D'narf look ill. Stupid bastard.

He jerks the pram violently.

PETE. Thass 'ow they 'ang yer – give yer a jerk.

MIKE. Reckon it'll grow up an idiot.

PETE. Or deformed.

BARRY. Look where it come from.

PETE. Little bleeder.

He jerks the pram violently.

  That knocked the grin off its face.

MIKE. Look! Ugh!

BARRY. Look!

COLIN. What?

They all groan.

PETE. Rub the little bastard's face in it!

BARRY. Yeh!

PETE. Less 'ave it!

He rubs the baby. They all groan.

BARRY. Less 'ave a go! I always wan'ed a do that!

PETE. Ain' yer done it before?

BARRY *does it. He laughs.*

COLIN. It's all in its eyes.

Silence.

FRED. There'll be a row.
MIKE. It can't talk.
PETE. 'Oo cares?
FRED. I tol' yer.
COLIN. Shut up.
BARRY. I noticed 'e ain' touched it.
COLIN. Too bloody windy.
FRED. Yeh?
PETE. Less see yer.
BARRY. Yeh.
PETE. 'Fraid she'll ruck yer.
FRED. Ha!

He looks in the pram.

  Chriss.
PETE. Less see yer chuck that.

PETE *throws a stone to* FRED. FRED *doesn't try to catch it. It falls on the ground.* COLIN *picks it up and gives it to* FRED.

MIKE (*quietly*). Reckon it's all right?
COLIN (*quietly*). No one around.
PETE (*quietly*). They don't know it's us.
MIKE (*quietly*). She left it.
BARRY. It's done now.
PETE (*quietly*). Yer can do what yer like.
BARRY. Might as well enjoy ourselves.
PETE (*quietly*). Yer don't get a chance like this everyday.

FRED *throws the stone.*

COLIN. Missed.
PETE. That ain't'!

He throws a stone.

BARRY. Or that!

He throws a stone.

MIKE. Yeh!
COLIN (*running round*). Where's all the stones?
MIKE (*also running round*). Stick it up the fair!
PETE. Liven 'Ampstead 'eath! Three throws a quid! Make a
  packet.
MIKE (*throws a stone*). Ouch!
COLIN. 'Ear that?
BARRY. Give us some.

He takes stones from COLIN.

COLIN (*throws a stone*). Right in the lug 'ole.

FRED *looks for a stone.*

PETE. Get its 'ooter.
BARRY. An' its slasher!
FRED (*picks up a stone, spits on it*). For luck, the sod.

He throws.

BARRY. Yyooowwww!
MIKE. 'Ear it plonk!

A bell rings.

MIKE. 'Oo's got the matches?

He finds some in his pocket.

BARRY. What yer doin'?
COLIN. Wan'a buck up!
MIKE. Keep a look out.

He starts to throw burning matches in the pram. BARRY *throws a stone. It just misses* MIKE.

Look out, yer bleedin' git!

COLIN. Guy Fawkes!

PETE. Bloody nutter! Put that out!

MIKE. No! You 'ad what you want!

PETE. Yer'll 'ave the ol' bloody park 'ere!

A bell rings.

BARRY. Piss on it! Piss on it!

COLIN. Gungy slasher.

MIKE. Call the R.S.P.C.A.

A bell rings.

FRED. They'll shut the gates.

PETE (*going*). There's an 'ole in the railin's.

BARRY. 'Old on.

He looks for a stone.

PETE. Leave it!

BARRY. Juss this one!

He throws a stone as PETE *pushes him over. It goes wide.*

Bastard!

To PETE. Yer put me off!

PETE. I'll throttle yer!

BARRY. I got a get it once more!

The others have gone up left. He takes a stone from the pram and throws it at point blank range. Hits.

Yar!

COLIN. Where's this 'ole!

MIKE. Yer bleedin' gear!

FRED. Chriss.

He runs down to the rod and boxes. He picks them up.

BARRY. Bleedin' little sod!

He hacks into the pram. He goes up left.

PETE. Come on!

A bell rings. FRED *has difficulty with the boxes and rod. He throws a box away.*

FRED. 'Ang on!

He goes up left.
They go off up left, making a curious buzzing. A long pause.
PAM *comes in down left.*

PAM. I might a know'd they'd a left yer. Lucky yer got
    someone t' look after yer. Muggins 'ere.

She starts to push the pram. She does not look into it. She speaks in a sing-song voice, loudly but to herself.
    'Oo's 'ad yer balloon. Thass a present from grannie. Goin'
    a keep me up 'alf the night? Go t' sleepies. Soon be 'ome.
    Nice an' warm, then. No one else wants yer. Nice an' warm.
    Soon be 'omies.

SCENE SEVEN

A cell. Left centre a box to sit on. Otherwise, the stage is bare.
A steel door bangs. FRED *comes in from the left. He has a*
mac over his head. He sits on the case. After a slight pause he
takes off the mac.

Silence. A steel door bangs. PAM *comes in left.*

PAM. What 'appened?
FRED. Didn't yer see 'em?
PAM. I 'eard.

FRED. Bloody 'eathens. Thumpin' and kickin' the van.

PAM. Oo?

FRED. Bloody 'ousewives! 'Oo else? Ought a be stood up an' shot!

PAM. You all right?

FRED. No. I tol' this copper don't open the door. He goes we're 'ere, the thick bastard, an' lets 'em in. Kickin' an' punchin'.

He holds up the mack.

Look at it! Gob all over.

He throws it away from him.

'Course I ain' all right!
Mimicking her. 'Are yer all right?'

PAM. They said I shouldn't be 'ere. But 'e was ever so nice. Said five minutes wouldn't matter.

FRED. Right bloody mess.

PAM. They can't get in 'ere.

FRED. I can't get out there!

PAM. I ain't blamin' yer.

FRED. Blamin' me? Yer got bugger all t'blame me for, mate! Yer ruined my life, thass all!

PAM. I never meant –

FRED. Why the bloody 'ell bring the little perisher out that time a night?

PAM (*fingers at her mouth*). I wanted a –

FRED. Yer got no right chasin' after me with a pram! Drop me right in it!

PAM. I was scared t' stay –

FRED. Never know why yer 'ad the little bleeder in the first place! Yer don't know what yer doin'! Yer're a bloody menace!

PAM. Wass it like?

FRED. They wan' a put you in, then yer'll find out. Bring any burn?

PAM. No.

FRED. Yer don't think a nothin'! Ain' yer got juss one?

PAM. No.

FRED. Yer're bloody useless.

PAM. What'll 'appen!

FRED. 'Ow do I know? I'll be the last one a know. The 'ole
thing was an accident. Lot a roughs. Never seen 'em
before. Don't arst me. Blokes like that anywhere. I tried
to chase 'em off.

PAM. Will they believe that?

FRED. No. If I was ten years older I'd get a medal. With a
crowd like our'n they got a knock someone. (*He goes right.*)
Right bloody mess.

PAM. Yer never bin in trouble before. Juss one or two woun-
din's an' that.

FRED. 'Alf murdered with a lot a 'and bags!

PAM. Yer wan' a arst t' see the doctor.

FRED. Doctor! They shouldn't let him touch a sick rat with
a barge pole. (*He walks a few steps.*) It's supposed a be
grub. A starvin' cat 'ld walk away. (*He walks a few more
steps.*) Wass bin 'appening?

PAM. Don't know.

FRED. On yer own?

PAM. What about them others?

FRED. What about 'em?

PAM. I could say I saw 'em.

FRED. That'd make it worse. Don't worry. I'm thinkin' it all
out. This way they don't know what 'appened. Not definite.
Why couldn't I bin tryin' a 'elp the kid? I got no cause t'
'arm it.

He sits on the box.

PAM. I tol' 'em.

FRED (*he puts his arms round her waist and leans his head
against her*). Yer'll 'ave t' send us letters.

PAM. I'm buyin' a pad on me way 'ome.

FRED. Pam. I don't know what'll 'appen. There's bloody gangs like that roamin' everywhere. The bloody police don't do their job.

PAM. I'll kill meself if they touch yer.

A steel door bangs. LEN *comes in left.*

I tol' yer t' wait outside.

LEN. I got 'im some fags. (*To* FRED.) I 'ad a drop 'em 'alf.

PAM. 'E still won't leave me alone, Fred.

LEN. I only got a minute. They're arstin' for a remand.

FRED. Chriss. That bloody mob still outside?

LEN. They've 'emmed 'em off over the road.

FRED. Bit bloody late.

PAM. Tell 'im t' go.

LEN. We both got a go. That inspector wants you.

FRED. Where's the snout?

LEN. Put it in yer pocket.

FRED (*to* PAM). See yer after.

She puts her arms round him before he can take the cigarettes.

PAM. I'll wait for yer.

FRED (*pats her back*). Yeh, yeh. God 'elp us.

LEN (*to* PAM). Yer'll get 'im into trouble if yer don't go.

FRED *nods at* PAM. *She goes out crying.*

FRED. 'Ow many yer got?

LEN. Sixty. I 'ad a drop 'em 'alf.

FRED. Will it be all right?

LEN. Give 'em a few like, an' don't flash 'em around.

FRED. She never 'ad none. I'll do the same for you sometime.

LEN. Put 'em in yer pocket.

FRED. I don't know what I'll get.

LEN. Manslaughter. (*Shrugs.*) Anythin'.

FRED. It was only a kid.

LEN. I saw.

FRED. What?

LEN. I come back when I couldn't find 'er.

FRED. Yer ain't grassed?

LEN. No.

FRED. O.

LEN. I was in the trees. I saw the pram.

FRED. Yeh.

LEN. I saw the lot.

FRED. Yeh.

LEN. I didn't know what t'do. Well, I should a stopped yer.

FRED. Too late now.

LEN. I juss saw.

FRED. Yer saw! Yer saw! Wass the good a that? That don't 'elp me. I'll be out in that bloody dock in a minute!

LEN. Nothin'. They got the pram in court.

FRED. Okay, okay. Reckon there's time for a quick burn?

LEN. About.

He gives FRED *a light.*

INTERVAL

SCENE EIGHT

The living-room.

HARRY *irons,* LEN *sits.*

LEN. Yer make a fair ol' job a that.

Pause.

Don't yer get choked off.

HARRY. What?

LEN. That every Friday night.

HARRY. Got a keep clean.

LEN. Suppose so.

Pause.

Yer get used t' it.

HARRY. Trained to it in the army.

LEN. O.

HARRY. Makes a man a yer.

MARY *comes in. She looks around.*

MARY *to* LEN. I wish yer wouldn't sit around in yer ol' work-clothes an' shoes. Yer got some nice slippers.

MARY *goes out.*

LEN. She won't let Pam.

HARRY. Eh?

LEN. She won't let Pam do that for yer.

HARRY. Don't take me long.

Long pause.

LEN. Yer could stop 'er money.

Slight pause.

Then she couldn't interfere.

HARRY. Don't take long. Once yer get started.

LEN. Why don't yer try that?

HARRY. That Pam can't iron. She'd ruin 'em.

LEN. Ever thought a movin' on?

HARRY. This stuff gets dry easy.

LEN. Yer ought a think about it.

HARRY. Yer don't know what yer talking about, lad.

LEN. No. I don't.

HARRY. It's like everthin' else.

LEN. 'Ow long yer bin 'ere?

HARRY. Don't know. (*He stretches his back. He irons again.*)
Yer mate's comin' out.

LEN. Yeh. Why?

HARRY. Pam's mate. (*He spits on the iron.*) None a it ain'
simple.

LEN. Yer lost a little boy eh?

HARRY. Next week, ain't it?

LEN. I got a shirt yer can do. (*Laughs.*) Any offers?

HARRY. She meet 'im?

LEN. Ain' arst.

HARRY. You?

LEN (*shrugs*). I'd 'ave t' get time off.

HARRY. O.

LEN. 'Ow d'yer get on at work?

HARRY (*looks up*). It's a job.

LEN. I meant with the blokes?

HARRY (*irons*). They're all right.

LEN. Funny, nightwork.

PAM *comes in. She has her hair in a towel. She carries a portable
radio. Someone is talking. She sits on the couch and finds a
pop programme. She tunes in badly. She interrupts this from
time to time to rub her hair.*

LEN (*to* HARRY). 'Ow about doin' my shirt?

He laughs. PAM *finishes tuning. She looks round.*

PAM. 'Oo's got my *Radio Times*? You 'ad it?

HARRY *doesn't answer. She turns to* LEN.

You?

LEN (*mumbles*). Not again.

PAM. You speakin' t' me?

LEN. I'm sick t' death a yer bloody *Radio Times*.

PAM. Someone's 'ad it. (*She rubs her hair vigorously.*) I ain'
goin' a get it no more. Not after last week. I'll cancel it.
It's the last time I bring it in this 'ouse. I don't see why I

'ave t' go on paying for it. Yer must think I'm made a money. It's never 'ere when I wan'a see it. Not once. It's always the same. (*She rubs her hair.*) I notice no one else offers t' pay for it. Always Charlie. It's 'appened once too often this time.

LEN. Every bloody week the same!

PAM (*to* HARRY). Sure yer ain' got it?

HARRY. I bought this shirt over eight years ago.

PAM. That cost me every week. You reckon that up over a year. Yer must think I was born yesterday.

Pause. She rubs her hair.

Wasn't 'ere last week. Never 'ere. Got legs.

She goes to the door and shouts.

Mum! She 'eard all right.

She goes back to the couch and sits. She rubs her hair.

Someone's got it. I shouldn't think the people next door come in an' took it. Everyone 'as the benefit a it 'cept me. It's always the same. I'll know what t' do in future. Two can play at that game. I ain' blinkin' daft. (*She rubs her hair.*) I never begrudge no one borrowin' it, but yer'd think they'd have enough manners t' put it back.

Pause.

She rubs her hair.

Juss walk all over yer. Well it ain' goin' a 'appen again. They treat you like a door mat. All take and no give. Touch somethin' a their'n an' they go through the bloody ceilin'. It's bin the same ever since –

LEN. I tol' yer t' keep it in yer room!

PAM. Now yer got a lock things up in yer own 'ouse.

LEN. Why should we put up with this week after week juss because yer too –

PAM. Yer know what yer can do.

LEN. Thass yer answer t' everythin'.

PAM. Got a better one?

HARRY. They was a pair first off. Set me back a quid each.
Up the market. One's gone 'ome, went at the cuffs. Worth
a quid.

LEN. Chriss.

Pause.

PAM. I mean it this time. I'm goin' in that shop first thing
Saturday mornin' an' tell 'im t' cancel it. I ain' throwin'
my money down the drain juss to –

LEN. Wrap up!

PAM. Don't tell me what t' do!

LEN. Wrap up!

PAM. Thass typical a you.
  She goes to the door and calls. Mum!
  To LEN. I ain' stupid. I know 'oo's got it.
  Calls. Mum! – She can 'ear.

HARRY. Ain' worth readin' any'ow.

LEN. Don't start 'er off again.

PAM (*to* LEN). You ain' sittin' on it, a course!

LEN. No.

PAM. Yer ain' looked.

LEN. Ain' goin' to.

PAM. 'Ow d'yer know yer ain' sittin' on it?

LEN. I ain' sittin' on it.

PAM (*to* HARRY). Tell 'im t' get up!

HARRY. Waste a good money.

PAM (*to* LEN). Yer'll be sorry for this.

LEN. I'll be sorry for a lot a things.

HARRY. Cuffs goin' on this one.

PAM (*by* LEN's *chair*). I ain' goin' till yer move.

HARRY. Lot a lies an' pictures a nancies.

PAM. Yer dead spiteful when yer wan'a be.

LEN. Thass right.

PAM (*goes to the couch, rubbing her hair*). 'E'oo laughs last. Fred's coming 'ome next week.

LEN. 'Ome?

PAM. 'Is ol' lady won't 'ave 'im in the 'ouse.

LEN. Where's 'e goin'?

PAM. Yer'll see.

LEN. 'E ain' 'avin' my room.

PAM. 'Oo said?

LEN. She won't let yer.

PAM. We'll see.

LEN. Yer ain' even arst 'er.

PAM. O no?

LEN. No.

PAM (*rubs her hair*). We'll see.

LEN. I'll 'ave one or two things t' say. Yer too fond a pushin' people about.

PAM. Must take after you.

LEN. I thought 'e'd be sharin' your room.

PAM. I ain' rowin' about it. 'E'll 'ave t' 'ave somewhere t' come out to. Chriss knows what it's like shut up in them places. It'll be nice an' clean 'ere for 'im when yer're gone.

LEN. 'Ave yer arst 'im yet?

PAM. I ain' rowin' about it. If 'e goes wanderin' off 'e'll only end up in trouble again. I ain' goin' a be messed around over this! We ain' gettin' any younger. 'E's bound a be different. (*She rubs her hair.*) Yer can't say anythin' in letters. Yer can't expect 'im to.

LEN. 'Ave yer arst 'im.

PAM. I don' wan' a talk about it.

LEN. You meetin' 'im?

PAM. Why? – You ain' comin'!

LEN. 'Oo said?

PAM. 'E don't want you there!

LEN. 'Ow d'yer know?

PAM. O let me alone!

LEN. 'E's my mate, ain' 'e?

PAM. I'm sick t' death a you under me feet all the time! Ain' yer got no friends t' go to! What about yer people? Won't they take yer in either?

LEN. Yer arst some stupid questions at times.

PAM. Yer can't 'ave no pride. Yer wouldn't catch me 'angin' round where I ain' wanted.

LEN. 'Oo ain' wanted?

PAM. I don't want yer! They don't want yer! It's only common sense! I don't know why yer can't see it. It's nothin' but rows an' arguments.

LEN. 'Oo's fault's that?

PAM. Anybody else wouldn't stay if yer paid 'em! Yer caused all the trouble last time.

LEN. I knew that was comin'.

PAM. None a that 'ld a 'appened if yer ain' bin 'ere. Yer never give 'im a chance.

LEN. Yeh, yeh.

PAM. Yer live on trouble!

LEN. That ain' what 'e told everyone.

PAM. Same ol' lies.

LEN. Listen 'oo's talkin'!

PAM. Yer start off gettin' 'im put away –

LEN. Don't be bloody stupid!

PAM. Jealous! An' now 'e's comin' out yer still can't let 'im alone!

LEN. *You* can't leave 'im alone yer mean!

PAM. Yer laughed yer 'ead off when they took 'im away.

LEN. Bloody stupid! You arst 'im!

PAM. Comin' 'ere an' workin' me up!

LEN. Yer wan'a listen t' yerself!

PAM. So do you.

LEN. Shoutin'.

PAM. 'Oo's shoutin'?

LEN. You are!

PAM. Yer 'ave t' shout with you!

LEN. Thass right!

PAM. Yer so bloody dense!

LEN. Go on!

PAM. Yer 'ave t' shout!

LEN. Yer silly bloody cow!

PAM. Shoutin' 'e says! 'Ark at 'im! 'Ark at 'im!

LEN. Shut up!

PAM. We ain' carryin' on like this! Yer got a stop upsettin' me night after night!

LEN. You start it!

PAM. It's got a stop! It ain' worth it! Juss round an' round.

A very long silence.

Yer can't say it's the kid keepin' yer.

A long silence.

It certainly ain' me. Thass well past.

Silence.

Yer sit there in yer dirty ol' work clothes. (*To* HARRY.) Why don't yer turn 'im out? Dad.

HARRY. 'E pays 'is rent.

PAM. Fred'll pay.

HARRY. 'As 'e got a job?

PAM. 'E'll get one.

HARRY. Will 'e keep it?

PAM. Thass right!

LEN. Now 'oo's startin' it?

PAM. You are.

LEN. I ain' said a word.

PAM. No – but yer sat there!

LEN. I got some rights yer know!

PAM. Yer're juss like a kid.

LEN. I'm glad I ain' yourn.

PAM. I wouldn't like t' 'ave your spiteful nature.

LEN. I certainly wouldn't like yourn!

PAM. Thass right! I know why yer sittin' there!

LEN. Yer know a sight bloody too much!

PAM. I know where my *Radio Times* is!

LEN. Stick yer bloody *Radio Times*!

PAM. I know why yer sittin' there!

LEN. That bloody paper!

PAM. Why don't yer stand up?

LEN. Yer don't even want the bloody paper!

PAM. As long as yer causin' trouble –

LEN. Yer juss wan' a row!

PAM. – then yer're 'appy!

LEN. If yer found it yer'd lose somethin' else!

PAM (*goes to* LEN's *chair*). Stand up then!

LEN. No!

PAM. Can't it a got there accidentally?

LEN. No!

PAM. Yer see!

LEN. I ain' bein' pushed around.

PAM. Yer see!

LEN. Yer come too much a it!

PAM. No yer'd rather stay stuck!

LEN. A sight bloody too much!

PAM. An' row!

LEN. Shut up!

PAM. Thass right!

LEN. I tol' yer t' shut up!

PAM. Go on!

LEN. Or I'll bloody well shut yer up!

PAM. O yeh!

LEN. Yer need a bloody good beltin'.

PAM. Touch me!

LEN. You started this!

PAM. Go on!

LEN (*he turns away*). Yer make me sick!

PAM. Yeh – yer see. Yer make me sick!

She goes to the door.

I ain' lettin' a bloody little weed like you push me around! *Calls.* Mum.

She comes back.

I wish I 'ad a record a when yer first come 'ere. Butter wouldn't melt in yer mouth. (*Calls.*) Mum!

HARRY (*finishing ironing*). Thass that, thank Chriss.

PAM (*calls*). Mum! – She can' 'ear.

(*Calls.*) You 'eard!

HARRY. Put the wood in the 'ole.

LEN. I'd like t' 'ear what they're sayin' next door.

PAM. Let 'em say!

LEN. 'Ole bloody neighbour'ood must know!

PAM. Good – let 'em know what you're like!

LEN. 'Oo wen' on about pride?

PAM (*calls through door*). I know yer can' 'ear.

MARY (*off*). You callin' Pam?

PAM (*to* LEN). One thing, anythin' else goes wrong I'll know 'oo t' blame.

MARY (*off*). Pam!

PAM. Let 'er wait.

MARY (*off*). Pam!

LEN (*calls*). It's all right! One a 'er fits!

PAM (*calls*). 'E's sittin' on the chair.

MARY (*off*). What?

PAM (*calls*). 'E's got my paper!

MARY (*off*). What chair?

PAM (*calls*). 'E 'as!

MARY (*off*). I ain' got yer paper!

PAM (*calls*). It don't matter!

MARY (*off*). What paper's that?

PAM (*calls*). It don't matter! You bloody deaf?

LEN. Now start on 'er!

HARRY (*piling his clothes neatly*). Didn't take long.

PAM (*to* LEN). Yer're so bloody clever!

LEN. If I upset yer like this why don't *you* go?

PAM. Thass what you want!

LEN (*shrugs*). You want *me* t' go!

PAM. I ain' bein' pushed out on no streets.

LEN. I'm tryin' t' 'elp.

PAM. Yer wouldn't 'elp a cryin' baby.

LEN. Yer're the last one a bring that up!

PAM. 'Elp? – after the way yer carried on t'night.

LEN. I lost me job stayin' out a 'elp you when yer was sick!

PAM. Sacked for bein' bloody lazy!

LEN (*stands*). Satisfied?

PAM (*without looking at the chair*). Yer torn it up or burnt it! Wouldn't put that pass yer!

PAM *goes out.* Silence. HARRY *finishes folding his clothes.*

MARY (*off*). Found it yet?

Pause.

HARRY. Wan'a use it?

LEN. No.

HARRY *folds the board.*

SCENE NINE

The living-room.
LEN *has spread a paper on the floor. He cleans his shoes on it.*
MARY *comes in. She is in her slip. She walks about getting ready.*

MARY. 'Ope yer don't mind me like this.

LEN. You kiddin'?

MARY. It's such a rush. I don't really wan'a go.

LEN. Don't then.

MARY. I said I would now.

LEN. Say yer don't feel up to it.

MARY. Yes. (*She goes on getting ready.*) Makes a change I
suppose.

LEN. Never know, it might be a laugh.

MARY. Yer got a do somethin' t' entertain yerself.

Pause.

I 'ope yer ain' usin' 'er *Radio Times*.

LEN. Ha!

MARY. She's got no patience. It'll land 'er in trouble one a
these days. Look at that pram. I told 'er t'wait. She should
a got two 'undred for that.

LEN. Easy.

MARY (*looks at her shoes*). This ain' nice. No, she 'as t' let it
go for fifty quid, the first time she's arst. Can't be told. Yer
couldn't give these a little touch up for me?

LEN. Sling 'em over.

MARY. Ta, dear.

LEN. What yer put on these?

MARY. That white stuff.

LEN *polishes her shoes in silence.*

Thinkin'?

LEN. No.

MARY. Whass worryin' yer?

LEN. Nothin'.

MARY. I expect yer're like me. Yer enjoy the quiet. I don't
enjoy all this noise yer get.

LEN. She said somethin' about my room?

MARY (*amused*). Why?

LEN. What she say?

MARY. That worried yer?

LEN. I ain' worried.

MARY. She's not tellin' me 'ow t' run my 'ouse.

She pulls on her stockings.

LEN. O. (*Holds up her shoes.*) Do yer?

MARY. Very nice. Juss go over the backs dear. I like t' feel nice be'ind. I tol' 'er there's enough t' put up with without lookin' for trouble.

LEN. Better?

MARY. Yes. I 'ad enough a that pair last time.

She steps into one shoe.

We're only goin' for the big film. She can do what she likes outside.

LEN (*gives her the other shoe*). Thass yer lot.

MARY. 'E wants lockin' up for life. Ta, dear. I don't expect yer t' understand at your age, but things don't turn out too bad. There's always someone worse off in the world.

LEN (*clearing up the polishing things*). Yer can always be that one.

MARY. She's my own flesh an' blood, but she don't take after me. Not a thought in 'er 'ead. She's 'ad a rough time a it. I feel sorry for 'er about the kid –

LEN. One a them things. Yer can't make too much a it.

MARY. Never 'ave 'appened if she'd a look after it right. Yer done a lovely job on these. What yer doin' t'night?

LEN (*sews a button on his shirt*). Gettin' ready for work.

MARY. Yer don't go out so much.

LEN. I was out Tuesday.

MARY. Yer ought a be out every night.

LEN. Can't afford it.

MARY. There's plenty a nice girls round 'ere.

LEN. I ain' got the energy these days. They want – somethin' flash.

MARY. Yer can't tell me what they want. I was the same that age.

LEN. I ain' got time for 'alf a 'em. They don't know what they got it for.

MARY. I thought that's what you men were after.

LEN. 'Alf a 'em, it ain' worth the bother a gettin' there. Thass a fact.

MARY. What about the other 'alf?

LEN. Hm!

MARY (*having trouble with her suspender*). Yer 'ave t' go about it the right way. Yer can't stand a girl in a puddle down the back a some ol' alley an' think yer doin' 'er a favour. Yer got yer own room upstairs. That's a nice room. Surprised yer don't use that. I don't mind what goes on, yer know that. As long as yer keep the noise down.

LEN. Ta.

MARY. It's in every man. It 'as t' come out.

Pause.

We didn't carry on like that when I was your age.

LEN. Pull the other one.

MARY. Not till yer was in church. Anyway, yer 'ad t' be engaged. I think it's nicer in the open. I do.

LEN. I bet yer bin up a few alleys.

MARY. You enjoy yerself. I know what I'd be doin' if I was you.

LEN. You meetin' a fella?

MARY. No! I'm goin' out with Mrs Lee.

LEN. Waste.

MARY. Don't be cheeky.

LEN. Yer look fair when yer all done up.

MARY. What you after? Bin spendin' me rent money?

LEN. Wass on?

MARY. Don't know. Somethin' daft.

LEN. Shall I look it up?

MARY. They're all the same. Sex. Girls 'angin' out a their dresses an' men bendin' over 'em.

LEN. It's one of them nudes. 'Eard the fellas talkin'.

MARY. Shan't go in.

LEN. Don't know what yer missin'.

MARY. Different for men.

LEN. Always full a tarts when I bin.

MARY. Thass where yer spend yer money.

LEN. Very nice. Big ol' tits bouncin' about in sinner-scope.

MARY. Don't think Mrs Lee'd fancy that.

LEN. I'll 'ave t' take yer one a these nights.

MARY. I'd rather see Tarzan.

LEN. Thass easy, come up next time I 'ave a bath.

MARY. Count the 'airs on yer chest?

LEN. For a start.

MARY. Sounds like a 'orror film.

LEN. I enjoy a good scrub. On me back.

MARY. Thass the regular carry-on in China.

LEN. No 'arm in it.

MARY. No.

Slight pause.

Pam's very easy goin' for a nice girl. I suppose yer miss that.

LEN. Takes a bit a gettin' used to.

MARY. 'Ow'd yer manage?

LEN. Any suggestions?

Slight pause.

MARY. Bugger!

LEN. Eh?

MARY. Thass tore it!

LEN. Wass up?

MARY. O blast! I caught me stockin'.

LEN. O.

MARY. That would 'ave to 'appen.

LEN. 'Ow'd yer do it?

MARY. Juss when I'm late. Bugger it.

She looks in the table drawer.

'Ardly worth goin' in a minute. Excuse my language. Never find anythin' when yer want it in this place.

LEN. What yer lost?

MARY. It's the only decent pair I got.

LEN. Thass a shame.

MARY. It'll run.

LEN. Less 'ave a shufties.

MARY. Caught on that blasted chair. It's bin like that for ages.

LEN. Yeh. Thass a big one.

MARY. Pam's got 'er nail-varnish all over the place except when yer wan'a find it.

LEN (*offers her the needle*). 'Ave a loan of this.

MARY. It'll run, y'see.

LEN. Less do the cotton.

MARY. I certainly can't afford new ones this week.

LEN (*threading the needle*). Not t' worry.

MARY. I'm no good at that.

LEN. Well, 'ave a bash.

MARY. It'll make it worse.

LEN. No it won't.

MARY (*puts her foot on the chair seat*). You do it.

LEN. Me?

MARY. I never could use a needle. I should a bin there by now.

LEN. I don't know if I –

MARY. Get on. It's only doin' me a good turn.

LEN. It ain' that. I –

MARY. Mrs Lee's waitin'. I can't take 'em off. I'm in ever such a 'urry. They'll run.

LEN. Yeh. It's dodgy. I don't wan'a prick –

MARY. Yer got steady 'ands your age.

LEN (*kneels in front of her and starts darning*). Yeh. (*He drops the needle*). O.

MARY. All right?

LEN. It's dropped.

MARY. What?

LEN. Me needle.

MARY. Yer're 'oldin' me up.

LEN (*on his hands and knees*). 'Ang on.

MARY. That it?

LEN. No.

MARY (*she helps him to look*). Can't a got far.

LEN. It's gone.

MARY. What's that?

LEN. Where?

MARY. That's it. There.

LEN. O. Ta.

MARY (*puts her foot back on the chair*). I ain' got all night.

LEN. I'll 'ave t' get me 'and inside.

MARY. You watch where yer go. Yer ain' on yer 'oneymoon
yet. Yer 'and's cold!

LEN. Keep still, or it'll jab yer.

MARY. You watch yerself.

LEN. I'll juss give it a little stretch.

MARY. All right?

LEN. Yer got lovely legs.

MARY. You get on with it.

LEN. Lovely an' smooth.

MARY. Never mind my legs.

LEN. It's a fact.

MARY. Some people'd 'ave a fit if they 'eard that. Yer know
what they're like.

LEN. Frustrated.

MARY. I'm old enough t' be yer mother.

HARRY *comes in. He goes straight to the table.*

    To LEN. Go steady!

LEN. Sorry.

MARY. You watch where yer pokin'. That 'urt.

LEN. I tol' yer t' keep still.

MARY. Yer'll make it bigger, not smaller.

HARRY *takes ink and a Pools coupon from the table drawer.*
He puts them on the table.

LEN. That'll see yer through t'night.

He ties a knot in the thread.

MARY. Wass up now?

LEN. Scissors.

MARY. Eh?

LEN. I 'ad 'em juss now.

MARY. Bite it.

LEN. Eh?

MARY. Go on.

LEN (*leans forward*). Keep still.

MARY. I can't wait all night.

LEN *bites the thread off.* HARRY *goes out.*

Took yer time.

LEN (*stands*). Ow! I'm stiff.

MARY (*looks*). Ta, very nice.

LEN. Ain' worth goin' now.

MARY. 'Ave I got me cigarettes?

LEN. Might be somethin' on telly.

MARY. I can't disappoint Mrs Lee.

LEN. I 'ad a feelin' 'e'd come in.

MARY. Yer'll be in bed time I get back.

LEN. She won't wait this long.

MARY. I'll say good night. Thanks for 'elpin'.

LEN. Stay in an' put yer feet up. I'll make us a cup of tea.

MARY. Can't let yer friends down. Cheerio.

LEN. Okay.

MARY *goes.* LEN *takes a handkerchief from his pocket. He*
switches the light off and goes to the couch.

SCENE TEN

A café.
  Furniture: chairs and three tables, one up right, one right and one down left. Apart from this the stage is bare.

LEN *and* PAM *sit at the table up right.*

LEN (*drinks tea*). Warms yer up.

Pause.

  These early mornin's knock me out. 'Nother cup?

Pause.

PAM. Wass the time?
LEN. Quarter past.
PAM. Why ain't they got a clock?

Pause.

LEN. 'Ave another one.
PAM. Thass the fourth time yer keep arstin.
LEN. Warm yer up.
PAM. Go an' sit on yer own table.

Pause.

LEN. Sure yer wrote the name right?
PAM. We'll look bloody daft when 'e finds you 'ere. Wass 'e goin' to say?
LEN. 'Ello.

Pause.

  Let me go an' find 'im.
PAM. No.
LEN. There's no use –

PAM. No!

LEN. Suit yerself.

PAM. Do I 'ave t' say everythin' twice?

LEN. There's no need t' shout.

PAM. I ain' shoutin'.

LEN. They can 'ear yer 'alf way t' –

PAM. I don't wan'a know.

LEN. Yer never do.

Silence.

PAM. Len. I don't want a keep on at yer. I don't know what's the matter with me. They wan'a put the 'eat on. It's like death. Yer'd get on a lot better with someone else.

LEN. Per'aps 'e ain' comin'.

PAM. They must 'ave all the winders open. It's no life for a fella. Yer ain' a bad sort.

LEN. Yeh. I'm goin' a be late in.

PAM. Don't go.

LEN. You make me money up?

PAM (*after a slight pause*). Why can't yer go somewhere?

LEN. Where?

PAM. There's lots a places.

LEN. 'Easy t' say.

PAM. I'll find yer somewhere.

LEN. I ain' scuttlin' off juss t' make room for you t' shag in.

PAM. Yer're a stubborn sod! Don't blame me what 'appens t' yer! Yer ain' messin' me about again.

LEN. I knew that wouldn't last long!

PAM. I'm sick t' death a yer. Clear off!

She goes to the table down left and sits. LEN goes out left. Pause. He comes back with a cup of tea. He puts it on the table in front of PAM. He stands near the table.

LEN. It'll get cold.

Pause.

Did 'e say 'e'd come?

Pause.

Did 'e answer any a your letters?

She re-acts.

I juss wondered!
PAM. I tol' yer before!
LEN. Thass all right then.

Pause.

PAM. It's like winter in 'ere.

There are voices off right. Someone shouts. A door bangs open.
MIKE, COLIN, PETE, BARRY, FRED *and* LIZ *come in.*

COLIN. 'Ere we are again.
BARRY. Wipe yer boots.
MIKE. On you!
BARRY. Where we sittin'?
MIKE. On yer 'ead.
BARRY. On me arse!
LIZ. Don't know 'ow 'e tells the difference.

She laughs.

FRED. This'll do.
PETE. All right?
LIZ. Can I sit 'ere?
MIKE. Sit where yer like, dear.
BARRY. What we 'avin'?
PETE (*to* FRED). What yer fancy?
FRED. What they got?
PETE (*looks left*). Double egg, bacon, 'am, bangers, double
    bangers, sper-gety –
BARRY. Chips.
FRED. Juss bring the lot.

PETE. Oi, ease off.

FRED. An' four cups a tea.

PETE. I'm standin' yer for this!

FRED. Make that twice.

BARRY. An' me!

PETE (*to* LIZ). Wass yourn, darlin'?

FRED. Now or later?

PETE. Now, t' start with.

BARRY. Tea and crumpet.

LIZ. Could I 'ave a coffee?

FRED. 'Ave what yer like, darlin'.

BARRY. Cup a tea do me!

COLIN. Wass she 'avin' later!

LIZ. Dinner.

MIKE. Teas all round then.

BARRY. Right.

MIKE (*to* FRED). Sit down, we'll fix it.

PETE, MIKE *and* COLIN *go off left.*

FRED. Where's all the burn?

LIZ. I only got one left.

FRED (*calls*). Get us some snout.

MIKE. Five or ten?

FRED *makes a rude gesture.* LIZ *offers him her cigarette.*

FRED. Keep it, darlin'. I'm okay.
He turns to LEN *and* PAM. Oi, 'ello then. 'Ow's it goin'?

He stands and goes down to their table. LEN *has already sat.*

PAM. 'Ello.

FRED. Thass right, yer said yer'd be 'ere. (*Calls.*) That grub ready? (*To* PAM.) Yeh.

BARRY (*to* FRED). Big gut!

COLIN (*off*). Give us a chance!

PETE (*off*). They didn't teach yer no manners inside.

FRED. Yer're arstin' for trouble. I don't wan'a go back juss yet.

PAM. You all right?

FRED. Yeh. You look all right.

LIZ. Don't yer reckon 'e looks thin?

PAM. I can't –

LIZ. Like a rake. I tol' yer, didn't I? Yer wan'a get some
meat on yer.

FRED. I will when that grub turns up.

BARRY *and* LIZ *are sitting at the table up right.* BARRY *bangs
the table.*

BARRY. Grub!

COLIN (*off*). Ease up, louse!

BARRY (*calls*). Make that two coffees. (*He puts on an accent.*)
I feel like a cup.

LIZ. Ain' what yer sound like.

PETE (*off*). Shut 'im up!

BARRY *makes a gesture.*

FRED. Why did the policewoman marry the 'angman?

LIZ. Eh?

FRED. They both liked necking.

They laugh.

PETE (*off*). Why was the undertaker buried alive?

LIZ. 'Is job got on top a 'im.

They laugh.

BARRY. Why did the woman with three tits 'ave quads?

MIKE. We 'eard it!

The rest groan.

COLIN (*off*). What about the sailor 'oo drowned in 'is bath?

FRED. 'Is brother was the fireman 'oo went up in smoke.

They laugh.

PETE (*off*). Didn't know they let yer 'ave jokes inside.

LIZ. Wass it like?

FRED. In there?

LIZ. Yeh.

FRED (*shrugs. To* LEN). 'Ow's the job?

LEN. Stinks.

FRED. It don't change. (*He sits at their table.*) Long time.

LIZ. Got a light?

FRED (*to* PAM). I got yer letters didn't I.

PAM. Yeh.

FRED. I ain' good at writin'.

PETE, COLIN *and* MIKE *shout and laugh, off.*

PAM. Where yer goin'?

FRED. I'm goin' to 'ave the biggest nosh-up a me life.

BARRY (*to* FRED). Did yer be'ave yerself inside?

PAM (*to* FRED). No, after that.

FRED. O yer know.

PAM. Yer fixed up?

FRED. 'Ow?

PAM. I'll take yer roun' our place.

FRED. O –

LEN. Yer can muck in with me a couple a nights. Give yerself
   time t' get straight.

FRED. Ta, I don't wan' a put –

LEN. Yer won't be in the way for a couple of days.

PAM. Mum'll shut up. It'll be nice and quiet. Thass what
   yer need.

FRED. Yer must be kidding!

BARRY (*to* LIZ). Arst 'im if 'e be'aved isself.

LIZ (*to* FRED). 'Ear that?

FRED. Yer know me.

BARRY. Not 'arf.

FRED. One day.

LIZ. Yeh.

FRED. This padre 'as me in.

BARRY. O yeh.

FRED. Wants t' chat me up. 'E says nothin that comes out a a man can be all bad.

BARRY. Whass that?

FRED. Then 'e 'ops out an' I 'as a little slash in 'is tea.

LIZ *and* BARRY *laugh* – LIZ *very loudly.*

LIZ. What 'appened?

FRED. 'E reckoned they ain' put the sugar in.

They laugh.

Another bloke –

LIZ. Yeh.

FRED. Stares at me. Keeps starin' at me. All day. It's 'is first day, see.

BARRY. Go on.

FRED. So I gets 'im on the landin' an' clobbers 'im.

BARRY. Bang!

FRED. An' it only turns out 'e'd got a squint!

They laugh.

LIZ. Wass it like inside?

FRED. I got chokey for the clobberin'. Bread and water!

BARRY. On yer jack.

FRED. Only good thing there's no one t' scrounge yer grub.

BARRY. Yer d'narf tell 'em.

FRED. Ain' my sort a life. Glad I done it once, but thass their lot. Ain' pinnin' nothin' on me next time.

LIZ. Wass it like?

FRED. In there?

LIZ. Yeh.

FRED. Cold.

LIZ. Eh?

FRED. Cold.

Silence. MIKE *comes in a few paces from the left.*

MIKE. Won't be 'alf a jik.

FRED. 'Bout time.

COLIN (*off*). 'E still moanin'?

COLIN *comes on and stands with* MIKE.

FRED. Eh?

COLIN. Bet yer couldn't carry-on in there.

FRED. Lot I couldn't do in there, if yer like t' look at it.

MIKE. We ain' got a treat yer everyday.

FRED. I'll pay for this if you like. (*To* LIZ.) Lend us ten bob.

PETE *comes in*.

PETE. 'Oo arst yer t' pay?

FRED. I reckon it's worth one lousy meal.

PETE. Yer made yer own decisions, didn't yer?

BARRY (*comes down*). Wass up?

PETE. We ain' got a crawl up yer arse.

COLIN. Grub smell all right, don't –

PETE. 'Ang on a minute, Col.

MIKE (*to* PETE). Nah, it's 'is first day out, Pete. Let 'im settle down.

COLIN. Come on.

He starts to go left.

PETE. 'E ain' swingin' that one on me.

PETE *and* COLIN *go out left*.

MIKE (*to* FRED). 'E got out the wrong bed this mornin'.

MIKE *follows them off. Slight pause.*

FRED (*laughs*). It's the ol' lag comin' out a me! (*Shouts.*) Whoopee!

BARRY. Ha-ha! Whoopee!

FRED.
    She was only a goalkeeper's daughter
    She married a player called Jack

It was great when 'e played centre forward
But 'e liked to slip round to the back.

(*He laughs.*) I used a lie in me pit thinkin' a that.

COLIN (*off*): What?

FRED: Nosh.

LIZ. That all?

FRED. An' tryin' a remember whass up your legs.

LIZ. I'll draw yer a picture. Give us a light.

FRED (*to* PAM). Give 'er a light.

He gives her a box of matches. She takes them to LIZ. *To*
LEN. Wass 'er game?

LEN. I don't wan'a get involved, mate.

FRED. Yeh? Yer should a read them crummy letters she
keeps sendin'. She ain' goin' a catch me round 'er place.

LEN. No. What was it like?

FRED. No, talk about somethin' else.

LEN. No, *before*.

FRED. Yer 'eard the trial.

PAM *comes back to the table.*

Go away, Pam.

PAM. I wan' a finish me tea.

LEN. Thass cold.

FRED. Can't yer take a 'int? Take yer tea over there.

PAM. Wass goin' on?

LEN. Nothin'!

FRED. No one's talkin' about you.

PAM (*going to sit down at the table*). I'd rather –

FRED. O Pam!

She goes to the unoccupied table and watches them.

'Er ol' people still alive? If yer can call it that.

LEN. Yeh.

FRED. Yer ain' still livin' there?

LEN. I'm goin' soon.

FRED. Yer're as bad as them. She won't get me there in a
   month a Sundays.

LEN. What was it like?

FRED. I tol' yer.

LEN. No, before.

FRED. Before what?

LEN. In the park.

FRED. Yer saw.

LEN. Wass it feel like?

FRED. Don't know.

LEN. When yer was killin' it.

FRED. Do what?

LEN. Wass it feel like when yer killed it?

BARRY (*to* LIZ). Fancy a record?

LIZ. Wouldn't mind.

BARRY. Give us a tanner then.

LIZ. Yer're as tight as a flea's arse'ole.

BARRY. An 'alf as 'andsome. I know. – Out a change.

LIZ *gives him sixpence. He goes off down right.* MIKE *brings on
two cups.*

MIKE. Comin' up.

FRED. Very 'andy.

BARRY (*off*). 'Ow about 'I Broke my 'Eart'?

LIZ. Yeh. Thass great.

BARRY (*off*). Well they ain' got it.

LIZ. Funny! What about 'My 'Eart is Broken'?

MIKE (*to* LIZ). One coffee.

BARRY (*off*). They got that.

LIZ (*to* MIKE). The sugar in it?

MIKE. Taste it.

MIKE *goes off left.*

LEN. Whass it like, Fred?

FRED (*drinks*). It ain' like this in there.

LEN. Fred.

FRED. I tol' yer.

LEN. No yer ain'.

FRED. I forget.

LEN. I thought yer'd a bin full a it. I was –

FRED. Len!

LEN. – curious, thass all, 'ow it feels t' –

FRED. No!

He slams his fist on the table.

LEN. Okay.

FRED. It's finished.

LEN. Yeh.

FRED (*stands*). What yer wan' a do?

The juke box starts.

LEN. Nothin'.

FRED. Wass 'e gettin' at?

LEN. It's finished.

PETE, MIKE, COLIN *and* BARRY *come on.* PAM *stands.* LIZ
still sits.

FRED. I were'n the only one.

LEN. I ain' gettin' at yer, skip.

PETE. Wass up?

FRED. Nothin' a do with you.

PAM. 'E was rowin'.

FRED. It's nothin'. Where's that grub?

PAM. I knew 'e'd start somethin'.

FRED. Forget it.

PAM. I tol' 'im not t' come.

FRED. Where's that flippin' grub? Move.

COLIN *and* MIKE *go off left.*

PAM. 'E won't let me alone.

FRED. I'm starvin' I know that.

PAM. 'E follers me everywhere.

FRED. Ain' you lucky.

PAM. Tell 'im for me! 'It 'im! 'It 'im!

FRED. It's nothin' a do with me!

PAM. It is! It is!

BARRY. She's started.

FRED. 'Ere we go!

He sits and puts his head in his hands.

PAM (*to* LEN). See what yer done?

FRED. Didn't take 'er long.

PAM. It's your place t' stick up for me, love. I went through
    all that trouble for you! Somebody's got a save me from
    'im.

FRED. Thanks. Thanks very much. I'll remember this.

He stands and starts back to his own table.

LIZ (*starting to click her fingers*). I can't 'ear the music!

PAM (*to* LEN). Don't bloody sit there! Yer done enough 'arm!

PETE 'Oo brought 'er 'ere?

FRED. Chriss knows!

PAM (*pointing to* LEN). 'E started this!

FRED. I don't care what bleedin' wet started it. You can stop it!

PAM (*to* LEN). I 'ate yer for this!

FRED. BELT UP!

PAM (*goes to* FRED, *who sits at his table*). I'm sorry. Fred, 'e's
    goin' now. It'll be all right when 'e's gone.

LEN *does not move.*

FRED. All right.

PAM (*looks round*). Where's 'is grub? 'E's starvin' 'ere. (*She
    goes to touch his arm.*) I get so worked up when 'e –

FRED. Keep yer 'ands off me! So 'elp me I'll land yer so bloody
    'ard they'll put me back for life!

PETE (*moving in*). Right. Less get ourselves sorted out.

COLIN *comes on left.*

PAM. It don't matter. I juss got excited. (*Calls*.) Where's 'is
   breakfast? It'll be time for –
FRED. Breakfast? I couldn't eat in this bloody place if they
   served it through a rubber tube.
PETE. Come on! (*Calls*.) Mike!
FRED. All I done for 'er an' she 'as the bloody nerve t' start
   this!
PETE. Come on, less move.
BARRY. She wants throttlin'.

MIKE *comes on left.* COLIN *and* FRED *go out right. The door
bangs.*

LIZ. I ain' drunk me coffee.
PETE. I said move!
MIKE. Flippin' mad'ouse.

MIKE *goes out right. The door bangs.*

LIZ. We paid for it!
PETE. Move!

LIZ *and* BARRY *go out right. The door bangs.*

   You come near 'im again an' I'll settle yer for good.
   Lay off.

PETE *goes out right. The door bangs.* LEN *still sits.* PAM *stands.
Pause.*

LEN. I'll see yer 'ome. I'm late for work already. I know I'm
   in the way. Yer can't go round the streets when yer're like
   that. (*He hesitates*.) They ain' done 'im no good. 'Es gone
   back like a kid. Yer well out a it. (*He stands*.) I knew the
   little bleeder 'ld do a bunk! Can't we try an' get on like
   before? (*He looks round*.) There's no one else. Yer only
   live once.

SCENE ELEVEN

The living-room.

On the table: bread, butter, breadknife, cup and saucer and milk.

MARY *sits on the couch.*

HARRY *comes in with a pot of tea. He goes to the table. He cuts and butters bread. Pause while he works.*

MARY *goes out.* HARRY *goes on working.* MARY *comes back with a cup and saucer. She pours herself tea. She takes it to the couch and sits. She sips.*

HARRY *moves so that his back is to her. He puts his cup upright in his saucer. He puts milk in the cup. He reaches to pick up the teapot.*

MARY *stands, goes to the table, and moves the teapot out of his reach. She goes back to the couch. Sits. Sips.*

MARY. My teapot.

Sips. Pause.

HARRY. My tea.

He pours tea into his cup. MARY *stands and goes to the table. She empties his cup on the floor.*

HARRY. Our'n. Weddin' present.
MARY (*goes to the couch and sits*). From *my* mother.
HARRY. That was joint.
MARY. Don't you dare talk to me!

HARRY *goes out.*

MARY (*loudly*). Some minds want boilin' in carbolic. Soap's too good for 'em. (*Slight pause.*) Dirty filth! Worse! Ha! (*She goes to the door and calls*). Don't you dare talk to me!

She goes to the couch and sits. HARRY *comes in.*

HARRY. I'll juss say one word. I saw yer with yer skirt up.
  Yer call me filth?

HARRY *goes out. Slight pause.* MARY *goes to the table and
empties his slices of bread on to the floor. She goes back to the
couch and drinks her tea.*

MARY. Mind out of a drain! I wouldn't let a kid like that touch
  me if 'e paid for it!

HARRY *comes in. He goes straight to the table.*

HARRY. I don't want to listen.
MARY. Filth!
HARRY. There's bin enough trouble in this 'ouse. Now yer
  wan'a cause trouble with 'im!
MARY. Don't talk t' me! You!
HARRY (*sees his bread on the floor*). Yer juss wan'a start trouble
  like there was before! (*He stoops and picks up the bread.*)
  Middle-age woman – goin' with 'er own daughter's left-
  overs – 'alf 'er age – makin' 'erself a spectacle – look at this!
  – No self control.
MARY. Filth!
HARRY. Like a child – I pity the lad – must want 'is 'ead
  tested.
MARY. There'll be some changes in this 'ouse. I ain' puttin'
  up with this after t'day. Yer can leave my things alone for
  a start. All this stuff come out a my pocket. I worked for it!
  I ain' 'avin' you dirtyin' me kitchin. Yer can get yerself
  some new towels for a start! An' plates! An' knives! An'
  cups! Yer'll soon find a difference!
HARRY. Don't threaten me –
MARY. An' my cooker! An' my curtains! An' my sheets!
HARRY. Yer'll say somethin' yer'll be sorry for!

*He comes towards her. There is a chair in the way. He trips over
it. The leg comes off.*

MARY. Don't you touch me!

HARRY. Two can play at your game! Yeh! I can stop your money t'morra!

MARY. Don't yer raise yer 'and t' me!

HARRY *goes back to the table. He starts cutting bread. Pause.*

I knew yer was stood outside when 'e was there. I 'eard yer through the door. I'd a bet my life you'd come in!

HARRY. Old enough t' be 'is mother. Yer must be 'ard up!

MARY. I seen you stuck 'ere long enough! You couldn't pick an' choose!

HARRY. One was enough.

MARY. No one else would a put up with yer!

HARRY. I can do without! Yer ain' worth it!

MARY. Ha! I saw yer face when yer come through that door. I bin watchin' yer all the week. I know you of old, Harry!

HARRY. Yer'll go out a yer mind one day!

MARY. Filth!

HARRY. I 'ad enough a you in the past! I ain' puttin' up with your lark again. I'm too old. I wan' a bit a peace an' quiet.

MARY. Then why did yer come in?

HARRY. Me pools was in that table.

MARY. Yer was spyin'! Yer bin sniffin' round ever since! I ain' puttin' up with your dirt! (*She picks up the teapot.*) Yer can bloody well stay in yer room!

PAM *comes in.*

PAM. Chriss. (*Calls.*) It's them!

HARRY (*cutting bread*). I ain' sunk so low I'll bother *you*!

MARY. Yer jealous ol' swine!

HARRY. Of a bag like you?

MARY. 'E don't think so! I could a gone t'bed, an' I will next time 'e arsts me!

HARRY. Now 'e's caught a sniff a yer 'e'll be off with 'is tail between 'is legs?

She hits him with the teapot. The water pours over him. PAM *is
too frightened to move.*

    Ah!
MARY. 'Ope yer die!
HARRY. Blood!
MARY. Use words t' me!
HARRY. Blood!
PAM. Mum!
HARRY. Ah!
LEN (*off*). Whass up?
HARRY. Doctor.
MARY. Cracked me weddin' present. 'Im.

LEN *comes in.*

LEN. Blimey!
HARRY. Scalded!
PAM. Whass 'appenin'?
HARRY. She tried t' murder me!
MARY. Yer little liar!
PAM. Are yer all right?
HARRY. Yer saw 'er.
MARY. 'E went mad.
LEN. It's only a scratch.
PAM (*to* MARY). Why?
MARY. 'Effin an' blindin'.
LEN. Yer'll live.
HARRY. Blood.
PAM (*to* MARY). Whass 'e done?
LEN. 'E's all wet.
MARY. Swore at me!
PAM. Why?
HARRY. Doctor.
MARY. There's nothin' wrong with 'im.
HARRY. Scalded.
MARY. I 'ardly touched 'im. 'E needs a good thrashin'!

LEN (*to* PAM). Get a towel.

HARRY. I ain' allowed t' touch the towels.

MARY. I kep' this twenty-three years. Look what 'e's done to it!

PAM. *What 'appened?*

LEN. Nothin'. They 'ad a row.

PAM. 'E called 'er a bag.

LEN. It's nothin'. I'd better be off t' work. They'll give us me cards. We juss seen Fred. 'E looks all right, well 'e don't look bad. It ain' Butlins. (*To* PAM.) Get 'im up t' bed. Put the kettle on. Yer could all do with a cup a tea.

PAM (*to* MARY). What made yer start talkin'?

MARY. Yer 'eard 'im call me a bag. (*To* LEN.) 'E went mad over catchin' you last week.

LEN (*looking at* HARRY's *head*). Yer'll 'ave t' wash that cut. It's got tealeaves in it.

HARRY *dabs at it with the tail of his shirt.*

PAM. Caught 'oo last week?

MARY (*pointing to* HARRY). 'Is filth. (*Points to* LEN.) Arst 'im!

PAM (*to* LEN). What 'appened?

LEN. Nothin'.

HARRY. I was cuttin' bread. (*He picks up the knife.*) She flew at me!

PAM (*to* LEN). I knew it was you! (*To* HARRY.) Whass 'e done?

LEN. Nothin'.

MARY. Filth!

HARRY. I found 'em both.

He points with the knife to the spot.

LEN (*pulling at* HARRY). No!

HARRY. She'll 'ave t' 'ear.

LEN (*he pulls at him*). No!

HARRY. She 'ad 'er clothes up.

PAM. No!

LEN. Yer bloody fool! Yer bloody, bloody fool!

LEN *shakes* HARRY. *The knife waves through the air.*

HARRY. Ah!

PAM. That knife!

MARY. Filth!

PAM. 'E'll kill 'im!

LEN. Bloody fool.

PAM (*screams*). Oh! No! – Whass 'appenin' to us?

She sits on the couch and cries. Pause.

HARRY. 'Im an' 'er.

PAM (*crying*). Why don't 'e go? Why don't 'e go away?
   All my friends gone. Baby's gone. Nothin' left but rows.
   Day in, day out. Fightin' with knives.

HARRY. I'm shakin'.

PAM (*crying*). They'll kill each other soon.

LEN (*to* PAM). Yer can't blame them on me!

PAM (*crying*). Why can't 'e go away!

HARRY (*removes his shirt*). Wet.

PAM (*crying*). Look at me. I can't sleep with worry.

MARY. Breakin' me 'ome.

PAM (*crying*). 'E's killed me baby. Taken me friends. Broken
   me 'ome.

HARRY. More blood.

MARY. I ain' clearin' up after 'im. 'E can clear 'is own mess.

PAM (*crying*). I can't go on like this.

LEN (*to* PAM). There was nothin' in it!

PAM (*crying*). I'll throw myself somewhere. It's the only way.

HARRY. Cold.

LEN *goes to* HARRY.

PAM (*sitting and crying*). Stop 'im! They'll kill each other!

LEN (*stops*). I was goin' a 'elp 'im.

PAM (*crying*). Take that knife. The baby's dead. They're all
   gone. It's the only way. I can't go on.

MARY. Next time 'e won't be so lucky.

PAM (*crying*). Yer can't call it livin'. 'E's pullin' me t' pieces. Nothin' but trouble.

LEN. I'm tryin' t' 'elp! 'Oo else'll 'elp? If I go will they come back? Will the baby come back? Will 'e come back? I'm the only one that's stayed an' yer wan'a get rid a me!

PAM (*crying*). I can't stand any more. Baby dead. No friends.

LEN. I'll go.

PAM (*crying*). No one listens. Why don't 'e go? Why don't they make 'im go?

MARY. 'E can stay in 'is own room after t'day.

LEN. I'll find somewhere dinnertime.

HARRY. Me neck's throbbin'.

PAM (*crying*). No 'ome. No friends. Baby dead. Gone. Fred gone.

SCENE TWELVE

LEN'S *bedroom.*

LEN *lies face down on the floor. The side of his face is flat against the floorboards. He holds a knife. There is an open suitcase on the bed. In it are a few things. Pause.*

The door opens. HARRY *comes in. He wears long white combinations and pale socks. No shoes. His head is in a skull cap of bandages. He comes up behind* LEN. LEN *sees him slowly.*

HARRY. Evenin'.

LEN. Evenin'.

HARRY. Get up. Yer'll catch cold down there.

LEN. 'Ow's yer 'ead?

HARRY (*touches it*). Don't know.

LEN. Thass a good sign.

HARRY. All right now?

LEN. I was listenin'.

He draws the knife between two boards.

Clears the crack. Yer can 'ear better.

HARRY. Thass a good knife.

LEN. She's got someone with 'er.

HARRY. Thought yer might like someone t' say good night.

LEN. Yer can 'ear 'er voice.

HARRY. No.

LEN. She's picked someone up. I couldn't get anywhere with me packin'.

HARRY. No, I saw 'er come in.

LEN. Could a swore I 'eard someone.

HARRY. Not with 'er!

LEN. She's still good lookin'.

HARRY. 'Er sort's two a penny. Lads don't 'ave t' put up with 'er carry-on.

LEN. I used t' 'ear Fred an' her down there.

HARRY. No more.

LEN. Kep' me awake.

HARRY (*sits on the bed*). Tired. Nice 'ere.

LEN. Seen worse.

HARRY. Quiet.

LEN. Sometimes.

Pause.

HARRY. She's cryin'.

LEN. O.

HARRY. In bed. I passed 'er door.

LEN. I knew I 'eard somethin'.

HARRY. Thass what yer 'eard.

LEN *puts a pair of socks in the case.*

Won't be the last time.

LEN. Eh?

HARRY. 'Owlin in bed.

LEN. O.

HARRY. She'll pay for it.

LEN. What?

HARRY. 'Er ways. Yer'll get yer own back.

LEN. I lost me case keys.

HARRY. Yer'll see.

LEN. Long time since I used it.

HARRY. Where yer goin'?

LEN. 'Ad enough.

HARRY. No different any other place.

LEN. I've heard it all before.

Pause.

HARRY. Thought yer'd like t' say good night.

LEN. Yeh. Ta.

HARRY. They're all in bed.

LEN. I get in the way, don't I?

HARRY. Take no notice.

LEN. Sick a rows.

HARRY. They've 'ad their say. They'll keep quiet now.

LEN. I upset every –

HARRY. No different if yer go. They won't let yer drop.

LEN. Different for me.

He puts a shirt in the case.

I never put a finger on your ol' woman. I juss give 'er a 'and.

HARRY. I known 'er longer'n you.

LEN. She reckoned she was late.

HARRY. Ain' my worry.

LEN. But yer 'ad a row.

HARRY. She 'ad a row.

LEN. You shouted.

HARRY. It ain' like that.

LEN. I 'eard yer.

HARRY. It clears the air. Sometimes. It's finished. – You shouted.

Pause.

LEN. I'll 'ave t' look for that key.

HARRY. I left 'er once.

LEN. You?

HARRY. I come back.

LEN. Why?

HARRY. I worked it out. Why should I soil me 'ands washin' an' cookin'? Let 'er do it. She'll find out.

LEN. Yer do yer own washin'.

HARRY. Eh?

LEN. An' cookin'.

HARRY. Ah, *now*.

Pause.

LEN. I can do without the key. I ain' goin' far.

HARRY. Bin in the army?

LEN. No.

HARRY. Yer can see that. Know where yer goin'?

LEN. Someplace 'andy. For work.

HARRY. Round Fred?

LEN. No.

HARRY. She won't see 'im again.

LEN. Best thing, too. Yer ain' seen what it done t' 'im. 'E's like a kid. 'E'll finished up like some ol' lag, or an' ol' soak. Bound to. An' soon. Yer'll see.

He moves the case along the bed.

That'll keep till t'morrow.

HARRY. It's a shame.

LEN. Too tired t'night. Wass a shame?

HARRY. Yer stood all the rows. Now it'll settle down an' yer –

LEN. I 'ad my last row, I know that.

HARRY. Sit 'ere.

LEN (*sits on the bed*). It's bin a 'ard day.

HARRY. Finished now.

A long pause.

LEN. I'd like t' get up t'morrow mornin' and clear right out.
There's nothin' t' keep me 'ere. What do I get out a it?
Jack it in. Emigrate.

HARRY. Yer're too young t' emigrate. Do that when yer past
fifty.

LEN. I don't give a damn if they don't talk, but they don't even
listen t' yer. Why the 'ell should I bother about 'er?

HARRY. It's juss a rough patch. We 'ad t' sort ourselves out
when you joined us. But yer fit in now. It'll settle down.

LEN. No one tells yer anything really.

Slight pause.

Was she all right?

HARRY. Eh?

LEN. In bed.

HARRY. Yer know.

LEN. No.

HARRY. Up t' the man.

LEN. Yeh?

HARRY. I 'ad the best.

LEN. Go on.

HARRY (*quietly*). I 'ad 'er squealing like a pig.

LEN. Yeh.

HARRY. There was a little boy first.

LEN. In the war.

HARRY. Then the girl.

LEN. On leave.

HARRY. An' back t' the front.

LEN. Go on.

HARRY. I saw the lot.

LEN. What was it like?

HARRY. War?

Slight pause.

Most I remember the peace an' quiet. Once or twice the 'ole lot blew up. Not more. Then it went quiet. Everythin' still. Yer don't get it that quiet now.

LEN. Not 'ere.

HARRY. Nowhere.

LEN. Kill anyone?

HARRY. Must 'ave. Yer never saw the bleeders, 'ceptin' prisoners or dead. Well, I did once. I was in a room. Some bloke stood up in the door. Lost, I expect. I shot 'im. 'E fell down. Like a coat fallin' off a 'anger, I always say. Not a word.

Pause.

Yer never killed yer man. Yer missed that. Gives yer a sense a perspective. I was one a the lucky ones.

Pause.

LEN. 'Oo tied your 'ead?

HARRY. I managed. I never arst them.

LEN. I'm good at that.

HARRY. No need.

Pause.

Nigh on midnight.

LEN. Gone.

He takes off his shoes and stands. He drops his trousers.

HARRY. Yer don't wan'a go.

LEN. Eh?

HARRY. Don't go. No point.

LEN (*his trousers round his ankles*). Why?

HARRY. Yer'd come back.

LEN. No use sayin' anythin' t'night –

HARRY. Don't let 'em push yer out.

LEN. Depends 'ow I feel in the mornin'.

He sits on the bed and pulls off his trousers.

HARRY. Choose yer own time. Not when it suits them.

LEN. I don't know anythin' t'night.

HARRY. I'd like yer t' stay. If yer can see yer way to.

LEN. Why?

HARRY (*after a slight pause*). I ain' stayin'.

LEN. What?

HARRY. Not always.

LEN. O, yeh.

He puts the case on the floor.

HARRY. Yer'll see. If I was t' go now she'd be laughin'. She'd soon 'ave someone in my bed. She knows 'ow t' be'ave when she likes. An' cook.

LEN. Yeh, yeh.

He slides the case under the bed and sits on the bed.

HARRY. I'll go when I'm ready. When she's on 'er pension. She won't get no one after 'er then. I'll be *out*. Then see 'ow she copes.

LEN. Ain' worth it, pop.

HARRY. It's only right. When someone carries on like 'er, they 'ave t' pay for it. People can't get away with murder. What 'd 'appen then?

LEN. Don't arst me.

HARRY. She thinks she's on top. I'll 'ave t' fall back a bit – buy a few things an' stay in me room more. I can wait.

LEN. 'Ead still 'urt?

HARRY. She'll find out.

LEN. I can let yer 'ave some aspirins.

HARRY. Eh?

LEN. Can yer move up.

Harry stands.

No, I didn't mean that.

HARRY. Yer should be in bed. We don't wan'a waste the light.

LEN. I won't let on what yer said.

HARRY. Eh?

LEN. You leavin'.

HARRY. She knows.

LEN. Yer told 'er?

HARRY. We don't 'ave secrets. They make trouble.

He goes to the door.

Don't speak to 'em at all. It saves a lot a misunderstandin'.

LEN. O.

HARRY. Yer'll be all right in the mornin'.

LEN. No work t'night?

HARRY. Saturday.

LEN. I forgot.

HARRY. Night.

LEN. Funny we never talked before.

HARRY. They listen all the time.

LEN. Will yer come up next Saturday night?

HARRY. No, no. Cause trouble. They won't stand for it.

LEN. I'd like t' tell 'er t' jump off once more.

HARRY. Sometime. Don't upset 'er. It ain' fair. Thass best all round.

LEN (*looks round*). It's like that.

HARRY. Listen!

LEN. What?

HARRY *holds up his hand. Silence.*

Still cryin'?

HARRY. She's gone quiet.

Silence.

There – she's movin'.

Silence.

LEN. She's 'eard us.

HARRY. Best keep away, yer see. Good night.
LEN. But –
HARRY. Sh!

He holds up his hand again. They listen. Silence. Pause.

HARRY. Good night.
LEN. 'Night.

HARRY *goes.*

SCENE THIRTEEN

The living-room.

PAM *sits on the couch. She reads the* Radio Times.

MARY *takes things from the table and goes out. Pause. She comes back. She goes to the table. She collects the plates. She goes out.*

Pause. The door opens. HARRY *comes in. He goes to the table and opens the drawer. He searches in it.*

PAM *turns a page.*

MARY *comes in. She goes to the table and picks up the last things on it. She goes out.*

HARRY's *jacket is draped on the back of the chair by the table. He searches in the pockets.*

PAM *turns a page.*

There is a loud bang (off).

Silence.

HARRY *turns to the table and searches in the drawer.*

MARY *comes in. She wipes the table top with a damp cloth.*

There is a loud bang (off).

MARY *goes out.*

HARRY *takes ink and envelope out of the drawer. He puts them on the table. He sits on the chair. He feels behind him and takes a pen from the inside pocket of his jacket. He starts to fill in his football coupon.*

A short silence.

PAM *quickly turns over two pages.*

Immediately the door opens and LEN *comes in. He carries the chair that* HARRY *tripped over and broke. He takes it down right and sets it on the floor. He crouches. His head is below the level of the seat. He looks under the chair. He turns it upside down. He fiddles with the loose leg.*

MARY *comes in. She straightens the couch. She takes off her apron and folds it neatly. She sits on the couch and pushes the apron down the side of the couch.*

Silence.

Stop.

LEN *turns the chair upright. He still crouches. He rests his left wrist high on the chair back and his right elbow on the chair seat. His right hand hangs in space. His back is to the audience. His head is sunk into his shoulders. He thinks for a moment.*

PAM *stands and goes to the door.*

LEN. Fetch me 'ammer.

PAM *goes out.* HARRY *writes.* MARY *sits.* LEN *presses his hand on the seat and the chair wobbles.* MARY *takes up the* Radio Times *and glances at the back page.* HARRY *takes a small leather folder out of the inside pocket of his jacket. He places the folder on the table.*

PAM *comes in and sits on the couch.*

LEN *turns the chair upside down and looks at it.*

MARY *puts the* Radio Times *back on the couch. She pats the pillow.* PAM *picks up the* Radio Times. *In one connected movement* LEN *turns the chair upright and stands to his full height. He has grasped the seat at diagonally opposite corners, so that the diagonal is parallel with the front of his body. He brings the chair sharply down so that the foot furthest from him strikes the floor first. It makes a loud bang. Still standing upright he turns the chair upside down and looks at the leg. He turns the chair upright and sets it down. He crouches. He places the flat of his palm on the seat. The chair still has a little wobble.*

PAM *folds the* Radio Times *and puts it down.*

HARRY *takes a stamp from the folder.* LEN *sits on the chair and faces front. He puts his head between his knees to peer under the chair.* HARRY *licks the stamp and silently stamps the envelope. He reaches behind him and puts the folder and the spare coupon in the inside pocket of his jacket.*

LEN *gets off the chair and crouches beside it. His back is to the audience. He bends over the chair so that his stomach or chest rests on the seat. He reaches down with his left hand and pulls the loose rear leg up into the socket.*

HARRY *reaches behind him and puts his pen into the breast pocket of his jacket. He puts the ink in the table drawer.*

LEN *slips his left arm round the back of the chair. His chest rests against the side edge of the seat. The fingers of his right hand touch the floor. His head lies sideways on the seat.*

MARY *sits.* PAM *sits.*

HARRY *licks the flap on the envelope and closes it quietly.*

The curtain falls quickly.

Early Morning

The events of this play are true

EARLY MORNING was first presented by the English Stage Society at the Royal Court Theatre, London, on 31 March 1968 with the following cast:

ALBERT	Nigel Hawthorne
DISRAELI	Malcolm Tierney
ARTHUR	Peter Eyre
GEORGE	Tom Chadbon
LORD CHAMBERLAIN	Roger Booth
LORD MENNINGS	Norman Eshley
QUEEN VICTORIA	Moira Redmond
FLORENCE NIGHTINGALE	Marianne Faithfull
LEN	Dennis Waterman
JOYCE	Jane Howell
JONES	Hugh Armstrong
GRISS	Harry Meacher
DOCTOR	Gavin Reed
GLADSTONE	Jack Shepherd
NED	Bruce Robinson

Directed by William Gaskill

CHARACTERS

PRINCE ARTHUR	20 years
PRINCE GEORGE, Prince of Wales	20 years
ALBERT, Prince Consort	45 years
DISRAELI, Prime Minister	50 years
GLADSTONE, Prime Minister	50 years
LORD CHAMBERLAIN	old
LORD MENNINGS	young
LEN, Joyce's boyfriend	18 years
CORPORAL JONES	35 years
PRIVATE GRISS	19 years
DOCTOR	50 years
NED, a drummer boy	16 years
QUEEN VICTORIA	45 years
FLORENCE NIGHTINGALE	20 years
JOYCE, Len's girlfriend	50 years

Mob, Courtiers, Footman, Officers, Soldiers, Wounded, Firing Squad, Ghosts, Jurors, Bodies etc.

Most of the smaller parts may be doubled, and played by some of the mob etc.

The play is in twenty-one scenes. It may be played in four parts, with intervals after scenes five, ten and fifteen: or in three parts, with intervals after scenes five and fifteen.

Very little scenery should be used, and in the last six scenes probably none at all. Whenever possible the place should be suggested by clothes and actions.

Scene One

A corridor in Windsor Castle. PRINCE ALBERT *and* DISRAELI *come on.*

ALBERT (*looks round*). This is safe.

DISRAELI. Victoria's going to announce the Prince of Wales' engagement. Victoria's not popular. She's frightened. She knows a royal wedding will pacify the people, so we must strike now.

ALBERT. Exactly.

DISRAELI. You've been saying exactly for five years.

ALBERT. It's my sons. Not George – when we kill Victoria he'll come to heel, he's just her tool – it's Arthur. I want him to join us.

DISRAELI. I hoped he would. He's heir after Prince George. It would have given our coup the appearance of legality. But there's no more time.

ALBERT. I'll talk to him.

DISRAELI. Again?

ALBERT. Tonight. I'll tell him about the engagement. That'll shock him.

DISRAELI. All right, but tomorrow I start secret mobilisation. Tonight I'll bring the black list up to date. I was going to shoot them – to demonstrate our military support, you understand. But I've decided on hanging – that will emphasise our respectability. I'll keep the numbers down.

ALBERT. How many?

DISRAELI. We don't know all our enemies till we start. So far, eight hundred and thirteen.

ALBERT. Make it fourteen. People are superstitious. (*Looks off. Loudly.*) I shouldn't be surprised if it doesn't rain.

They go.

Scene Two

Windsor Castle. The Princes' bedroom. Dark. GEORGE *isn't seen till he wakes up.* GEORGE *and* ARTHUR *in bed.* ALBERT *comes in. He carries a candle.*

ARTHUR. George is asleep.

ALBERT. If I could talk to you alone for once – just for five minutes – we'd clear up all our misunderstandings.

ARTHUR. Be quick!

ALBERT. It's not easy, Arthur. Help me. Try to –

ARTHUR. Sh! (ALBERT *starts to go.*) No, he's asleep.

ALBERT. He spoke.

ARTHUR. He wants some water. He thinks he's in a desert. He always dreams that when he's frightened.

ALBERT. Why's he frightened?

ARTHUR. He's getting married.

ALBERT (*annoyed*). Who told you?

ARTHUR. Who's the woman?

ALBERT. We don't know. Disraeli's going to mobilise. I can't put him off any longer.

ARTHUR. He wants to make himself dictator.

ALBERT. Of course. But we can use him for a time. Your mother's the first danger. We must stop her before she causes the wrong revolution. She should have been a prison governess. She's afraid of people. She thinks they're evil. She doesn't understand their energy. She suppresses it.

ARTHUR. If you give Disraeli his head, he'll end up by standing us all against the wall.

ALBERT. No. Let him establish the new constitution, and then blame him for using force – because force is going to be necessary, let's be realistic – and stage a counter revolution. But you must be in from the start. You must accept responsibility. I mean personally, between ourselves. That's what I want.

ARTHUR. How many will you kill?

ALBERT. A few. Every time you open a bridge you know people will throw themselves off it.

ARTHUR. A purge.

ALBERT. No.

ARTHUR. Mother?

ALBERT. A place in the country.

ARTHUR. And George?

ALBERT. That's up to you.

ARTHUR. He'd have to accept it.

ALBERT. Good.

ARTHUR. So, have your revolution, get rid of Disraeli when he's done the dirty work, and make yourself Regent. I won't interfere.

ALBERT. No, you don't understand. I'm not doing this because I hate your mother. Hate destroys, I want to build. The people are strong. They want to be *used* – to build empires and railways and factories, to trade and convert and establish law and order. I know there'll be crimes, but we can punish them. The good will always outweigh the bad – in the end perhaps there won't be any bad, though I don't believe that. Arthur I can't do this alone. That would be tragic. You must promise to carry on my work.

ARTHUR. The trouble with the world is it's run by politicians.

ALBERT. I'm going to tell Disraeli you've joined us. That will give you time to think, and when you decide to join us – we need a code – you must say you've solved the riddle!

GEORGE *sits up in bed. He drinks some water.*

GEORGE. I thought I was in a desert. (*He sees* ALBERT.) Who's that?

ALBERT. I'm tying my shoe.

GEORGE. You're wearing slippers.

ALBERT. They don't fit. Goodnight. (ALBERT *goes out*.)

GEORGE. I shall have to tell mother about this.

ARTHUR. He has these little talks because he's jealous of you
    and mother. She should stop sending you notes.

GEORGE. They're state secrets. Goodnight. (*He lies down*.)

ARTHUR. We shouldn't quarrel. It can't be all my fault, and –

GEORGE. I try, I shall keep trying, but you'll never respond.

ARTHUR. That's not true! I always give way if it helps. I
    try to put myself in your shoes: it's not easy being Prince of
    Wales . . . One day you'll have to marry.

GEORGE. Yes.

ARTHUR. I shan't object.

GEORGE. Thank you!

ARTHUR. *I* can't marry! Have you thought of that?

GEORGE. That's up to you.

ARTHUR (*angrily*). No, it isn't! How could I involve a woman
    in this unless I was forced to? (*Slight pause*.) When you do
    marry we must stop quarrelling. She'll have enough to put
    up with without –

GEORGE (*suddenly realizing*). You know!

ARTHUR. You talked about it in your sleep.

GEORGE. I did not! I've trained myself not to talk in my sleep.
    He told you!

ARTHUR. Who is she?

GEORGE. That's no concern of yours.

ARTHUR. This is impossible!

GEORGE. Goodnight!

ARTHUR (*angrily*). I have no rights – not even the right to
    surrender. I'm sick of secrets and arguments. I'd like to be
    happy – just for the experience! That's all. And if that's all
    you wanted there wouldn't be any trouble. Instead I'm
    trapped!

GEORGE. . . . Water . . .

Scene Three

Windsor Castle throne room. The LORD CHAMBERLAIN, LORD
MENNINGS, *a* FOOTMAN, *other* LORDS *etc.*

CHAMBERLAIN. Her Majesty will be here directly.

MENNINGS. This trial should be a real jazz. Is it true the
woman's a lot older than him?

CHAMBERLAIN. Yes.

MENNINGS. You can't get tickets. The black market's sold
out.

CHAMBERLAIN. I'm as modern as anyone, but I'm all for
holding trials in secret and executions in public. That
simplifies government and satisfies the people. We should
never have abolished hanging. It was something to live up to.

ALBERT *comes in. Bows.*

FOOTMAN. The Prince Consort.

DISRAELI *comes in.*

FOOTMAN. The Prime Minister.

ALBERT (*quietly to* DISRAELI). Why's she summoned us
here?

DISRAELI. I don't know.

FOOTMAN. The Prince of Wales and Prince Arthur.

ARTHUR *and* GEORGE *come on. It is seen that they are siamese
twins. Bow.*

ALBERT. Have you solved the riddle?

GEORGE. What riddle? (*To* ARTHUR.) Well?

ARTHUR. What burns in water, drowns in fire, flies through the ground, and lies in the sky?

GEORGE. Well what?

ARTHUR. I don't know.

FOOTMAN. The Queen.

VICTORIA *comes in. Bows.*

VICTORIA. Albert, dearest, where have you been since breakfast?

ALBERT (*kisses her cheek*). My love.

VICTORIA. Thank you. You've cured my headache. (*She makes a formal address.*) Our kingdom is degenerating. Our people cannot walk on our highways in peace. They cannot count their money in safety, even though our head is on it. We cannot understand most of what is called our English. Our prisons are full. Instead of fighting our enemies our armies are putting down strikers and guarding our judges. Our peace is broken. You know that the Prince of Wales poses certain constitutional questions. Because of this the anarchists and immoralists say that the monarchy must end with our death, and so they shoot at us. They are wrong. Our son will follow in our footsteps, with his brother at his side, and in time his son will follow him. Our line began at Stonehenge, and we shall not fall till Stonehenge falls. We shall not abandon this kingdom to anarchy. That is why our son will have a normal marriage. His bride will be Miss Florence Nightingale.

FLORENCE NIGHTINGALE *comes in. She curtsies to* VICTORIA *and then to* GEORGE. VICTORIA *gives a note to her and a note to* GEORGE.

GEORGE (*reads his note*). Dear Miss Nightingale, I welcome you to Windsor and hope you will be happy here.

FLORENCE (*reads her note*). Thank you.

VICTORIA. Miss Nightingale is an expert sanitarian. We believe that to be a branch of eugenics.

ARTHUR. Why wasn't I warned?

VICTORIA. Warned is not diplomatic. Gentlemen, you may go.

MENNINGS. May I say how delighted –

VICTORIA. Thank you.

The others go. VICTORIA, ALBERT, GEORGE, ARTHUR, DISRAELI *and* FLORENCE *are left.*

VICTORIA. I will not permit family bickering in public! (*To* ARTHUR.) Of course this will call for some slight personal adjustment. But the country must come first. (*To* DISRAELI.) He'll make that girl's life a tragedy – and one day she'll hate me, poor child.

DISRAELI (*going with* VICTORIA). Ma'am, you wear a crown of thorns.

DISRAELI *and* VICTORIA *go out.* ALBERT *follows them. Slight pause.*

GEORGE. I'd better show you the castle.

ARTHUR. He's inspired.

FLORENCE. Why don't you cut . . .

ARTHUR. We can't. I have the heart – he hasn't got one.

GEORGE. There was a mistake. I'll show you the castle.

ARTHUR. I'm not in a sightseeing mood.

GEORGE. Well we are! (*He tries to pull* ARTHUR *with him. A brief, silent struggle. He stops.*) You! . . . He wants you to think I'm impotent without him.

FLORENCE. Isn't it nice here!

ARTHUR. I'm going to sit down. Join me. Talk. I won't listen. You'd better decide how many children you're going to have. Then you can warn me.

GEORGE. Bastard.

ARTHUR. Did mother tell you he swore?

FLORENCE. I'm so pleased to be here. I ought to tell you something . . . I love you.

ARTHUR. Another note.

FLORENCE. I was eleven when it happened. You were going down the street in a big carriage. You wore a sailor suit. You looked very . . . clean and kind and lonely. I prayed for you. I dream about you . . . I'm sorry.

ARTHUR (to GEORGE). Don't get too excited. It's bad for my heart.

GEORGE (holds her hands). Mother's clever. I knew she'd choose best.

ARTHUR. Warn me if you're going to kneel.

FLORENCE (to ARTHUR). I hope I won't get in your way.

ARTHUR. Break off your engagement. That's the best advice you've had since you got engaged. You don't know what you're letting yourself in for.

FLORENCE. I do – I'm a nurse. Can we look at the castle?

Slight pause.

ARTHUR (unsmiling). If you like.

They go out.

Scene Four

Windsor Castle throne room. The stage is bare except for some chairs, or a bench, upstage, and downstage two chairs or a smaller bench, by an open trap. DISRAELI and ALBERT alone.

DISRAELI. Next Monday there's a picnic in the Great Park. I'll dress my soldiers as servants. During the picnic the Queen will be shot together with anyone who helps her. I hope Prince Arthur –

ALBERT. He sees himself as a shrewd politician. He's not going to join us till we've seized power. But one thing: he'll never accept our hand in the killing. He's peculiar about his mother. It must look as if some stray fanatic kills her. We just step in to keep the peace. We close the ports and airfields, take over the power stations, broadcast light classics and declare martial law. The important thing is she mustn't recover: she must be shot dead.

DISRAELI. Well, shoot her more than once. Who's the assassin? You wanted to pick him. (ALBERT *puts his hands on the back of one of the chairs by the trap.*) Congratulations.

ALBERT. Oddly enough Arthur was talking about him. He said he'd murder his mother for five shillings, if he hadn't done it already for the experience. Victoria will tear him to pieces today – and I shall promise him his freedom. It gives us a motive – revenge – and it guarantees a good job.

The LORD CHAMBERLAIN *comes in. He has a pile of old clothes, tagged as exhibits. He puts them down.*

CHAMBERLAIN (*calls*). Bring up the prisoner.

LEN *and* JOYCE *are brought up through the trap by* JONES *and* GRISS.

MENNINGS. There he is!
CHAMBERLAIN. Rise.

VICTORIA, FLORENCE, GEORGE, ARTHUR *and* DOCTOR *come on. They sit upstage.* VICTORIA *is in the centre.*

VICTORIA (*to* FLORENCE). Pass me that hat, dear. I'm sitting in a draught. (FLORENCE *hands her the black hanging cap. She puts it on.*) Black's my lucky colour. (*To* LORD CHAMBERLAIN. Read the charge. Place?

CHAMBERLAIN. Outside the State Cinema, Kilburn High Street.

VICTORIA. Day?

CHAMBERLAIN. A week last Wednesday.

VICTORIA. Time?

CHAMBERLAIN. Evening.

VICTORIA. What happened?

CHAMBERLAIN. The accused killed Joseph Hobson, and then
   ate him.

JOYCE. 'E pushed in the queue.

LEN. I –

VICTORIA. Silence.

JOYCE (to LEN). What did I tell yer? I tol' yer wait, ain I?
   Yer can't take 'im nowhere.

VICTORIA. If he'd listened to you before he wouldn't be here.

JOYCE. Thanks, lady. I'll shut 'im up for yer. (To LEN.) Shut
   it. – Me best bet's ask for a separate trial.

LEN. I –

VICTORIA. Silence.

JOYCE. You tell 'im, dearie. (To LEN.) An' keep it shut.

VICTORIA. I shall proceed to sentence.

LEN (to JOYCE). 'Ere, I thought yer said I'd get me say?

JOYCE. Well, what yer wan'a go an' antagonise 'er for?

VICTORIA. Put him on oath, but don't let him touch the
   Bible. King James would turn in his grave. (LORD CHAM-
   BERLAIN holds the Bible in front of LEN.)

LEN. I swear to tell the truthwholetruthnothingbuttruth.

CHAMBERLAIN. Amen.

JOYCE. Go on.

LEN. We –

JOYCE. Louder.

LEN.
JOYCE. } We was stood in the queue for the State –

LEN. T' see 'Buried Alive on 'Ampstead 'Eath' –

JOYCE. No, 'Policeman in Black Nylons'. 'Buried Alive' was
   the coming attraction.

LEN. Fair enough. We was stood in the queue for –

LEN. ⎫
JOYCE. ⎭ 'Policeman in Black Nylons' –

JOYCE. – an I'd like t' know why chair accommodation ain'
provided. They don't wan'a know yer in this country. Thass
'ow yer get yer trouble. Yer pays enough. Not that I pay.
Me entertainments never cost me a penny, not that I wan'a
boast. Well, next thing this fella's pushed in up front. 'E
weren't there when we looked before, was 'e?

LEN. Never looked.

JOYCE. Don' I always tell yer count the queue in front? That
could 'ang yer.

LEN. 'E –

JOYCE. 'E crep' in with 'is 'ead in 'is paper.

VICTORIA. This? (LORD CHAMBERLAIN *holds up a blood
stained newspaper*.)

LEN. Picture a Manchester United page six?

JOYCE. Seven.

VICTORIA. The page doesn't matter.

LEN. Course it matters, it's United.

CHAMBERLAIN. There's a football team on page eight.

JOYCE. I was thinking a the earlier edition.

VICTORIA. Does he recognise the blood?

JOYCE (*sniffs*). 'Is.

VICTORIA. Go on.

LEN. We'd bin stood there 'ours, and me guts starts t' rumble.
'Owever, I don't let on. But then she 'as t' say I ain' arf
pecky'.

JOYCE. Thass yer sense a consideration, ain it! I'd 'eard your
gut.

LEN. I 'ad an empty gut many times, girl. That don't mean
I'm on the danger list. But when you starts rabbitin' about
bein' pecky I –

JOYCE. Now don't blame me, love.

LEN. Truth ain' blame, love.

JOYCE. Then wass all this 'she says' for? Anyway the 'ole

queue turned round for a good look! 'Ow'd they know it
ain' me? O, no, I ain' –

LEN. Wrap it!

JOYCE. I never 'eard that.

LEN. You're a rabbitin' ol' git! 'Ear that?

JOYCE. O, it's different names when he puts the light out.

VICTORIA. We'll leave that for the medical report.

LEN. Look, we're stood outside the State for 'Buried Alive on
'Ampstead 'Eath' – right? – me gut rumbles and there's
this sly bleeder stood up front with 'is 'ead in 'is paper –
right? – so I grabs 'is ears, jerks 'im back by the 'ead, she
karate-chops 'im cross the front of 'is throat with the use of
'er 'andbag, and down 'e goes like a sack with a 'ole both
ends – right? – and she starts stabbin' 'im with 'er stilletos,
in twist out, like they show yer in the army, though she
ain' bin in but with 'er it comes natural, an 'e says ''Ere,
thass my place', an then 'e don't say no more, juss bubbles
like a nipper, and I take this 'andy man-'ole cover out the
gutter an drops it on 'is 'ead – right? – an the queue moves
up one.

JOYCE. 'Policeman in Black Nylons'.

LEN. Yer can't win.

JOYCE. Me catch went. They don't 'ave the workmanship in
'em. I paid best money.

VICTORIA. Who cut him up?

LEN. Don't remember. (*To* JOYCE) You remember? It was
my knife. She 'ad the wishbone.

JOYCE. I know I stripped him. I kep' 'is knickers on. I don't
'old with this rudery yer get. Speak ill a the dead, but 'e
weren't worth the bother. Still, it makes a change. Yer
don't know what t' get in for a bit of variety. I suppose you
don't 'ave 'ouse-keepin problems. 'E 'as t' 'and 'im round, a
course.

LEN. Yer can't nosh an not offer round, can yer? Some a the
fellas off the queue give us a 'and, an' I 'ad a loan a this

'atchet from some ol' girl waitin' t' cross the street. Yer 'ad t' offer 'im.

JOYCE. 'Oo said anythin' about the queue or the ol' lady? I don't begrudge no pensioners. All I say is, there was a leg on the pavement one minute and when I turned round it's gone. Someone goin up the street 'ad that an' dodged round the corner, sharpish. Thass was wrong. They ain' even paid t' go in!

LEN. Then the commissionair blows 'is whistle and the queue starts t' move.

JOYCE. Thievin' ol' grabber. I know 'oo 'ad the pickins when we was gone. Anyway, I played it crafty. I drops a few bits in me 'andbag an' we 'as a little nosh when the lights went down. I don't 'old with that stuff they bring round on sticks. Give yerself a nasty mouthful a splinters in the dark.

CHAMBERLAIN. That's our case.

VICTORIA. I shall sum up.

ARTHUR. Where's the defence?

VICTORIA. Silence.

ALBERT. It would look better.

VICTORIA. Albert, you are always right. (*She turns to* ARTHUR.) You defend them.

ARTHUR. Has a doctor seen them?

ALBERT. Yes.

The DOCTOR *is nudged. He stands. His stethoscope is in his ears. Pause.*

ARTHUR. Have you seen these two? (*Someone removes his stethoscope.*) Have you seen these two?

DOCTOR. I have examined the accused. Loosely speaking one was male and the other was – I made a note of it at the time ... (*He finds his note. He stares at it. He realises that he is reading it upside down. He turns it up the right way.*) I see, it's a diagram ... female.

VICTORIA. That explains most crimes. (*Appreciative laughter.*)

MENNINGS. There are others. (*A frozen silence.*)

ARTHUR. But did you find anything that would help us?

DOCTOR. Most definitely. Both the accused have stomachs.

ARTHUR. Yes?

DOCTOR. That suggests – I wouldn't care to put it any higher than that – that the accused would experience from time to time . . . (*To his stethoscope.*) What? I'm so sorry, I thought you spoke . . . Pangs.

VICTORIA. Exactly!

DOCTOR. I protest! I was forcibly prevented from making an autopsy. Had I been given full academic freedom my evidence would have hanged them. (*He sits.*)

VICTORIA. I shall sum up: guilty.

LEN. Leave t' appeal.

VICTORIA. Granted.

LEN. I put the man'ole cover back.

JOYCE. It *was* 'Policeman in Black Nylons'. I remember because I like a good musical.

VICTORIA. Appeals dismissed. The sentence of the court upon you is that you be taken from this place to a lawful prison and that you be there kept until you are dead, and that your bodies be afterwards handed over to the doctors, and your souls to our lady novelist royal.

PARSON (*low*). Eureka.

LEN. ⎫ Lord George hanged my father
JOYCE. ⎭ Dad fell through the trap
       But he started bouncing
       Dad's neck wouldn't snap
       Lord George said to father
       Play the game, my lad
       But he kept on bouncing
       You can't hang my dad.

There is a scuffle.

VICTORIA. Put them down.

LEN *and* JOYCE *are forced apart. It is seen that they are handcuffed together.*

ARTHUR. No! (*He goes towards them.* GEORGE *moves reluctantly.* ARTHUR *stops by the pile of exhibits.*) You're handcuffed together!

LEN. She likes t' keep an eye on me.

ARTHUR. Why did you kill him?

LEN. 'E pushed in the queue.

ARTHUR. Why?

LEN. It's 'is 'obby.

FLORENCE. George is too close.

VICTORIA. Don't be frightened, Florence. I'll take care of you.

ARTHUR. Why did you kill him –

LEN. No fancy questions. I ain' being mucked about!

ARTHUR. You're sure these are his clothes?

LEN. Yeh!

JOYCE. Mr 'Obsons.

ARTHUR. Shoes. Socks. Trousers. Pants. Vest. Shirt. Mac. No tie. The cuffs are gone.

JOYCE. Thass 'im.

ARTHUR. Why did you kill him –

LEN. I said it ain' I? 'Is shirt! 'Is shoes! 'Is vest! (*He kicks the exhibits at* ARTHUR.) I done it! Thass that! Get, mate, get! They're 'is! 'Is! I got a right a be guilty same as you! An you next, matey! You ain' out a reach!

Some of the exhibits fall on ARTHUR. *He's draped in them.*

ARTHUR. Why did you kill him –

FLORENCE. George!

VICTORIA. You're trembling. You're so young. Let me take you away.

JOYCE. Be'ave. Yer'll land yerself in trouble one day.

FLORENCE. My arm!

VICTORIA. Darling, I won't hurt you.

VICTORIA *goes out with* FLORENCE. LEN *and* JOYCE
are bundled down the trap. LEN *sings 'Lord George' as he
goes.* ARTHUR, GEORGE *and* ALBERT *are left alone.*

GEORGE (*referring to* ARTHUR). Typical.

ARTHUR (*holds mac*). Can I keep this for a while?

ALBERT. I suppose you can.

ARTHUR. Mother will ban queues.

ALBERT. And films. (*He starts to go out through the trap.*)

ARTHUR. I've solved the riddle.

ALBERT (*surprised*). I thought you would.

FLORENCE (*off*). George!

GEORGE (*calls*). Yes!

ALBERT. Don't go to the picnic.

GEORGE. I'm going!

ARTHUR (*to* ALBERT). Why not?

ALBERT. Nothing. I didn't mean anything . . . (ALBERT *goes
out through the trap.*)

FLORENCE (*off*). O!

ARTHUR. I feel as if I'd eaten too much.

GEORGE (*he starts to go. Calls*). Florence?

They go out.

Scene Five

Windsor Great Park. A picnic chair. A hamper with a rug on it. The men wear flannels, blazers and boaters, except for the servants and the LORD CHAMBERLAIN. *He wears regalia or a uniform.* FLORENCE *wanders on.*

FLORENCE (*distraught*). I'm changed. Queen Victoria raped me. I never dreamed that would happen. George will know. I'll disgust him . . . I've started to have evil thoughts. Her legs are covered in shiny black hairs.

LORD MENNINGS *comes in. He carries a silver hip flask. Distant shots.*

FLORENCE. What was that?

MENNINGS. Shots. Aren't you well?

FLORENCE. Yes, yes.

MENNINGS. I like picnics. (*Laughs.*) Drink?

FLORENCE. No. No.

MENNINGS (*he pours himself a drink from the hip flask*). Bottoms up!

FLORENCE (*before he can drink*). I want that chair.

MENNINGS (*surprised*). Yes. (*He brings the chair to her. She sits.*) You're tired.

FLORENCE. Give me that. (*He hands her his drink. She takes off her shoe and pours the drink into it.*)

MENNINGS (*on his knees*). I knew it! (*He kisses the shoe on her other foot*). Governess!

FLORENCE. You dare touch me before you've earned permission! I own all the shoes in the world!

MENNINGS. I'm evil.

FLORENCE. Don't make excuses. You're a grovelling little pervert. I'll cauterise your lips where they touched me.

MENNINGS. O shoe-boss!

FLORENCE. Deposit my marching weapon on the floor. (*He does so.*) Drink. (*He starts to drink like a dog. Immediately.*) Did you say grace?

MENNINGS. I've sinned.

FLORENCE. I shall withdraw all shoes.

MENNINGS. No. No. More! One drop!

FLORENCE. I might allow you half a drop.

MENNINGS. O ma'am-boss-miss! (VICTORIA *and the* LORD CHAMBERLAIN *come on upstage behind* FLORENCE *and* LORD MENNINGS.) May – may –

FLORENCE. Stuttering?

MENNINGS. MayIdrinkitfromthetoe?

FLORENCE. If it comes in three. (*She holds the shoe over his mouth, with the open toe point downwards.*) One. Two. Thr – (*It trickles into his mouth. He is convulsed.*)

VICTORIA. That reminds me I'm thirsty.

FLORENCE *stands.* LORD MENNINGS *lies on the ground.*
VICTORIA *comes down and takes the shoe.*

VICTORIA (*to* FLORENCE). Please pour.

FLORENCE. I'd like to go home. I've had a fainting spell.

VICTORIA. I'm thirsty. (FLORENCE *fills the shoe.*)

CHAMBERLAIN. Ma'am, I can fetch a cup.

VICTORIA. Lord Chamberlain, you are like the bishop who always said amen after he'd lain with his wife. She became frigid. (*To* FLORENCE.) Cheers. (*She drinks and throws the shoe over her shoulder.*)

FLORENCE. My shoe ... (*She goes upstage and looks for her shoe.*)

MENNINGS (*watches* FLORENCE *on his hands and knees*). My shoe ...

VICTORIA. Lord Mennings, they're coming. I'll have you flogged.

MENNINGS. Thank you, ma'm; sir. By the shoe owner . . .

VICTORIA. Disgraceful. (*She swats a fly with a flyswat.*) Eighteen.

ALBERT, GEORGE *and* ARTHUR *come on.* ALBERT *carries a rifle, and* GEORGE *dead birds.*

ALBERT. Is there enough shade for you, dearest?

VICTORIA. It's perfect. (LEN, JONES *and* GRISS *come on dressed as rustics.* VICTORIA *clasps* ALBERT's *hands to her breast.*) Such pretty costumes! (*The rustics lay the picnic.*)

ARTHUR. Why is Florence limping? She's only been with us a week.

VICTORIA. She's lost her shoe.

ARTHUR. D'you dance?

FLORENCE. Dance?

ARTHUR (*sarcastically*). You dance with one shoe and I dance with four legs. It's called the hobble.

FLORENCE. I don't know that one.

ARTHUR. It's a new dance in honour of your engagement. She's very well brought up. She only dances to hymn tunes.

FLORENCE. Why is he rude to me?

ARTHUR (*surprised*). Rude?

FLORENCE. I can't find my shoe. (*She goes upstage.* ARTHUR *and* GEORGE *go to* ALBERT, *by the hamper, and* GEORGE *puts down the birds.*)

VICTORIA (*loudly*). I think it went over here . . . (*She takes* FLORENCE *aside.*) Freddie –

FLORENCE. George will –

VICTORIA. Darling.

FLORENCE. No.

VICTORIA. Call me Victor.

FLORENCE. Not here.

VICTORIA. Tonight.

FLORENCE. No.

VICTORIA. I've never had a girl with such deep feelings –
you've seen my maids of honour.

FLORENCE. Victor.

VICTORIA. I shall cherish that moment when I felt you were
a virgin. Will you do something for me?

FLORENCE. Yes, yes.

VICTORIA. Kill my husband.

FLORENCE. Why?

VICTORIA. He wants to kill me.

FLORENCE. That's wicked!

VICTORIA. O, you look for it in a husband. (*She swats a fly.*)
Twenty. He'll propose the loyal toast in a minute – that's one
of his pompous habits. You hand him his drink – and pour
the powder from this earring into it. (*She takes off an
earring and gives it to* FLORENCE.) No one will suspect you.
You look so innocent.

FLORENCE. It's pretty.

VICTORIA. Wear it, and I'll wear the other. That will make us
blood brothers.

FLORENCE. Victor, is it right to kill?

VICTORIA. You'll always be attractive because you're so pure.

GEORGE (*calls*). Florence, what are you doing?

VICTORIA (*calls back*). Lady's talk. (*To* FLORENCE.) Till
tonight. (VICTORIA *and* FLORENCE *join the others. Loudly.*)
It's hot. You must all be thirsty. (LEN *passes. He whistles
'Lord George'.* ARTHUR *notices this.*)

GEORGE. Florence, did the trial upset you?

FLORENCE. Yes.

GEORGE. Is that why mother took you out?

FLORENCE. I fainted.

GEORGE. But why did you scream?

VICTORIA (*interrupting* GEORGE, *swats*). Twenty-one! O,
twenty and a half. I once scored 187. (*Swats.*) Twenty-one.

ALBERT. I want to give you a toast. (*He holds a filled glass.*)

VICTORIA. Dearest, drink it from Florrie's shoe.

GEORGE. No!

ALBERT. Of course! You youngsters don't understand romantic gestures.

FLORENCE *holds the shoe and a rustic fills it.*

VICTORIA. Full. (*The rustic puts more in.* FLORENCE *poisons it and takes it to* ALBERT. *Swats.*) Twenty-three! Two at one go!

ALBERT. Ladies and gentlemen, I offer you the loyal toast – and Florence. And then we will pass the shoe round, like a loving cup. (VICTORIA *chokes. He drinks.*) Victoria. (*He offers her the shoe.*)

VICTORIA. I've signed the pledge. I'm teetotal. Drink is the ruin of the country.

ALBERT. But you must drink to our daughter-in-law!

LORD MENNINGS *runs to* ALBERT. *As he passes the rustics* LEN *whips out a pistol.* LORD MENNINGS *snatches the cup and drinks.*

MENNINGS. Nightingales! Eagles!

FLORENCE. He's drunk it all. (*Laughter.* LEN *tries to hide the pistol.*)

GEORGE. That man's armed!

VICTORIA. Treason!

LEN. Keep still a minute.

ALBERT (*goes to* LEN). Please give me that gun. (*Aside.*) Shoot her, you fool!

LEN. Well, make up yer mind!

ARTHUR *stands in front of* VICTORIA.

JONES. Contact base, sir?

ALBERT. Base?

GRISS. Wilco. (*He converts the hamper into a radio set by*

pulling out an aerial and plugging in earphones.) Dead Queen
to base. Are you receiving me? Over.

CHAMBERLAIN. It's highly organised.

JONES (*to* GRISS). Gettin' anythin'?

GRISS. Dead Queen t' base.

LEN (*to* ARTHUR). Move, sonny.

ARTHUR (*to* ALBERT). You said you wouldn't kill her!

ALBERT. But I knew nothing about this! You heard me ask
for his gun. He's crazed with revenge.

VICTORIA. Liar! This is your doing!

GRISS. Dead Queen to –

ALBERT. Put that bloody thing away!

JONES. O, 'e's got a make contact, sir.

GRISS. They're all 'anging on down the other end.

VICTORIA (*quietly*). George, keep him talking.

ALBERT (*quietly to* LEN). Shoot her – or I'll have you court
martialled!

LEN. 'Ow can I shoot 'er with 'im stuck in front? Yer said
don't touch 'im.

VICTORIA. I'm ready to die. I shall make a final speech. I need
thirty minutes to arrange my thoughts.

ALBERT. Arthur, I'm your father. Help me!

ARTHUR. You're a liar!

ALBERT. I'm running a revolution. You have to lie. (*He looks
at his watch*). I'm not well.

VICTORIA. At last! You've been poisoned.

MENNINGS. The shoe!

FLORENCE. That's not possible.

ALBERT (*staggers*). It hurts.

GRISS. Dead Queen to base.

JONES. Try the other channel.

ALBERT *falls.*

VICTORIA. Take off his garter.

CHAMBERLAIN (*goes to* ALBERT). I beg your pardon. (*He

tries to take the garter sash from ALBERT. ALBERT *struggles, and the* LORD CHAMBERLAIN *hits him with his hat.*) I only want to look after it for you, sir. (*He takes the sash.*)

GRISS. I'm getting somethin'.

VICTORIA (*swats*). Twenty-four. (LORD MENNINGS *falls.*) I shall pass my highest score. (ALBERT *tries to crawl away.*)

CHAMBERLAIN. Shall I put my foot on him, ma'am?

VICTORIA. Let him crawl, it circulates the poison. You can't crawl out of your hearse.

GRISS (*to* LEN). You any good with these things?

LEN *holds one headphone against his ear.*

ALBERT (*still crawling*). Shoot her, you –

LEN (*listening to the set*). You nutter! Thass Radio One!

VICTORIA (*comes from behind* ARTHUR). I don't like to see them linger – I'm a patron of the RSPCA. (*She strangles* ALBERT *with the garter sash.*)

ARTHUR (*tries to pull* VICTORIA *off.* GEORGE *tries to stop him*). No! No! Stop it!

LEN (*listens to the set. Clicks his fingers*). Thass my favourite number!

ALBERT. O dear. (*Dies.*)

VICTORIA. Let that be a lesson to you. (*Examines her swat.*) He broke my swat!

ARTHUR *kneels by* ALBERT. DISRAELI *comes on and stands behind* LEN *and the two* SOLDIERS.

GRISS (*listening to the earphones*). Dead Queen to base!

DISRAELI. She isn't dead!

GRISS. I got 'em! I got 'em! (*Into set.*) Spot of tech' trouble, sir. Delay in –

DISRAELI. I'm here!

LEN *and the* SOLDIERS *turn to face* DISRAELI. *They come to attention.* GRISS *salutes.* VICTORIA *picks up* ALBERT's *rifle. She points it at* DISRAELI's *back. She fumbles with the catch.*

LEN *sees her with the rifle, drops his pistol and puts up his hands.*
There are no other weapons on stage.

LEN. Permission to speak sir.

DISRAELI. Parade, shun!

ARTHUR (*takes the sash from* ALBERT's *neck.*) You stupid little
fool.

LEN. Permission t' –

DISRAELI (*to* JONES). Parade, report!

JONES. Dead Queen reportin', sir, all present an –

DISRAELI. But she's not dead yet!

JONES. Set konked out, sir.

LEN. Permission t' –

JONES. Battery went.

DISRAELI. I shall have something to –

LEN. 'Scuse me, sir, she's pointin' 'er gun at yer.

DISRAELI (*turns to face* VICTORIA). A counter attack. I'll
fetch reinforcements. (DISRAELI *goes out.*)

VICTORIA (*points to* LEN's *pistol on the floor*). He dropped his
gun! Get it! (LEN *and* GEORGE *both go for the pistol at the*
same time. VICTORIA *fires the rifle at* LEN. *It clicks.*)

GEORGE. Push the safety catch!

LEN *and* GEORGE *reach the pistol at the same time. There is a*
scuffle between LEN, GEORGE *and* ARTHUR. *They interlock in a*
bundle.

VICTORIA. Where's the safety catch? (VICTORIA *and* FLOR-
ENCE *examine the rifle. The* SOLDIERS *pack up the radio set.*)

FLORENCE. Is that it?

VICTORIA. Yes. (*She pulls the trigger. The rifle fires over the*
soldiers.)

GRISS. They're closin' in.

JONES. Better warn the others. (JONES *and* GRISS *go out.*)

GEORGE, ARTHUR *and* LEN *mill slowly round.* VICTORIA
walks round them trying to aim the rifle at LEN. FLORENCE
tries to swat at him with the broken swat.

CHAMBERLAIN (*brushes his regalia with a small pocket brush*).
I'll be with you in a minute. The late prince unintentionally
soiled my clothes when I was giving him artificial respira-
tion. If you don't go into battle neat and clean you never
win. One guardsman with polished boots is worth fifty
American rockets.

Off. A whistle blows.

VICTORIA (*prodding*). Is that you, George?

*There is a shot inside the group. They stop struggling. They fall
apart.*

ARTHUR (*groans*). Pain.
FLORENCE. Arthur's shot!
LEN (*looks for the* SOLDIERS). They bloody scarpered! (*He
goes out.*)
VICTORIA. Is George all right?

GEORGE *is holding his head in his hands.* ARTHUR *lifts it up. It
is covered in blood. Off: a whistle blows.*

ARTHUR. He's shot. I feel his pain.
DISRAELI (*off*). Double! Double!
VICTORIA. I knew it was going too well! (ARTHUR *winces
harshly. To* FLORENCE.) We must run.
FLORENCE. I can't leave George!
VICTORIA (*hustling* FLORENCE *out*). Quickly. We'll be shot!

Off: a whistle blows. VICTORIA *and* FLORENCE *go out.*

MENNINGS (*he holds the shoe to his mouth*). If you're dying
you might as well enjoy it. The last drop.
CHAMBERLAIN. My job is to serve the head of the country.
But who is the head? Uncertainty always leads to ineffective-
ness. I shall go to bed for a few weeks. By then my duty
should be clear. (*He bows to* GEORGE *and goes out.*)

GEORGE *is unconscious with pain. His head is on* ARTHUR's

chest. ARTHUR *has his eyes shut. Several* SOLDIERS *come on.*
They carry rifles. DISRAELI *comes on.*

MENNINGS (*diminuendo*). Shoe. Shooe. Shoooe. (*Dies.*)
DISRAELI. The day's catch?

Scene Six

A room in Windsor Castle. DISRAELI, DOCTOR, GEORGE,
ARTHUR. *The* DOCTOR *has a field dressing case with a red*
cross on it. GEORGE *and* ARTHUR *sit.*

DOCTOR. The Prince of Wales is dying.
DISRAELI. What about Prince Arthur?
DOCTOR. I shall cut him free.
ARTHUR (*looks at* GEORGE). He'll die.
DOCTOR. Yes. I give you my word.
ARTHUR. And I'll live? (DISRAELI *makes a sign to the* DOC-
     TOR.)
DISRAELI. Yes?

An OFFICER *comes in.*

OFFICER. Sir, the mob's collecting outside.
DISRAELI. Good.
OFFICER. Sir. Permission to fire.
DISRAELI. No. Don't knot the sack till it's full. I'll be down
     soon. (*The* OFFICER *starts to go.*) Have you found the
     Queen?
OFFICER. Sir, not yet.
DOCTOR. He's coming round. (DISRAELI *gestures to the*
     OFFICER *to go.*)
OFFICER. Sir. (*He goes out.*)

DOCTOR. Watch my finger. (*He moves his finger in front of* GEORGE's *face.*)

GEORGE (*snaps at the finger. Misses*). Bone.

DOCTOR. His brain's gone.

DISRAELI. Good. He'll be better off out of his misery. (*To* ARTHUR.) So you're King. The mob's outside. I'll read the riot act in your name.

The crowd is heard in the distance.

ARTHUR. I won't cut my brother off.

DISRAELI (*an angry pause. Calls*). Officer. (*To* ARTHUR.) You always said you wanted to get rid of him!

The OFFICER *comes in.*

DISRAELI. What's happening?

OFFICER. They're throwing stones.

DISRAELI. I'll come down. Doctor, stay and look after your patients. (*To* OFFICER.) Put more sentries on this door. We must protect their highnesses.

OFFICER. Sir. (DISRAELI *and the* OFFICER *go out. The* DOCTOR *opens his satchel.*)

DOCTOR. I'll give you an injection.

ARTHUR. No.

DOCTOR. You're in pain.

ARTHUR. It's gone.

DOCTOR. As your doctor I – (*Breaking glass. The mob sounds nearer.*) What's that?

ARTHUR. Glass.

DOCTOR. O.

ARTHUR. They'll break the doors next.

DOCTOR. They sound like animals.

ARTHUR. They'll be all right once they've lynched someone.

DOCTOR. If they're lynching they'll need death certificates. Is there a back way out?

ARTHUR. Down the corridor.

DOCTOR. The sentries will look after you.

The DOCTOR *goes out.*

GEORGE (*frightened*). Cut.

ARTHUR. No.

GEORGE. Breadboard.

ARTHUR. Walk.

GEORGE. Knifeboard.

ARTHUR. We'll slip out through the secret passage.

GEORGE. Cut.

ARTHUR (*opens trap*). You'll be all right. It's easy. (*He sits on the edge of the trap. Winces.*) O God. (*He climbs down.*)

GEORGE (*going down*). Cut ... Cut ... Cut (ARTHUR *helps him. They go.*)

Scene Seven

Forest clearing. A large flat gravestone. Otherwise the stage is bare.

GEORGE *and* ARTHUR *come on.* GEORGE *looks white.*

GEORGE. Eat.

ARTHUR. There was a battle. Bang field, yes? We must keep going.

GEORGE. Eat. (*He stops.*)

ARTHUR. No. (GEORGE *won't move.* ARTHUR *is too tired to struggle much.*) All right. I haven't heard the guns for an hour. Sit down. (*They sit on the gravestone.* ARTHUR *takes a cake from his pocket.* GEORGE *snatches.*) Wait! (ARTHUR *breaks the cake and gives some to* GEORGE.) Slowly! (GEORGE *gulps at it. Immediately his mouth slackens. Cake dribbles down his chest.*) Eat.

GEORGE. Sleep.

ARTHUR. You were hungry!

GEORGE. Sleep.

ARTHUR. If you don't eat you can't walk! (*He picks up the cake that* GEORGE *dribbled on the floor. He eats this. He puts fresh cake in* GEORGE's *mouth.* GEORGE *leaves it there.*) It's good cake. A lot of people are starving.

GEORGE. Sleep.

ARTHUR (*looks round*) ... I'm tired too. (*He scoops the cake from* GEORGE's *mouth with his finger. He holds it in his hand.* GEORGE *lies down.*) Goodnight. At least it's quiet here. (*He covers* GEORGE *with a coat. He eats the cake in his hand. He stares in front of him and chews slightly.*)

GEORGE. Hic ... Cold. Pain. Sleep. Eat. Sick. Cut. Die. Hic. Jacet.

ARTHUR. Hic jacet ... (*He reads the gravestone.*) This is our father's grave. (*He half rises, but* GEORGE *won't move.*) We've walked in a circle. (*He tries to stand.*)

GEORGE. Cold! Cold!

ALBERT *comes out of the grave. He wears a brown shroud.*

GEORGE. ... Wha'? ... (*He sees* ALBERT.) Death here! Death come! Run!

ALBERT. Shut up. – Arthur, no flowers? I've waited a long time.

GEORGE. Run!

ALBERT. Listen to it! (*He gestures* ARTHUR *to the open grave.*) That's the pit. I lie there and you tramp round and round on top of me. There's no peace. The living haunt the dead. You will learn that. (*He lifts his arms. Heavy chains run from them into the grave.*) I dragged these with me. Help me.

ARTHUR. How? How?

ALBERT. Kill the Queen. Make yourself King. Let the country live in peace. Let us die in peace.

ARTHUR. George is King!

ALBERT. Kill him too!

ARTHUR. No!

ALBERT. This is why you came here.

ARTHUR. No! It was an accident. We came in a circle –

ALBERT. You came so that I could cut him off! (GEORGE *whimpers.* ALBERT *comes slowly down from the gravestone as he talks.*) I had a state funeral. The Queen changed my will – I didn't know. It said I was to lie with my hands on my stomach holding a bible. So they laid me out like that. But when they closed their eyes to pray I reached out and took my sword. You can't face heaven with a bible in your hands. (*He takes his sword from under his shroud. There is no scabbard.*)

ARTHUR. No.

ALBERT. You were first in the womb. Your mother screamed and struggled and your brother thrashed his way out in front.

GEORGE. Run!

ALBERT *groans and shakes his shroud and lunges with the sword. The chains still run back into the grave and hamper him. He stamps and lunges.*

ARTHUR (*to* GEORGE). My arm! Keep still!

GEORGE (*shouts*). Cut! Cut!

ALBERT *lunges round* GEORGE. *Some of the lunges seem to hit him.*

ALBERT. Die! Die! Die!

GEORGE. Cock-a-cock-aroo!

ALBERT. Kill!

GEORGE. Cock-a-cock-aroo!

ALBERT (*stands on his grave. He gathers his shroud round him*). Cock crow!

ARTHUR. It's him.

ALBERT. Cock crow! (*He flays with his sword.*)

GEORGE. Ding-dong. Ding-dong.

ALBERT. Bells! (GEORGE *giggles with fright.*) Bells! Bells! My sword . . . My sword won't . . . (*It droops in his hands.*)

ARTHUR. It's him! Father, don't go!

GEORGE. Cock-cock-creewww! (ALBERT *goes down into the grave.* GEORGE *looks down into it.*) Ding-dong-bell, pussie's in the – (ALBERT's *arm comes out of the grave. He reaches towards* GEORGE.)

ALBERT (*off*). I'll frighten him to death! (*His arm goes down out of sight.* GEORGE *tries to pull away.*)

ARTHUR. Come here! He's gone!

GEORGE (*gasping. Struggling*). No!

ARTHUR. Don't pull!

GEORGE. You!

ARTHUR. He's gone.

GEORGE. Kill.

ARTHUR. No!

GEORGE. Let – let – go!

ARTHUR (*shouting ironically*). Let go! Let go!

GEORGE. You – glad – doctor – kill – me – but scared – Dis – Disra' – kill you – you run – save *you* – not me – you hate – always.

ARTHUR. Keep still! Father can't hurt you! He's dead!

GEORGE. Dead. (*Dies.*)

Pause.

ARTHUR (*looks up*). .... How long have I been here? I must cut him off. Your blood's like ice. I'm free. Tomorrow I'll look at a map. I must sleep. (*He lies down on the grave.*)

Scene Eight

Windsor Great Park. A lynching mob comes in. GLADSTONE, JOYCE, JONES, GRISS *and* LEN. LEN's *arms are tied behind him. His feet are shackled. He hobbles and jumps along.*

GRISS. Wass best?

JONES. The lot.

JOYCE. The lot plus extras.

GLADSTONE. This tree was made for it.

JONES. Oo's got the ball a string?

GLADSTONE. 'Old it, brothers. Trial first.

GRISS. Stick yer trial.

GLADSTONE. Yer 'ave t' 'ave yer trial t' make it legal. Yer
don't wan' a act like common criminals. Trial first, death
after: yer got a copy a the book. Wass the charge?

JONES. 'E – (*He pushes* LEN.) let that bitch scarper – (*He
pushes* LEN.) when we –

GRISS. 'Ere-'ere!

JONES. – 'ad 'er teed up nice for 'im. (*He pushes* LEN.)

GLADSTONE. So, brother, less 'ear your side. Speak out – we
don't tolerate no totalitarian larkins 'ere. Only keep it sharp.
We don't want our brothers on overtime. They need their
leisure same as you.

JOYCE. I was a virgin mother a nine an' 'e seduced me. 'E
showed me the bright lights an' I neglected me offspring.
Five died. Give me back me babies.

GLADSTONE. An old story.

JOYCE. 'E ought a be castrated.

GRISS. Castrated as well.

JOYCE. By the offended party.

JONES. This I got a see.

GLADSTONE. Is it in the book, brothers?

GRISS. Stick the book!

GLADSTONE. Now, brothers, don't get excited. Rules are
made t'abide by. One foot off the straight an narrer an yer
never know what yer'll tread in. The proper procedure is
vote an amendment. 'Ands up for castration.

All except LEN *put their hands up.*

GRISS. My vote's as clean as the next man's.

JOYCE. One woman one vote.

GLADSTONE (*counts the hands silently*). Castration in. Rule 98.

JOYCE. By offended party.

GLADSTONE (*counts the hands silently*). In. Sub rule 98 little i. Right, brothers. The book now gives us a clear guidance. (*To* LEN.) Well, less 'ear yer plead.

GRISS. 'E'll *plead* all right.

GLADSTONE. All right, brother. It's a good joke – don't spoil it by over indulgin'. Yer get too worked up. (*To* LEN.) Well, brother? (LEN *spits at him.* JONES *knocks him down and puts his boot across his mouth.*)

JONES. Spit on that. It could do with a clean.

GLADSTONE. Thank yer, brother. Spit I don't mind – it's a natural expression a feelin' – but yer're quite right t'protect the dignity a the court. Well, 'e's put the block right on. Yer can't 'ang 'im till yer've 'eard 'is version. Rule 53. (*He turns to* LEN.) Brother – (LEN *spits at him again.*) I'll 'ave yer spitting out a the ends a yer finger tips before I done. (*To* JONES.) Explain the legal situation to 'im, brother.

JONES. Will do, dad. (*He stands* LEN *on his feet and starts kicking his legs.*)

GLADSTONE (*strolls round the stage*). Life! Life! The sparrer falls, the mountain turns t'dust, we spit into the wind, an the ash blows back into our face. (GRISS *gives* LEN *a kick.*) Do my mincers see right? Yer can't do that, brother. Where's yer uniform?

GRISS. What uniform? I got a right a do me duty same as 'im. Change the rules.

GLADSTONE. Not twice in one day, brother. Rule nineteen. Drive slow an yer'll never bump into yerself comin' back. 'Oo uses a nose rag. (JOYCE *gives him a handkerchief.*) Thank yer, sister. I like me women folk t'be clean in their 'abits. (*He ties the handkerchief round* GRISS's *arm.*) Yer'll do now yer got yer armband up, brother.

GRISS. Cor thanks, pop. (*He salutes.*)

GLADSTONE. Now less see yer get stuck into a bit a team work. Four feet is one more than a yard. (GRISS *and* JONES *start kicking* LEN *again.* GLADSTONE *strolls round the stage.*) Time! Time! Suddenly the birds come, it's spring, suddenly they mate, suddenly they 'atch, the young fly, a few days and they're gone, the sickle's already in the corn, the fruit falls, the old man leans on 'is 'oe, suddenly 'e looks up, it's winter, and the skull's already on the window-sill.

JOYCE. 'E ought t' be on telly. (LEN *groans.*) 'E'd give a lovely epilogue.

GLADSTONE. 'E speak?

GRISS. Nah. Somethin' broke.

GLADSTONE. I ain' the one t'criticise the workin' man, as yer well know, brothers. But yer're too excitable. Yer lack yer discipline. Let an old 'and show yer – or should I say an old boot?

JOYCE. 'E's 'ysterical!

GLADSTONE: The secret is: move from the thigh an' let the weight a the tool do the work. That economises yer effort so yer can keep it up longer. (*He demonstrates without touching* LEN.) Watch that toe. Keep a good right angles t' the target. The other way looks good but it's all on the surface. Yer don't do yer internal damage. Study yer breathin': in when yer go in, out when yer come out. Got it? (*He swings his boot back.*) Out – thigh – toe – in! (*He kicks* LEN *once.*) Child's play.

GRISS. Gor, 'e travelled 'alf a yard!

JOYCE. I'll give yer a 'and.

GLADSTONE. Dodgy, darlin'.

JOYCE. Fair shares for –

GLADSTONE (*explaining*). It's the uniform, ain' it?

JOYCE. I ain' got no arm band, but I got a leg band. (*She shows him the top of her stockings.*)

GLADSTONE. It's stretchin' a point, but it'll do for an emergency.

GRISS. It'll do for my emergency.

GLADSTONE. Can yer squeeze in a little one?

JONES. I could squeeze in somethin'.

JOYCE (*lining up*). Ain' it a giggle?

GLADSTONE. One, two, three!

They kick LEN. ARTHUR *and* GEORGE *come in.* GEORGE's *skin is white and looks wet.* ARTHUR *supports him.*

GLADSTONE. 'Old up.

JOYCE (*kicking*). Yer pus-brained, murderous git! There won't be nothin left t'castrate.

GLADSTONE. Later, sister.

They stop kicking.

ARTHUR. 'Morning. (*Points ahead of him.*) Which way is this? (*Sees* LEN.) Ah. What's wrong with him?

JONES. Nothin' yet.

GRISS. We're killin' 'im.

GLADSTONE. Allow me t'introduce meself. William Ewart Gladstone. You're wanted for war crimes.

ARTHUR. Don't touch me. I've got Porton Plague.

GLADSTONE (*steps back*). It's a try-on.

ARTHUR. I caught it on your battlefields. My brother's died of it.

GLADSTONE. Leave off.

JOYCE. No – they look like that. I was late out for bingo one night an' I 'ad t' smother three a me nippers. I never 'ad time t'get 'em t'bed. They look juss like that when I come 'ome next week. I'll get the doctor. (*She goes out.*)

JONES. I'll see she's all right.

GLADSTONE. Stay put.

JONES (*taking off his belt*). Yer got a protect the ladies. Never know 'oo's roamin' about. (*He throws the belt to* GRISS.) Cop 'old a that. (*He goes out.*)

GRISS. I'd better give 'im a 'and. (*He goes out, undoing his flies.*)

GLADSTONE (*calls*). I'll court-martial the lot a yer!

ARTHUR. Help him up.

GLADSTONE. Let him lie. 'E's my son. Ain' many could a took 'is 'ammerin'. When 'e dies I'll be the first t'cry. I ain' ashamed a tears. Till then he lives by the book. Rule 5. Me an' brother Disraeli's formed a national government. We want you – so take my advice an' scarper. I can't nab yer on me jack, but I'll be back an' yer'll need yer runnin' pumps t'dodge me then. I'll see yer later. (*He goes out.*)

ARTHUR. Get up.

LEN (*sways to his feet*). O, Laws a cricket is it? Don't shoot till the umpire's scratched 'is balls. (*He tries to stand in a fighting pose.*) Less 'ave yer. (*Sways, looks round.*) Where's all the rocks? . . . (*His arms fall to his sides.*) Chriss, guv, be quick. Finish us off, guv. I 'ad enough. Be quick.

ARTHUR. I'm glad it's you. I had something to ask you. Why did you kill that man?

LEN. What man?

ARTHUR. Go home.

LEN. 'Ome?

ARTHUR. He's fetching troops.

LEN. Turn me back an' yer knife's in it. I 'eard a you blokes: can't look yer in the eye when they do it.

ARTHUR (*going. To* GEORGE). We must find somewhere for the night, George.

LEN (*realises*). You're a gent, guv! I won't forget yer, sir. (*He touches his cap.*) You'll need a 'and someday – an' I 'ope I'm in reachin' distance. God bless yer, guv.

ARTHUR *goes out, still supporting* GEORGE.

LEN (*coughs blood*). I've landed on me feet 'ere! If I was t' go t' the Queen an' tell 'er I knows where 'er boys is – thass worth two quid any day! Three if I play me cards right! Four if me luck's in! (*Slyly.*) . . . an then if I was t' . . . (*Gestures left.*) . . . an then if I was t' (*Gestures right.*) . . . I'd

be rollin' in clover – if me internal 'aemorrhagin' 'olds out . . .
(*He goes out cunningly after* ARTHUR *and* GEORGE.)

Scene Nine

Windsor Castle. VICTORIA *and* FLORENCE. VICTORIA *sits and knits a union jack.* FLORENCE *stands beside her dressed as John Brown.*

FLORENCE (*in her own voice*). The Lord Chamberlain's here.
VICTORIA. I'll see him.

FLORENCE *goes out. She returns immediately with the* LORD CHAMBERLAIN. *She now walks and talks as John Brown.*

FLORENCE. The ol' wuman'll see ye noo.
CHAMBERLAIN (*bows*). Congratulations, ma'am. I hear the enemy's been driven into Wales. They won't be any more trouble, they'll go native. The doctor says I should be in bed. But I've been away from my post long enough.
VICTORIA. John keeps an eye on me. (FLORENCE *and* LORD CHAMBERLAIN *exchange nods.* VICTORIA *knits.*) Lady Flora says you got her with child.
CHAMBERLAIN. Accidently, ma'am. It was dark. My wife and I don't converse during intimacy, apart from the odd remark about the weather. It was only afterwards that I discovered she was not my wife. (*Aside to* FLORENCE.) What's up that kilt?
FLORENCE. Did ye address me, laddie?
VICTORIA. John, I'm out of wool.
FLORENCE. Theer's enough sheepies heer in yon baggie tay nat wavies far yeer 'hae armee, wuman. As ma faither sayed; eek muckle the wuman, an the nattin wull sluther. That's wisdum.

VICTORIA. Help me wind.

FLORENCE (*holds the skein of wool on her wrists.* VICTORIA *winds the wool*). Wend, wend, wend, the loom a' leef a' wendit. If yor brack yeer thrud, aluck! ye'll nayer ment it. That was ma maither's constant reply.

VICTORIA. Thank you, John. Your thoughts are a comfort. I wonder if they'd make you archbishop.

CHAMBERLAIN (*aside to* FLORENCE). What's up that kilt? Am I your type?

VICTORIA (*drops the ball of wool*). It's dropped. (FLORENCE *bends to pick it up.*)

CHAMBERLAIN (*aside to* FLORENCE). What's up that kilt? When's your night off?

LEN *is brought in by a* SOLDIER. *His hands and feet are shackled again. He hobbles and jumps.*

VICTORIA (*still winds the wool, but looks at* LEN). Good! You've caught him. Dear Albert stood in front of me and took the bullet. You were tried in absentia and sentenced to be shot.

LEN. I never ment t' shoot yer, lady. I was going t' miss. I can prove it. I juss give meself up. 'Ow about a pardon an' five nicker?

VICTORIA (*stops winding*). Why should I give you money?

LEN. I know where yer boys is, luv.

VICTORIA. Where?

LEN. I need the money t' pay me legal expenses.

VICTORIA. Only a hero could find the Prince of Wales. You're pardoned. (*She counts out the money.*) D'you mind all silver? One, two, three, four. I'll owe you one. (*The* SOLDIER *unties* LEN. *To* LORD CHAMBERLAIN.) When he's shot see my money's returned to me. (*To* LEN.) How is George? (*To* LORD CHAMBERLAIN.) And don't let him spend any in the meantime.

LEN. 'E's dead.

VICTORIA (*stands. Her knitting falls to the ground. To* FLOR-
ENCE.) Pick up my knitting. (*She goes upstage.* FLORENCE
stoops and starts to gather up the knitting.)

CHAMBERLAIN. Allow me. (*He helps her*). You're a fine figure
of a scotsman. What's up that kilt? D'you know that one
about the horizontal sporran? I can introduce you to a lot
of nice people.

VICTORIA (*upstage*). The court will go into mourning.

Scene Ten

Near Bagshot. A cave. GEORGE *and* ARTHUR *sit on a box.*
GEORGE's *skin is wet and blotchy, and he is set in an awkward,
hunched position. The* SOLDIERS *are formed in a firing squad
on the other side. Their rifles point at* ARTHUR. *The breeches are
open. The* OFFICER *goes along the line and puts a bullet
into each rifle. After he has done so the* SOLDIER *closes the bolt.
There is silence except for the noise of the closing bolts.*

DISRAELI *takes a few steps towards* ARTHUR.

DISRAELI. I shall protect your name for history. Your
mother's assassins shot you. Your last words were 'St
George and Disraeli for England'.

The Firing Squad takes aim.

ARTHUR (*to* GEORGE). Ignore them and they'll go away.

GRISS (*listening on headphones*). Forward party's sighted
Queen.

DISRAELI. Good. My plan works. This can wait. (*To* GRISS.)
Remind the men to keep under cover. We'll ambush her
when she's inside. (*To* ARTHUR.) If you warn her, I'll put

a bullet through your brother's head. (ARTHUR *shudders slightly*.)

DISRAELI *and his men hurry out.* ARTHUR *and* GEORGE *are alone. Immediately* VICTORIA, FLORENCE *and the* LORD CHAMBERLAIN *hurry in.*

VICTORIA. So, you've finally killed my heir.

ARTHUR. He's got the queen's evil.

FLORENCE. What the devil's that?

ARTHUR. An old disease. Once the queen cured you. She kills.

FLORENCE. I mind noo I heard tell a yon. Try it some day, wuman. I'm awful partial tay experimentation.

VICTORIA. I'm a constitutional monarch, so far as medicine is concerned.

ARTHUR. Try.

VICTORIA. What am I supposed to do? He's dead.

ARTHUR. And now you'll kill me.

VICTORIA. The law does.

ARTHUR. Cure him. Try! – What's the use? You never –

VICTORIA. That's not true. You hate me, so you think I have no feelings. He was born first, but they said he'd have to die. Kill that poor little boy? I wouldn't let them, and you've never forgiven me. You exploited your position to come between us. You set Albert against me. I had to find happiness where I could: d'you think I like that?

ARTHUR (*to* GEORGE). I'll tell you a riddle. What drowns in water, burns in fire, lies in the ground and falls out of the sky?

VICTORIA (*dabs at her eyes. She reaches out to* GEORGE *and touches his shoulder*). Arise, my son! George, this is mother, I want you back. (*Slight pause.*) Good. (*To* ARTHUR.) You've been tried and I've dismissed your appeal.

ARTHUR. Blindfold him. (*He ties the scarf round* GEORGE's *head.* LEN *comes on.*)

LEN. All set? (VICTORIA *nods. He gestures to the offstage. The* OFFICER *marches back with the firing squad.*)

OFFICER. Squad halt. Right turn. Order arms.

ARTHUR (*at the same time*). She answers riddles. Who came first, the man or his shadow? The shadow, of course. I undressed a shadow once: it was white underneath and cried: it was cold.

GEORGE. Where am I?

FLORENCE. Take it off! (*She removes his blindfold.*)

GEORGE. Who are you?

FLORENCE. It's Florence! Florence! You were dead.

GEORGE. Why's she got a moustache?

VICTORIA. George, congratulations. I knew everything would come out all right. I hope you cut your father.

GEORGE. Why are you wearing those clothes?

FLORENCE. It's fancy dress.

VICTORIA. We're going to a party. To raise money for war wounded.

ARTHUR. What was it like? It's better than here?

VICTORIA. Be quiet. Let him thank me.

FLORENCE. I'm so happy again!

GEORGE (*touches his head*). My head. (*Tries to stand. Realizes.*) O. I forgot.

ARTHUR. We'll both stand.

GEORGE (*to* VICTORIA). Did you do this?

VICTORIA. Yes.

GEORGE. You had no right to!

VICTORIA. Arthur said –

GEORGE. Of course! It's you! Only you would drag me back to this misery!

ARTHUR. Misery?

GEORGE. Misery! You taught me that, why can't you learn it? – and let me die in peace! (*To* VICTORIA) You should have made him cut me off! (*To* ARTHUR.) Help! – look at my head! that's blood!

FLORENCE. I'll stop it.

GEORGE. I don't want it stopped! I want to die!

VICTORIA. That's enough. You haven't benefited from your experience. (*She turns away.*) Government must continue. Arthur must be shot.

FLORENCE. Not now!

VICTORIA. The court found he'd poisoned Albert's champagne. I'd like to pardon him, but Governments must keep their word. Officer! (*She takes* FLORENCE *aside.*) Listen, Florence. I'll tell them not to hit George.

FLORENCE. If Arthur dies he dies!

VICTORIA. Will he? The doctors say he will – that means he probably won't. And if he does I'll bring him back to life.

FLORENCE. But he's got no heart!

VICTORIA. He's got yours.

FLORENCE. Yes. I'll always love you – but I still love him.

VICTORIA. You did right to tell me. (*She turns away and goes to the squad.*) Splendid turnout. How's Mrs Smith?

OFFICER. Mrs Jones, ma'am?

VICTORIA. I thought so, Major Jones.

OFFICER. Captain, ma'am.

VICTORIA. Nonsense, I've just promoted you. I have a favour to ask in return. Shoot them both. (*Aside.*) I shan't resurrect him. I'll say my power's gone. Florence has only herself to blame. I can't share her – certainly not with my son. It's worse than incest, and I'm head of the church.

LEN. Could I have a loan a yer pistol, mum?

VICTORIA. Why?

LEN. Give 'im the last rites in the back a the neck.

VICTORIA. Yes, you might as well earn your five pounds. (*She laughs without opening her mouth. She gives her pistol to* LEN.) On your marks. (*The squad point their rifles at* ARTHUR.) Get set. Fire. (*The squad point their rifles at* VICTORIA.) . . . Let me warn you: I fire the last shot.

DISRAELI *comes on.*

DISRAELI. Good morning, ma'am.

VICTORIA. Private Jones, you're cashiered . . .

DISRAELI (*gives* LEN *money.*) Well done. I'll make you a life peer. Line them up. Ma'am, I trust we part friends. You stare death in the face magnificently. It must flinch.

The SOLDIERS *move* VICTORIA, GEORGE, ARTHUR *and* FLORENCE *upstage.*

CHAMBERLAIN. I shouldn't be out. I'll fetch my doctor's certificate. It won't take –

JONES. Up. (*He moves the* LORD CHAMBERLAIN *up with the others.*)

FLORENCE (*to* GEORGE). I'm afraid.

ARTHUR (*looks at her*). Try not to scream.

VICTORIA (*to the other prisoners*). Play for time. Something always turns up. (*To* DISRAELI.) I have the right to die like a queen. I shall give the orders. On your marks. (*Pause.*) Get set. (*Pause.*) God save the Queen. (*Pause.*) Rule Britannia. (*Pause.*) Unaccustomed as I am. (*Pause.*) In moments of crisis. (*Pause. She shrugs.*) Fire! (*Silence.*) Mutiny even now!

JONES. She makes yer piss run cold.

DISRAELI. On your marks. Get set. Fire! (*They shoot him.*) Betrayed! (*He falls dead.*)

GLADSTONE *comes in.*

GLADSTONE. Mornin', all. Morning, ma'am.

VICTORIA. We are not amused.

GLADSTONE. Tyranny shall be cast down. Beware thy left 'and in the night.

LEN. Squad shun!

GLADSTONE. Thankyer son, I knew yer'd see yer ol' dad right. (*Gives* LEN *money.*)

LEN. Three cheers for the people's William! 'Ip-'ip!

They cheer.

GLADSTONE. One's enough. We'll celebrate after openin' time.

VICTORIA. Dear Mr Gladstone –

GLADSTONE. Did yer know 'e wore corsits, ma'am? I ain' ambitious, but I thought no man in a corsit, 'oo puts 'is 'air in curlers, ain' good enough for Britain, even for the tories.

VICTORIA. William – may we call you William? – come over to our side and we'll drive together to St Paul's –

GLADSTONE. No drives, ol' lady. It's the chopper.

VICTORIA. I have one card left to play: prayer. (*She kneels in prayer.*)

CHAMBERLAIN. Bill – it is Bill, isn't it? My doctor says fresh air is bad for me, so I'll just –

GLADSTONE. Our's is a complete cure, brother. I'll address me army. (*He turns to the squad.*) Brothers, yer're now owned by the people's William. Up from the gutter, selfmade, shine like a new penny. Me secret is take it slow. Take it calm. Take it natural. The slower yer go the sooner yer get there.

VICTORIA. Amen. (*Slight pause while the prisoners look at GLADSTONE.*) O.

ARTHUR. Her gift doesn't work in reverse. A pity – that would be more useful to a politician.

VICTORIA. I never abandon God. (*She prays.*)

GLADSTONE. Remember me motto, boys: moderate it. What yer spend on beer yer can't spend on riney, but yer still get yer money's worth if yer take yer time. William knows. (*The squad laugh.*)

LEN. Three cheers for the people's William. 'Ip- 'ip! (*They cheer.*) 'Ip-'ip! (*They cheer.*) –

GLADSTONE. Two'll do, bretheren. Moderate it. Ready then.

Nice and slow. Never run through the door, it might be locked ... Steady aim ... Comfy grip ... Wait on the word ... One ... Two ... Two-an'-a-'alf –

He falls dead.

LEN (*goes to* GLADSTONE). 'Is 'eart! (*He puts his pistol on the ground and looks in* GLADSTONE'*s pockets.*) Where's yer pills, yer silly ol' bugger? Dad? I tol' 'im the cheerin' would go to 'is 'ead. – He's landed us right in it!

VICTORIA (*goes to* GLADSTONE). Authority shall be lifted up. The sun rises on the Lord's dead.

GEORGE *picks up* LEN'*s pistol.*

JONES. Watch 'im. 'E's nicked a gun.

GRISS. We're surrounded.

LEN. Best warn our mates.

JONES, GRISS, *the rest of the squad and* LEN *go out.*

FLORENCE. Don't George! Please!

ARTHUR (*holds* FLORENCE *off*). Let him do it! (GEORGE *shoots himself.*)

FLORENCE. O God!

GEORGE. Death again. (*He slumps.*)

FLORENCE. It's happened! It's happened!

VICTORIA. No time to cry! They'll be back.

FLORENCE (*sobs*). George! No hope! Nothing to live for.

VICTORIA. Now, now – we must count our blessings.

VICTORIA *tries to take* FLORENCE *out.* FLORENCE *breaks away and runs out ahead of her.* VICTORIA *follows quickly.*

GEORGE (*dying*). Yes, I remember ... We weren't joined together there, we were free ... when you die *you*'ll be ... free and happy ... when you die. (*Dies.*)

Scene Eleven

A clearing. The stage is bare, but there is something down left that looks like a pile of old clothes. ARTHUR *comes in.* GEORGE *is still attached to him, but he is now a skeleton.* ARTHUR *and* GEORGE *sit on a box, or can, and talk.*

ARTHUR. I did not give your foot to the dog! – Well why say I did? The dog took it. – I did not give it to him! I'd have given him a leg! (*Pause.*) All right, I'm sorry. I'm tired. You're not easy to carry. – I didn't say it's easy to walk on one foot. . . . You don't eat. That's your trouble. . . . At least you sleep. (*He drapes a coat round* GEORGE.) You're good at that. And you're wrong about the dog. (*Pause. Suddenly.*) I know I gave your clothes away! They were beggars! They'd been fighting. They were cold. – I did not! (*Pause.* GEORGE's *head is pointing down left.*) What are you staring at? (ARTHUR *stands, goes down left, stops, looks, turns, goes back to his box, and sits. Calmly.*) It's a body. (*Slight pause.*) We'll take turns to sleep. I'm not being blamed if you lose your other foot. (*Softly.*) Don't stare. Would you like to be stared at? . . . Is it someone we know? (ARTHUR *goes to the body. He stoops and looks closely at it.*) Him. I thought they'd get him. Undo his flies. (*He does so.*) She got her souvenirs. He wouldn't like that. (ARTHUR *has accidently uncovered* LEN's *face. His features are blurred. His hair is plastered. He doesn't grin. His eyes are shut.* ARTHUR *turns and starts to walk back to his box. He stops.* LEN *has spoken to him.*) I'm sorry. (*He goes to* LEN *and fastens his flies.*) I thought you wouldn't mind. – I know it's a liberty. Is that better? – Could we sit with you? Thank you. (*He sits. Pause.*) Travelling mostly. It's nice to hear some

intelligent conversation. (*He looks at* GEORGE. *In tears.*)
So many bones to be broken . . . (*To* LEN.) He can't hear.
I pretend he hears because I'm lonely. – You noticed?
Sh, I gave it to a dog. I woke up and this brute was slinking
off with its tail down and its ears back and his foot in its
mouth. I threw a stone and it dropped it . . . Then I thought
no. So I called it back and gave it to him. I'm a limited
person. I can't face another hungry child, a man with one
leg, a running woman, an empty house. I don't go near
rivers when the bridges are burned. They look like the
bones of charred hippopotamuses. I don't like maimed cows,
dead horses, and wounded sheep. I'm limited. (*He looks at*
GEORGE.) He won't miss it. (*Longer pause.*) I talk too much
– D'you dream? – So do I. D'you dream about the mill?
There are men and women and children and cattle and
birds and horses pushing a mill. They're grinding other
cattle and people and children: they push each other in.
Some fall in. It grinds their bones, you see. The ones pushing
the wheel, even the animals, look up at the horizon. They
stumble. Their feet get caught up in the rags and dressing
that slip down from their wounds. They go round and round.
At the end they go very fast. They shout. Half of them run
in their sleep. Some are trampled on. They're sure they're
reaching the horizon. . . . Later I come back. There's a dust
storm. White powder everywhere. I find the mill and
it's stopped. The last man died half in. One of the wooden
arms dropped off, and there's a body under it. (*He looks
off right.*) We're being watched. (*Slight pause.*) Some of my
dreams are better. In one, each man slaughters his family and
cattle and then kills himself.

The DOCTOR *comes in. He is covered with oil and smoke stains.
His clothes are torn. His satchel is dirty and empty. The flap is
open.*

ARTHUR. Doctor.

DOCTOR (*going*). No supplies. Keep still. Try to sleep.

ARTHUR. Is this the way to Windsor?

DOCTOR (*points*). There.

ARTHUR. Who won?

DOCTOR. We're regrouping. (*He walks round the stage, looking off.*)

ARTHUR. Was Napoleon there?

DOCTOR. I didn't see him.

ARTHUR. Hitler? Einstein?

DOCTOR. Try to sleep.

ARTHUR. Doctor, you're a medical man. Why do men hate life? Is it the light? Is it more comfortable to be mud and ashes? (*The* DOCTOR *crosses to the other side and looks off.*) Why do the good men work for the bad men? Doctor? (*He turns to* LEN.) Not many people rise to the heights of Hitler. Most of them only nurse little hates. They kill under license. Doctor, Hitler had vision. He knew we hated ourselves, and each other, so out of charity he let us kill and be killed.

DOCTOR. No supplies. (*He crosses the stage and looks off.*)

ARTHUR. Heil Hitler! Heil Einstein! Hitler gets a bad name, and Einstein's good. But it doesn't matter, the good still kill. And the civilized kill more than the savage. That's what science is for, even when it's doing good. Civilization is just bigger heaps of dead. Count them.

DOCTOR (*crossing the stage*). Try to sleep.

ARTHUR. It's unfair to Hitler. With his insight he could have killed himself at twenty. Instead, he stayed alive and did his duty. He must have known it would lead to misunderstandings. Well, saints expect the cross. Doctor, why don't you ask me something? Ask me why doesn't everyone just kill himself? That's simplest. But you see, they don't just hate their own life – they hate life itself. It's a matter of conscience, like duty in the blood: they stay alive to kill. They can't die in peace till they've seen the world dead first.

That's why they have doctors and drugs and anti-famine weeks and scientists and factories and comfort to keep them alive – when their only happiness is being dead. It's tragic. But not for long. They're clever. They'll soon learn how to grant their own wishes. (*He sees that the* DOCTOR *has gone.*) Pity. I wanted to tell him why I'm going back to Windsor. The world's been lucky: there's always been enough dictators to ease its misery. But even Hitler had his limitations. He pretended – in my dark moments I even think he pretended to himself – that he killed for the sake of something else. But I've discovered the logical thing for men to do next. It's a real step in human progress. For the first time in my life I can be useful. Hitler protected his own people. What we need now is the great traitor: who kills both sides, his and theirs. I'm surprised no one's seen it. It lets you kill twice as many. He wants to congratulate me. (*He takes* GEORGE's *hand*). First I'll take over the mob – it's easy now they've lost their old leader. Then we'll go on to Windsor. Shake. (*He shakes* GEORGE's *hand.*)

Scene Twelve

The Long Walk at Windsor. Three corpses hang on a gallows upstage. Another corpse is tied to a gallows-post. And two other corpses to the other gallows-post. These last three have been blindfolded and shot. VICTORIA *and* FLORENCE.

FLORENCE. I was better today. It's a question of taking it calmly and getting all your things ready beforehand. Like cooking.

VICTORIA. You make me proud.

FLORENCE (*looks off*). What does Arthur want?

VICTORIA. We'll soon know. I've told the sentries to bring

him straight up. Florrie, you're not wearing your kilt
again.

FLORENCE. No.

VICTORIA. I wish you would.

FLORENCE. I can't do the accent.

VICTORIA. Try. If they knew you were a woman there'd be
a scandal.

ARTHUR *comes on.* GEORGE *is still attached to him, but a leg,
an arm and half the ribs are gone.*

VICTORIA. I got your letter. I don't usually receive war
criminals.

ARTHUR (*looks at the gallows*). Who were they?

VICTORIA. They were all called Albert. I can't take chances.

FLORENCE. I didn't shoot the ones on the posts, but I hanged
the others.

ARTHUR (*looks across at them*). Good, good.

FLORENCE. I'm the first hangwoman in history – public
hangwoman, that is. It's part of our war effort. We take over
any man's job that's suitable.

ARTHUR. I'm sure *they* prefer it.

FLORENCE. Victoria knits the hoods.

VICTORIA. I run a knitting circle for ladies. They like to be
useful.

FLORENCE. I use a new hood each time. It adds that little
touch of feminine sensibility. That's very precious in war.

ARTHUR. What d'you charge?

FLORENCE. Just pin money.

ARTHUR *goes to the gallows. He unblindfolds one of the shot
men. He looks at him. A long silent pause.* FLORENCE *tip-toes
to the gallows. She takes hold of the feet of one of the hanging men
and swings the body so that it kicks* ARTHUR.

FLORENCE. Penny for them.

ARTHUR. Just admiring . . .

VICTORIA. You call yourself King.

ARTHUR. Yes.

VICTORIA. And you tell your men they're winning.

ARTHUR. I want to betray them.

VICTORIA. Why?

ARTHUR. You were right and I was wrong. I had no political experience. Now I've learned that justice depends on law and order, unfortunately. The mob's sadistic, violent, vicious, cruel, anarchic, dangerous, murderous, treacherous, cunning, crude, disloyal, dirty, destructive, sadistic –

FLORENCE. You said that.

VICTORIA. Foulmouthed.

ARTHUR. Yes.

VICTORIA. And unwashed. I'm delighted! There's nothing like political responsibility for educating a man.

ARTHUR. The animals would blush to call him brother. The earth isn't his – he stole it, and now he messes in it. Even lice crawl off him, like rats abandoning a doomed ship. He has no pity. He can't see further than his own shadow. He eats his own swill and makes his own night and hides in it. That's what's wrong with the world: it's inhabited. To live! Live is evil spelt backwards. It is also an anagram of vile.

VICTORIA. Yes. We must keep a sense of proportion. Hate is an anagram of ... Death is an anagram of ... I'm always kind when I can be. It makes you liked. Your letter mentioned a plan.

ARTHUR. I've brought a long rope. I'll arrange a tug of war between our armies. We'll say it's the final effort. We'll put everyone on the rope: every man, woman, child, horse, dog, cat, bird – even the sick. I'll choose a site and line my side up with a precipice behind them. We'll start pulling in the normal way, and when everyone's pulling flat out I – or you – give a signal. Immediately everyone on your side drops the rope. My side will be pulling flat out. They'll rush back over the precipice and be killed. It's very deep.

VICTORIA. It sounds sensible.

ARTHUR. I said I was going for a stroll. They'll miss me. Let me send you the details later. (*Suddenly, to* FLORENCE.) Why are you staring at him? Didn't you like him?

FLORENCE. Yes.

ARTHUR (*hesitates*). He always talks about you. It's irritating. (*He goes out.*)

VICTORIA. I prayed for this to happen! He's mad. But that doesn't matter. If we can just get his side together, we'll beat them. And perhaps he *will* get rid of them – and then we'll get rid of him. This is what I've dreamed of: peace.

FLORENCE. I'm going to the front.

VICTORIA. No.

FLORENCE. That's why I've been unhappy. I knew it when I saw those bones. Men are dying.

VICTORIA. I need you! (FLORENCE *starts to go.*) Florrie! Fred! You'll be killed! You're all I live for. (FLORENCE *goes out.*) Again, again! Things seem to go better, and then suddenly I lose everything. Freddie, don't leave me! Don't Don't!

VICTORIA *follows* FLORENCE *out*.

Scene Thirteen

Slough. A hospital ward. The stage is bare. Men lie in blankets on the floor. NED, *a drummer boy,* JONES *and other soldiers.* GRISS *is being brought in.*

JONES. What copped you, mate?

GRISS. Leg off.

NED. Juss the one?

GRISS. Yeh.

NED. So far.

GRISS. That true?

JONES. About this ward?

GRISS. Yeh!

NED. It's true. But she don't let yer in till you're down for dyin'.

GRISS. What a way t' go.

NED. I'm 16, but I'll die 'appy.

GRISS. Wass 'e lost?

JONES. 'Is cherry.

NED. So long as you ain' 'ad it, yer grotty ol' 'oodlum. (*He drums a roll.*) I got a lot a give thanks for. If I was 'ome I'd still be developin' the muscles in me right wrist. 'Ere I've 'ad more 'ole than the ol' fella ever 'ad off the ol' lady, an' they're celebratin' their silver bung-up. (*He drums a roll.*)

FLORENCE *comes on. She carries a lamp.*

VOICES. Bless yer mum. God bless yer mum. Angel a Mons. Angel a mercy. 'Underneath the lamp light dum-di-dum-di-dum.'

FLORENCE. Good evening, boys. (*To* GRISS.) You're the new man?

GRISS. Permission t' touch yer skirt, lady.

NED. ''Or! They're scrapin' the barrel – they're sendin' out fetishists. Another one t' jerk off in 'er shadder.

FLORENCE. Ned.

NED. It still hurts.

FLORENCE. Where?

NED. Give us yer 'and an' I'll take yer on a guided tour.

FLORENCE. I have a letter from the Queen.

NED. Don't ask me t' stand by me bed. There'd be sensation.

JONES. We wouldn't notice, sonny.

FLORENCE (*reads*). Dear men, I want you to know you are always in my thoughts, night and day. I too have made my sacrifice to this war, and I know what suffering is. (*She holds the letter nearer the lamp*). I can't see.

NED. Won'a loan a bigger wick?

FLORENCE. I have planned a tug-of-war against the enemy. You will all take part. (*Groans.*) Crutches and wheel chairs will be provided. After the victory you may go home. (*Cheers, laughter, whistles.*) I have a large stock of knitted material, and this is being made into bed-jackets for you. (*A wolf-whistle.*) Miss Nightingale has you in good hands. (*Groans.*) God bless you all, Victoria RI.

GRISS. Could I keep it, mum. (FLORENCE *gives him the letter.*)

NED. 'Ere, 'e's a sentimentalist under all that dirt.

JONES. Wrap up.

NED. Watch it. I'll be over there and stick me drumsticks where yer 'ide yer wallet. Both of 'em. (*He drums a roll.*)

JONES (*immediately*). I'm still waitin'.

GRISS. An' me, mate.

NED (*to* GRISS). O matey, you wan' a watch yerself. 'E fancies one-legged corpses. 'E ought to be in quarantine. (*He drums a roll.*) Remember the drummer boy! (*To* FLORENCE.) Come on, luv, less 'ave the names out the 'at. (*He gives her a military cap.*) 'Oo's first bash t'night. Give it a good shake. (*He drums a roll as she picks out a twist of paper and unfolds it. He stops and she reads the name.*)

FLORENCE. Ned.

JONES. Stone me!

NED. She's chuffed! Thass what we like. A drop a keenness is like salt on chips.

JONES. Don't know what yer see in 'im, ol' girl. Yer got me 'ere.

NED. I take 'er mind off 'er murky past.

FLORENCE. He's the purest person I know. He has most of the virtues of Christ, and none of his vices.

NED. An' I do it all on one ball. The Light Brigade charged

over the other one. Could a bin a lot worse. Could a bin the 'Eavy Brigade. Less 'ave the light out.

JONES. 'Old on, give 'er time to read the other names.

FLORENCE (*reads*). Ned, Ned, Ned –

GRISS. 'E's put 'is bleedin' monica on every bleedin' slip. The scabby little –

JONES (*To* GRISS). All right, lad. We'll write the names t'morra.

JONES *lowers the lamp as* FLORENCE *goes to* NED. *She stands by him. The light is almost out. She goes back to* JONES.

FLORENCE. Give me the lamp. (*He gives her the lamp. She turns it full up and goes back to* NED. *She looks at him.*) He's dead . . .

Silence.

GRISS. Stroll on . . .

JONES. The silly little . . . 'Ow many times I told 'im take it easy?

FLORENCE. I'll tell the men to –

JONES. No. Let 'im be. 'E's all right for a bit. It's cold in the corridor.

Scene Fourteen

Beachy Head. Bare stage. The two sides are lining up on the rope. Some are on crutches and in splints. GEORGE *is still attached to* ARTHUR, *but he is now only a skull and a few bones, like a ragged epaulette, on* ARTHUR's *shoulder.*

VICTORIA (*upstage*). Let us thank God for granting us victory.

HER MEN. Amen.

JONES. 'E ain't give us it yet.

ARTHUR (*downstage. He talks to the skull*). Have you guessed?
    This riddle isn't hard. When my men go over the side what
    will hers do? What can you trust them to do? What would
    you expect them to do? What's the natural thing, the normal
    thing, the human thing to do? Run to the edge and watch
    the others die. Her whole army will stand along the edge.
    That's why I chose it. It's weak, it'll give, and her men will
    fall down on top of my men and they'll all be killed, both
    lots together. Don't grin, she'll see.

FLORENCE *takes her place on the rope.*

ARTHUR *to* VICTORIA. They know the signal.

VICTORIA. Yes. They let go when I shout peace.

ARTHUR. Good. One – two – pull!

VICTORIA. Pull! (VICTORIA *and* ARTHUR *shout 'pull' while
    the teams pull.*)

HERS. Pull.

HIS. Heave.

HERS. Groan.

HIS. Grunt.

HERS. Onward!

HIS. Forward!

HERS. Upward!

HIS. To the future!

HERS. The dawn!

HIS. Freedom! Justice!

HERS. Culture! Democracy!

HIS. Science! Civilisation!

HERS. Our future! Our past!

HIS. Our children! Our home!

HERS. Fraternity! Brotherhood! Love! Mankind!

VICTORIA. Peace!

VICTORIA's *side let the rope go.* ARTHUR's *side run backwards
over the cliff. For a moment* VICTORIA's *side stand in silence.*

Then they cheer, and rush to the edge. They stand along it. They look down, laugh, wave, the cliff roars and gives.

Scene Fifteen

Foot of the cliff. The stage is littered with bodies. Some of these are broken dummies. A rope curls round the stage, and under and over and between the bodies. ARTHUR *comes down. He has lost the skull, but the bones are still on his shoulder.*

ARTHUR. Over. Finished. Now I can die in peace. (*He takes out a pistol.*)

FLORENCE *comes in. She is dirty and untidy. She carries the red cross satchel.*

ARTHUR. Why didn't you fall?

FLORENCE. Victoria ran to the edge, so I stayed behind.

ARTHUR. I ought to kill you. It's not fair to leave you out. George would think I hate you. But I've done enough good for one life. Will you do something for me?

FLORENCE. What?

ARTHUR. Close my eyes.

FLORENCE. Why?

ARTHUR. I have some weaknesses. (*A line of ghosts rises up-stage. They are in black cowls. They stand close together.*) Look. Ghosts. (*The ghosts move down a few steps. They stop.*) Don't stop. I'm not afraid. Look. (*He shoots himself.*) Ah! That's blood. Nearly spot on: it won't take long ... (*To the ghosts.*) ... I feel better now. Stand here. Hup! Hup! Salute! I'm proud. I've lived a good life. Arthur the Good. I set you free. You'll always be free. (*The ghosts move apart. They are joined together like a row of paper cut-out men.*) No! That's not true! That's a lie! No! I killed you! You're free! – This is all right, my mind's going, I'm seeing things ... You've no right to come here like this! Florence, stop them!

FLORENCE. Who?

ARTHUR. Them!

FLORENCE. They're dead!

ARTHUR. No, no. Help them.

FLORENCE. It's burning oil from tanks.

ARTHUR. O god! The pit! The pit! Give them the kiss of life! Him! Him! (*He breathes into a man's mouth.* GEORGE *comes from the line of ghosts. He holds himself as if he was still attached to* ARTHUR.) My blood! Give them my blood! (*He wets his hand on his head.*) My – (*He sees* GEORGE. *He steps back. He falls down.*)

FLORENCE. He's dead.

GEORGE *goes to* ARTHUR. *He bends down and starts to fasten himself to* ARTHUR. ARTHUR *shudders and groans.*

ARTHUR (*groaning*). No. No. No. No. No.

Scene Sixteen

Heaven. The stage is bare. The wheeled hamper, which is used several times in the remaining scenes, is a trolley with two large hamper-baskets on it. It has a handle for pushing and pulling. The whole cast except VICTORIA, ALBERT *and* FLORENCE. ARTHUR *and* GEORGE *sit downstage. They are joined as before. The others are upstage, under a pulley.*

ARTHUR (*repeats in surprise*). Where?

GEORGE. Heaven.

ARTHUR. What d'you do?

GEORGE. Nothing. We're all happy in heaven.

ARTHUR. We're still joined.

GEORGE. Till the trial.

ARTHUR. What trial?

GEORGE. Everyone's tried. Then they cut us free.

ARTHUR. I saw some men chained together.

GEORGE. Imagination! – that's just a habit.

ALBERT *and* VICTORIA *come on.*

ALBERT. Arthur, this is nice!

VICTORIA. Yes, I'm surrounded by my family again. But you're very late – we were here long ago. Let's start the Trial.

ALBERT (*to* ARTHUR). The father prosecutes and the mother defends.

VICTORIA. Arthur v God.

During the trial people, including the JURY, *wander backwards and forwards between the court and the pulley. At one time all the* JURY *are under the pulley. There are bursts of noise and laughter from the people at the pulley.*

ARTHUR (*points to the pulley*). What's that?

VICTORIA. What's the charge?

The LORD CHAMBERLAIN *whispers in* VICTORIA's *ear.*

VICTORIA. O. Well, we have the perfect defence. (*She brings out a huge pile of papers.*)

ALBERT. Swear the jury.

The JURORS *raise their hands one after the other and say one of the following lines. Some say more than one line, but not two lines consecutively. They smile and nod at* ARTHUR *while they speak. One waves.*

He rapes little girls.

He rapes little boys.

He rapes grey haired grannies.

He rapes grey haired grandads.

He rapes dogs.

He rapes anything.

He rapes himself.

He likes to flog.

He gives babies syphilis.

He drinks before breakfast.

He wastes electricity.

He's mean.

He gives gonorrhoea syphilis.

He kills.

He's a nose-picker.

He looks at dirty pictures.

He picks his nose while he looks at dirty pictures.

He kills.

He can't control his natural functions.

He's only got unnatural functions.

He kills.

He eats dirt.

He is dirt.

He dreams about killing.

They ought to name a venereal disease after him.

VICTORIA. No objections.

ALBERT. First witness.

LEN *comes down from the group under the pulley.*

LEN. I admit that when 'is brother wen' a kill 'is-self 'e reckons let 'im. An' whass more, 'e poisoned 'is cake. (*The* JURY *clap.*) But – when 'is brother died 'e wen' an' dragged 'im back t' life! – I'm top a the queue. (*He goes upstage to the pulley.*)

ARTHUR. I wanted to make him happy. (*The* JURY *laugh.*) I was confused.

FOREMAN. The accused must not speak out of turn.

VICTORIA (*to* ARTHUR). Hush. (*To* FOREMAN.) No questions. (*She sorts her papers.*)

ALBERT. A last word. I can smell his finger-prints from here.

VICTORIA. We call no evidence. (*She grabs her papers.*) Members of the jury, we speak to the mothers among you. (*They are all men.*) My son used to be a disappointment to me. Then he killed us all. For the first time I was able to call him son. The defence confidently asks for a verdict of guilty. (*She puts her papers away.*)

ALBERT. Members of the jury, your verdict. (*The* JURY *put their heads together.*)

FOREMAN. We order trial by ordeal.

ARTHUR. This is –

VICTORIA. The usual formality.

The LORD CHAMBERLAIN *comes down from the pulley with* ALBERT's *sword. The* FOREMAN *tests the blade.*

FOREMAN. White hot.

ALBERT. Let me unbutton your shirt.

ALBERT *undoes* ARTHUR's *shirt. The people under the pulley have been making a steady noise. They now chant: 'Heave-heave-heave.'*

ALBERT *sticks the sword into* ARTHUR. ARTHUR *does not react. A slight pause.* ALBERT *pulls the sword out.*

VICTORIA (*sniffs*). Do I smell burning?

ALBERT. The verdict?

FOREMAN. Guilty and admitted to Heaven.

ALBERT *cuts* ARTHUR *from* GEORGE *with the sword. There are loud shouts from the crowd at the pulley.* LEN *runs downstage carrying a leg. It is torn off at the thigh and still wears its sock and shoe. The stump is ragged and bloody.* LEN *chews it. The crowd fight round him like sparrows.*

CROWD. Me! Me! Me!

LEN (*fights them off by kicking at them, and by swinging the leg*).
Lay off! 'Ang about! Get the other one! (*He chews.*)

ALBERT. You're interrupting a trial.

VICTORIA. It's disgraceful. If you must make that noise
make it elsewhere.

CROWD. Me! Me! Shares!

LEN. 'Old on, 'old on. (*He turns to* ARTHUR.) Yer once did me
a good turn. Welcome t' 'eaven. It's all yourn – (*He wrenches
a bite from the leg.*) – wass left of it. (*He puts the leg into*
ARTHUR's *hands and steps back shyly. Then he shyly rubs the
palms of his hands on the seat of his trousers. Shyly and
pleasantly.*) An' I 'ope it chokes yer.

JOYCE. O – I didn't know 'e 'ad it in 'im. (*Some of the crowd
pat him on the back.*)

ALBERT. In heaven we eat each other.

VICTORIA. It doesn't hurt.

ALBERT. And it grows again.

GEORGE. Like crabs.

VICTORIA. Nothing has any consequences here – so there's
no pain. Think of it – no pain. Pain is just a habit. You
forget all your habits here. Bon appetite. (*She sniffs sus-
piciously.*) I could have sworn I smelt burning.

*A one-legged man stands up under the pulley. He has a rope
round his neck. The other end is slung over the pulley. He pulls it
free.*

VICTORIA (*sniffs*). I could have sworn –

*The one-legged man starts to hop out. The rope hangs from his
neck and dances along behind him.*

LEN. 'E's off.

CHAMBERLAIN. Bring him down!

GEORGE. Talley-ho!

They shout and chase the man out. ARTHUR *is alone. He has
been in one position since the leg was put in his hand. He holds it*

vertical with the stump up. Slight pause. He seems to whisper.
Then he speaks with difficulty.

ARTHUR. I'm not dead. O God, let me die.

Scene Seventeen

Heaven. GEORGE *writhes on the floor with his knees up.*
VICTORIA *brings* ALBERT *in.*

VICTORIA. It's his second attack today.
ALBERT. Perhaps he's eaten something that disagreed with him.
VICTORIA. I hoped you'd say something sensible! – I know what's behind this. (*She turns away.*) I haven't seen Arthur since the trial, and that was weeks ago.

FLORENCE *comes on.*

VICTORIA. Florence!
ALBERT. How nice!
VICTORIA. We were just talking about you. How did you get here?
FLORENCE. O, after the catastrophe I had to earn my living. (VICTORIA *clicks her tongue.*) I opened a brothel, and business was so brisk I didn't have time to get up. I catered for ministers, probation officers, WVS hierarchy, women police chiefs. – Well, there I was, in bed with Disraeli and Gladstone. They always shared a booking. They got very excited as usual and just then Gladys (a nom d'amour) said 'Listen'. There was a newsboy shouting in the street. Mafekin had been relieved. That on top of the rest was too much. They got over excited – and here I am.

VICTORIA. I'm pleased about Mafekin.

GEORGE. Hungry.

VICTORIA. George, you can't feel pain in heaven! (*She takes* FLORENCE *aside.*) I'm giving a little garden party, dear. I expect it of myself. My other guests will be here soon. I've managed to store a little food away, but I didn't tell George.

ARTHUR *comes on and crosses upstage.* GEORGE *immediately goes and stands by him.*

VICTORIA. Arthur.

ARTHUR (*turns vaguely*). Florence . . .

VICTORIA. Arthur. (*He turns to her.*) George isn't well. He's hungry. Are *you* hungry? (*Slight pause.*) Arthur, dear?

ARTHUR. No.

VICTORIA. I've got some sweets left from when I was alive.

ARTHUR (*his hands shoot out*). Yes! (*The others stare at him.* GEORGE *groans.*)

VICTORIA. So you're not eating! That's what's making George hungry.

GEORGE (*still standing next to* ARTHUR). Starving!

VICTORIA. Aren't you happy here?

ALBERT. Of course he is! It's heaven. Anyway, you only die once. He can't starve himself to death.

GEORGE. For God's sake eat! You couldn't stand this agony.

ARTHUR. I feel it too.

VICTORIA. Arthur. What's wrong? Is there something you don't like? Some little thing we've overlooked? Is it me? Don't be afraid to tell me.

ARTHUR *goes out.*

GEORGE (*following* ARTHUR *closely*). Eat! Eat! (*He goes out.*)

VICTORIA. Good – they'd have spoiled my party. Albert, go and keep an eye on them, and don't let them back till it's over.

ALBERT. But I was . . .!

The mob start to come on. ALBERT *goes out. The mob's clothes are not rags, but most of them are worn and dirty.* VICTORIA *greets them, but they ignore it.*

VICTORIA. I'm so glad you could come.

LEN. Glad t' do a favour.

VICTORIA. I'm so glad you could come.

GRISS. Where's the grub?

FLORENCE (*to* VICTORIA). You're upset. You should have cancelled it.

VICTORIA. I died fighting. I won't give in now. – I'm so glad you could come.

LEN. Whass this garden-whass-it caper?

JOYCE. Picnic.

GRISS (*at the hamper*). This the grub? (*Opens the hamper. Surprised.*) She must be runnin' 'er own farm! (*Sniffs.*) Don't it pong, though?

LEN (*sniffs*). Thass off!

VICTORIA. It's game.

GRISS. Game?

VICTORIA. It's hung – to give it flavour.

JOYCE. Naturally. (*To* LEN.) Thass game. (*To* VICTORIA.) Ta, luv. (*Eats.*) It's all right, en it? It *is* person?

VICTORIA. O yes.

GRISS. English.

VICTORIA. Well, British.

GRISS. I wouldn't fancy no black and yeller imported muck.

LEN. Well, it's freeman's. (*Eats.*) Strewth. (*Eats.*)

GRISS. 'S all right if yer 'old yer nose an swaller quick.

ARTHUR *comes on.* GEORGE *follows him closely.*

VICTORIA. I wanted you to stay away!

GEORGE (*to* ARTHUR). Eat!

JOYCE. Wass up?

GEORGE. Eat! Eat!

ARTHUR (*in pain*). O God.

LEN. Whass 'is caper?

GEORGE (*sees the others eating*). Food! (*He runs to the hamper and takes food.*) Ah!

As GEORGE *eats* ARTHUR *starts to retch and this automatically makes* GEORGE *retch.*

GRISS. 'Oo you shuvin'?

GEORGE *rolls on the floor and eats and retches. The mob stare at them.*

JOYCE. 'Ere! They're poisoned.

GRISS. Do what?

LEN. I knew it tasted funny.

GRISS. You kiddin'?

JOYCE. No, me ol' gran was 'avin a knees-up one night when I wanted a watch telly. I 'ad t' put drain-cleaner in 'er meths t' quieten 'er down. She rolled down the stairs juss like that.

GEORGE (*eating and retching*). Arthur, stop it! Let me eat!

LEN (*drops his food*). 'Er word's good enough for me!

GRISS (*drops his food*). Me gut!

VICTORIA. You can't be poisoned in heaven!

GEORGE. Aahh! Arthur!

ARTHUR. I can't eat!

GRISS. 'E can't eat!

JOYCE. Thass yer confirmation! (*The mob groans and doubles up.*)

VICTORIA *and* FLORENCE *run out.*

JOYCE (*alarmed*). Whass goin' a 'appen to us?

LEN. It's worse'n the double cramps!

JOYCE. We ain' goin' a die again? We ain' goin' a lose all this?

ALBERT *comes in. He sees* GEORGE *and* ARTHUR.

ALBERT. There you are! But where's Victoria? (*He takes a piece of body from the hamper.*)

JOYCE. 'E's one a 'em! (*The mob stops.*)

GRISS. Out the same sty! (*The mob surrounds* ALBERT.)

JOYCE. Take 'is bone away! (GRISS *takes the food from* ALBERT.)

ALBERT. I thought my wife was here. I'd better –

GRISS. Up the pulley!

GRISS *takes a rope from his shoulder. The mob push* ALBERT *into the hamper and tie the rope on him.* GRISS *walks away tugging on the rope. The mob crowd round the hamper holding* ALBERT *in. They shout.* GRISS *tugs.* GEORGE *runs between* GRISS *and the mob encouraging and trying to help.*

GEORGE. Food! Food!

ARTHUR (*Quickly. In pain*). No! No! No more pain, no more war, no more suffering – we're in heaven!

JOYCE (*calling to* ARTHUR). All right, luvy, we'll settle 'im for yer!

ARTHUR. Why can't I let them alone in peace!

LEN (*calling to* ARTHUR). Yeh, yer deserve a gong for flushin' 'im out!

ARTHUR (*Quickly*). Let me die! (*The mob shouts, the rope slackens, and* GRISS *sits down with a thump.*) Stop it! No more! I'll eat! I'll eat! (GEORGE *runs from the hamper, eating a piece of* ALBERT. ARTHUR *takes a piece of* ALBERT *from the hamper. He bites from it.*)

ARTHUR. I'll eat! I'll be good! Good! Good!

JOYCE (*at the hamper*). Drag 'im up our end.

LEN (*helping her*). 'Ow's yer gut?

JOYCE. Bit better.

LEN. We'll eat 'er next. She'll purge it for yer!

They drag the hamper out. The trolley is left on stage. GEORGE *sits alone and eats.*

ARTHUR (*eats*). Eat and be good. Be good and die. Die and be happy. (*They chew in silence for a few moments.*) O God, let me die. Let me die – and everyone will be happy.

Scene Eighteen

Heaven. VICTORIA *and* FLORENCE *come on.* FLORENCE *looks over her shoulder.* VICTORIA *has a black eye. Her hair is undone.*

VICTORIA (*stops*). Rest for five minutes.

FLORENCE (*looks back*). They should keep up. It's dangerous. (*Calls.*) George!

VICTORIA. If there's pain in heaven, why isn't there love? (*After reflection.*) I can't say I love you. D'you love me?

FLORENCE. No.

VICTORIA. D'you feel pain?

FLORENCE. No.

VICTORIA. Nor do I. Nor does the mob. Crowds believe anything.

GEORGE *wheels* ALBERT *in on the trolley.* ALBERT *has no legs.*

GEORGE (*groans*). I can't go on. (*Stops pushing.*) It's getting worse! I thought it would go when he started to eat.

VICTORIA. He must have stopped again. We can't keep running away. We must do something.

ALBERT. Yes.

VICTORIA. There was peace in heaven till Arthur got here. He doesn't belong! He hasn't got the gift of happiness. We must get rid of him. (GEORGE *is groaning.*)

ALBERT (*defeated*). You can't kill people in heaven.

VICTORIA. We could eat him.

ALBERT (*shrugs*). He'd grow again.

VICTORIA. We could eat him again. Keep his bones, and chew off every sign of life the moment it appears.

ALBERT. That's a brilliant idea!

VICTORIA. But we can't do it.

ALBERT. Why not?

VICTORIA. You'd never catch him. The mob protects him. He's infected them with his lunacy – they *all* think they're in pain. He's their messiah.

GEORGE. Use Florence.

VICTORIA. What?

GEORGE. She could put a ring through his nose and bring him here on his knees.

FLORENCE. Could I?

VICTORIA. I see. I've just understood something. (*To* GEORGE). I've underrated you. (*To* FLORENCE.) Get him away from the mob – take him for a walk. Then it'll be four against one.

FLORENCE. No. I'm afraid of the mob.

GEORGE. He won't let them touch you. (*Groans.*)

VICTORIA. At least you'll stand a chance. If we go on like this we'll all be caught. And think what it means; peace.

FLORENCE. I'll try.

VICTORIA (*going*). Let's go back.

FLORENCE. Now?

VICTORIA. Now! I feel lucky again.

GEORGE (*groans*).

They go out.

Scene Nineteen

Heaven. ARTHUR *sits upstage.* LEN, JOYCE, JONES *and* GRISS
sit a little apart from him. They moan. ARTHUR *has long,
dirty hair and a long, dirty beard. He wears rags. The others
are not so dirty and ragged.* FLORENCE *stands downstage.
She looks at* ARTHUR.

ARTHUR. Yes?
FLORENCE. I wasn't sure it was you.
LEN (*stands*). Whass 'appenin'?
ARTHUR. Sit down. (LEN *sits*.) How's my brother?
FLORENCE. Can we go somewhere?
LEN. 'E ain' t' be bothered.
GRISS. I got pain all over.
JOYCE. This ain' 'eaven. It's prison.
JONES. We want civilised grub.
ARTHUR. I'd like a walk.
LEN (*shrugs*). On yer pins then. (*He helps* ARTHUR *to stand*.)
ARTHUR. I'll be back soon.

ARTHUR *and* FLORENCE *walk downstage. All the others go out.*

ARTHUR. Sit here. (*Sits*.)
FLORENCE. Not here.
ARTHUR. I'm tired.
FLORENCE (*sits*). Why aren't you happy?
ARTHUR. I'm in pain.
FLORENCE. I'm sorry, you can't be. Not in heaven.
ARTHUR. You don't feel pain.
FLORENCE. Sometimes I'm hungry. That's all. – They ate my
    arm. It didn't hurt. Eat me. Part of me.

ARTHUR. No.

FLORENCE. You do eat. Sometimes George's pain's a bit better.

ARTHUR. I eat myself.

FLORENCE. O.

ARTHUR. When it's too bad. I eat my arm. (*He moves the back of his forearm across his mouth and chews.*)

FLORENCE. Does it hurt?

ARTHUR. Less than hunger.

FLORENCE (*pause*). You're old.

ARTHUR. My beard grew overnight. The night I ate my father. I ate some of him. I don't know what. When I woke up I was old. My hair was white and I had a beard. It was white when it came, and wet – I must have been crying. I felt very tired, as if I'd been born with a beard. (*A slight pause.*) Why did you come?

FLORENCE. I'm not sure.

ARTHUR. I'm going to ask you something. First, I'm not staying in heaven.

FLORENCE. There is nowhere else.

ARTHUR. I'm not staying here. (*He reaches for her hand. She stands and looks round.*) What is it?

FLORENCE. What were you going to ask me?

ARTHUR. Don't eat.

FLORENCE. I –

ARTHUR. Most people die before they reach their teens. Most die when they're still babies or little children. A few reach fourteen or fifteen. Hardly anyone lives on into their twenties.

FLORENCE. Thank God.

ARTHUR. Bodies are supposed to die and souls go on living. That's not true. Souls die first and bodies live. They wander round like ghosts, they bump into each other, tread on each other, haunt each other. That's another reason why it's better to die and come here – there *must* be peace when you're dead. Only I'm not dead.

FLORENCE. You are! Just believe in yourself!

ARTHUR. No. Not quite. I've tried, but I can't die! Even eating didn't kill me. There's something I *can't* kill – and they can't kill it for me. Pity – it must be nice to be dead. Still, if I can't die I must live. I'm resigned to my curse! I accept it. I'll probably even end up being happy. (FLORENCE *moves*.) O God, don't go! You're looking for something.

FLORENCE. I'm hungry! I'm hungry!

ARTHUR. Don't go back to my family!

FLORENCE. I must!

ARTHUR. Come with me.

FLORENCE. Where?

ARTHUR. Somewhere.

FLORENCE. There is nowhere!

ARTHUR (*desperately*). We'll find somewhere!

FLORENCE. What good is that? You still won't eat!

ARTHUR. We'll eat ourselves!

FLORENCE. No!

ARTHUR. We'll eat each other!

FLORENCE. You said you wouldn't!

ARTHUR. Well – well – yes if you stay!

FLORENCE. You won't! You know you won't! You talk about life when you mean pain! That's why you cause trouble – you can't let them die in peace. The mob, your mother – wherever you go – someone will always want to kill someone, and they can't and so it goes on and on! I'm hungry! They're hungry! You're hungry! We're all dead and hungry! And it's the same wherever you go!

ARTHUR. You keep me alive.

FLORENCE. You're not alive! This is heaven! You can't live or laugh or cry or be in pain! You can't love! You can't torture people! Let me alone! You're a ghost! Ghost! Ghost! You're haunting me – O, stop it!

ARTHUR. You're crying.

FLORENCE. No, no, no, no.

ARTHUR. My hand's wet.

FLORENCE. Too late. Why didn't you tell me this before?
What d'you think I did while I waited? I'm not crying.
Perhaps I'm alive, perhaps we needn't be like this. I'm
trying to think.

VICTORIA *runs in.*

VICTORIA (*calls*). Albert! We've got him!

FLORENCE (*trying to make* VICTORIA *leave*). We must go.
The mob's here.

VICTORIA. No. The moment he left they went hunting for
food.

ALBERT *and* GEORGE *come on.* ALBERT *has legs again. He
limps.*

VICTORIA (*takes hold of one of* ARTHUR's *arms. To* ALBERT).
Take that arm.

GEORGE (*rubs his hands together*). I told you!

VICTORIA (*to* GEORGE). Keep watch! (GEORGE *goes upstage.*
ALBERT *limps across to* ARTHUR.)

ARTHUR. Florence, help me!

GEORGE. I'm hungry!

VICTORIA. Albert, don't just stand there –

GEORGE (*goes to* ARTHUR). Food! –

VICTORIA (*to* GEORGE). Go and keep watch.

GEORGE (*going upstage*). Hurry!

VICTORIA. Now, Albert, we'll –

ARTHUR (*to* FLORENCE). Help me!

ALBERT. They'll hear!

FLORENCE. We can't eat him!

VICTORIA (*to* ALBERT). Gag him!

ALBERT. But I didn't bring any –

ARTHUR. Florence!

VICTORIA. Strangle him!

ALBERT. But I didn't bring any –

VICTORIA. With his beard!

ALBERT. His –!

VICTORIA. Beard! Like this. (*She winds the beard round* ARTHUR'*s throat.*) And so. Two. Three. (*To* ARTHUR.) This is for *your* good. Six. Seven. Eight.

GEORGE (*upstage, looking off*). Be quick!

VICTORIA. Nine. Ten. (*She stops strangling.*) He'll be out for a good ten minutes.

GEORGE (*going back to the others*). They must have heard!

VICTORIA. Keep calm! Calm. (*To* ALBERT.) Put him across your back.

VICTORIA *and* GEORGE *help* ALBERT *to get* ARTHUR *on to his back.*

FLORENCE (*walking round*). He feels pain, you see . . .

VICTORIA. Walk. Don't run.

ALBERT *starts to carry* ARTHUR *out.*

GEORGE (*groans*). I'm starving!

ALBERT, GEORGE *and* VICTORIA *go out.*

FLORENCE. Why didn't he talk to me before? You have to pay for waiting.

FLORENCE *follows the others out.*

Scene Twenty

Heaven. VICTORIA, ALBERT *and* FLORENCE *resting.* FLOR-
ENCE *sits on the hamper.*

ALBERT. Where's George?

FLORENCE. Picking up the bones.

VICTORIA. He left a trail of them behind us. He hopes he'll
find some meat on them.

ALBERT (*licks his fingers*). He won't find much.

GEORGE *comes on. He chews a bone, and he has a stack of bones
under his arm.*

GEORGE. I'm still starving!

VICTORIA. It should have gone when we ate him.

GEORGE (*chews and groans*). It didn't.

VICTORIA. Give me those bones. (*He gives her the bones, but
keeps the one he is chewing.*) And that.

GEORGE. I'm hungry.

VICTORIA. And that. (*He gives her the bone.*) We must keep
them together. (*She stands them in a large box and arranges
them like flowers.*) Where's his head?

GEORGE. I haven't got it. (*He picks his teeth and chews hungrily.*)

VICTORIA. Florence?

FLORENCE. No.

VICTORIA. Albert?

ALBERT. No.

VICTORIA. You don't just lose a head.

ALBERT. O lor'.

VICTORIA (*annoyed*). That's why you're still in pain.

GEORGE (*stands by the bones and eyes them*). It can't have gone
far.

VICTORIA (*to* FLORENCE). You're not sitting on it, dear?

FLORENCE. No.

VICTORIA. Well who remembers eating it?

GEORGE. I don't.

VICTORIA. You wouldn't.

GEORGE (*groans*). That's not fair! Starving's bad enough
    without –

VICTORIA. Well, we'll have to search. It's got to be found.
    He might sprout a new body!

FLORENCE. Can he?

VICTORIA. It's the sort of perverse thing he would do. We'd
    end up with two Arthurs on our hands. I couldn't cope.
    (*To* ALBERT *and* GEORGE.) Come on. – Florence.

FLORENCE. I'll stay and mind the bones.

VICTORIA (*going*). You don't just lose a head.

GEORGE *groans.* GEORGE, ALBERT *and* VICTORIA *go out.*
FLORENCE *waits. Then she uncovers her lap.* ARTHUR's *head
is in it.*

FLORENCE. O dear.

ARTHUR. Don't. I love you.

FLORENCE. They're looking for you.

ARTHUR. I know.

FLORENCE (*shudders*). O dear.

ARTHUR. This is the first time I've been happy. I'm not
    hungry now.

FLORENCE. Something's going to fall in your eyes. (*She
    removes it.*)

ARTHUR. It's a hair.

FLORENCE. Keep still.

ARTHUR. My beard. Mother tore it out when she strangled
    me.

FLORENCE. Why are you smiling?

ARTHUR. It's nice here.

FLORENCE. What?

ARTHUR. In your lap?

FLORENCE. O.

ARTHUR. Don't shake. When they cut off a man's leg he still
feels it. I'm like that. They've cut off my body – but I'm
alive. I could make love to you. Now. I can feel it. Hard.
That's why I like it in your lap.

FLORENCE (*laughs. Bewildered*). I don't know what to do.

ARTHUR. You keep worrying because you ate me.

FLORENCE. Victoria was watching.

ARTHUR. It's all right. I love you.

FLORENCE. But what can I do?

ARTHUR. Don't eat.

FLORENCE. You always say that! –

ARTHUR. Tell Victoria you love me. She won't stand for that:
it's treason. She'll make them eat you, and then you'll be
like me.

FLORENCE. What good is that?

ARTHUR. You'll be alive.

FLORENCE. Where? How?

ARTHUR. With me.

FLORENCE. But you're nothing. They've eaten you.

ARTHUR. I'm alive. Or I'm beginning to live!

FLORENCE. Where? How?

ARTHUR. I don't know. I can't tell you, you must find out.
I'm like a fire in the sea or the sun underground. I'm alive.
You love me.

FLORENCE. It's too late. Love, love – I don't know what it
means now. You talk about sun and fires – and I'm hungry!

ARTHUR. Of course you are! The dead are always hungry!

FLORENCE. I've told you, I don't understand.

ARTHUR. You do!

FLORENCE. I want to, but I don't.

ARTHUR. It's why you're hiding me.

FLORENCE. I don't know why!

ARTHUR. I'm in your lap! That's proof!

FLORENCE. I'll see. I'll try. I'll try.

ARTHUR. Kiss me.

FLORENCE. Let me think.

ARTHUR. Kiss me! Lift my head in your hands and hold it against your mouth. Then it will be all right. We'll be alone, and happy.

FLORENCE. Yes . . . Yes. (*She slightly bends her head towards him. She takes his head in her hands and starts to raise it.*)

VICTORIA (*off*). You don't just lose a head.

FLORENCE *covers* ARTHUR's *head.* VICTORIA *comes in.*

FLORENCE. Did you find it?

VICTORIA. I will.

ALBERT *and* GEORGE *come on.* ALBERT *has his hands in his pockets.* GEORGE's *pain is obviously worse. He chews a bone.*

ALBERT. Tch, tch, tch!

GEORGE. O God! (*He drops the bone in the tin.*) A microbe couldn't feed on that. (*He hunts through the other bones.*) If we had a fire we could boil soup.

VICTORIA. You don't just lose a head.

FLORENCE. I expect it's rolled off on its own somewhere. It doesn't matter.

VICTORIA (*to* GEORGE). Put those bones down. (*She takes the tin to* FLORENCE.) I'm not losing any more. Albert, you can't think with your hands in your pockets. No wonder we lost his head. (*To* FLORENCE.) Look after those, dear.

FLORENCE. Yes. (*She puts the tin on the floor.*)

ALBERT. Dear-o-dear-o-lor!

GEORGE (*suddenly*). I can't stand it! Ah! (*He rolls on the floor.* ALBERT *looks at him.*)

VICTORIA. He's just trying to attract attention. Florence, we'll go for a walk.

FLORENCE. It's nice here.

VICTORIA. It's nicer walking.

ALBERT (*looking at* GEORGE). Victoria, this is serious. I didn't realise how bad he was!

VICTORIA (*looks at* GEORGE). Hm. – Florence, come and look at him.

FLORENCE. I don't think I could help.

VICTORIA. Nonsense, you're a nurse. (*She bends down and looks at* GEORGE. FLORENCE *starts to walk towards them.*)

ALBERT. Shall I rub his wrists?

VICTORIA. Put something between his teeth. George, we're going to put something between your teeth. (*To* FLORENCE.) Fetch a bone, dear.

FLORENCE. What?

VICTORIA. A bone. To put between his teeth.

FLORENCE. Yes. (*She starts to walk back to the hamper.*)

VICTORIA. George, try saying the National Anthem backwards. It calms the nerves.

FLORENCE (*stops. To* ARTHUR *under her skirt*). Stop it! (*She smacks him.*)

VICTORIA. What, dear?

FLORENCE. I twisted my back. (FLORENCE *starts to walk again.*)

VICTORIA. What's wrong with your legs?

FLORENCE. They went to sleep. (*She reaches the tin of bones. She takes out a bone and starts walking back to* VICTORIA. VICTORIA *is saying the National Anthem backwards.*)

ALBERT. Take off his shoes.

VICTORIA. Why?

ALBERT. You always take the shoes off the sick.

FLORENCE. Stop it! (*She slaps* ARTHUR's *head under her skirt. She wriggles and grimaces.*)

VICTORIA. Is that your leg, dear?

FLORENCE. My leg?

VICTORIA. It went to sleep.

FLORENCE. It's worse. I'll sit down. (*She turns to go.*)

VICTORIA. Try jumping.

FLORENCE. I don't think I –

VICTORIA. It helps the circulation.

FLORENCE. I've got a headache.

VICTORIA. It's invaluable for headaches and for twisted
backs. Up you go! (FLORENCE *jumps once.*) You call that
up? Again. Higher. Up! (FLORENCE *jumps once.*) Nurses
never look after themselves. I'll massage it.

FLORENCE (*moves quickly away*). It's gone now.

VICTORIA. There you are. Jumping cures everything.

ARTHUR *laughs.* FLORENCE *slaps him under her skirt.*

VICTORIA. George, don't laugh. You're supposed to be ill.

GEORGE (*points at* FLORENCE). I didn't laugh. It was –
(FLORENCE *puts the bone in his mouth. He talks through the
bone.*) – bla bla bla.

VICTORIA. And don't talk with your mouth full.

GEORGE (*pointing at* FLORENCE). Bla bla bla!
(FLORENCE *backs away from* GEORGE. *She trips over the
hamper. She falls with her feet in the air.* VICTORIA *sees
the head between her legs. She grasps* FLORENCE'*s legs and
holds them up. She twists her head round so that it is in line
with* ARTHUR'*s head.*)

VICTORIA. Arthur! I said you don't just lose a head.

GEORGE (*takes the head*). Meat!

VICTORIA. Give that back!

GEORGE. No!

GEORGE *takes a bite from the head.* ARTHUR *laughs loudly.*

GEORGE (*stops*). He laughed!

VICTORIA. George give me that head!

GEORGE. No. (*He puts the head under his jacket.*)

VICTORIA. Albert, speak to him.

ALBERT. George –

GEORGE *runs upstage. He takes a bite from the head.* ARTHUR
laughs loudly.

GEORGE: O!

GEORGE *runs out with the head. Silence.*

FLORENCE. Why did Arthur laugh?
VICTORIA (*to* ALBERT). Pick up the bones.
ALBERT (*to* VICTORIA). It's no use being bitter. We've all had
   a trying day.

GEORGE *runs on with the head. It is half eaten.*

GEORGE (*chewing*). It's a miracle! My pain's going!
VICTORIA. Albert!
ALBERT. George, I'm very cross with –

GEORGE *goes out.*

FLORENCE. Why did he laugh when George ate him?

GEORGE *runs back. He carries a skull.*

GEORGE. My pain's gone! Gone! All gone!
ALBERT (*takes the skull from* GEORGE). And when he grows
   again you won't have one bite!
GEORGE. I'm free! I'm free! (*He runs out.*)
VICTORIA. He won't grow again.
ALBERT. Why not?
VICTORIA. He's dead.
ALBERT. How?
VICTORIA. If George's pain is gone, Arthur's gone.
FLORENCE. Where?
VICTORIA. I don't know. I don't want to know. He's dead –
   that's good enough for me. Give me his skull. (ALBERT
   *gives her the skull. She puts it in the tin, on top of the
   other bones.*) Now we've got a complete set.

GEORGE (*off*). Yippee!

ALBERT. What will happen?

VICTORIA. We'll wait and see.

FLORENCE. Will he grow again?

VICTORIA. He might. But it'll be dead meat. Not fit for human consumption. And there'll be no more pain.

GEORGE (*off*). Yippee!

VICTORIA. We must keep him quiet. I don't want to face the mob till I can show them the body.

They all go out. The bones are left onstage in the tin.

Scene Twenty-One

Heaven. ARTHUR *is lying with one foot in the tin. The bones are gone.* JOYCE *sleeps near him.* VICTORIA, ALBERT, GEORGE *and* FLORENCE *come on.*

ALBERT. He's grown.

VICTORIA (*pokes* ARTHUR). But he's dead. (*To* GEORGE.) And you're not in pain?

GEORGE. No.

VICTORIA. Good. Fetch a coffin. (GEORGE *and* FLORENCE *go out.*)

VICTORIA (*shakes* JOYCE). Wake up, dear!

JOYCE. You killed the master!

VICTORIA. He said you'd say that. Run and fetch your friends, dear.

JOYCE. I will! (JOYCE *runs out.*)

ALBERT. What are you going to do?

VICTORIA. Settle it.

GEORGE *and* FLORENCE *come in with a coffin. They set it down by* ARTHUR.

VICTORIA (*to* ALBERT). Get the food, but don't bring it on till I go like this. (*She makes a gesture.*)

JOYCE (*off*). Yoooeee!

VICTORIA (*to* FLORENCE). Hammer? (FLORENCE *goes out.*) I have to think of everything. It'll be interesting to see if she brings the nails.

JOYCE, LEN, JONES, GRISS *and the rest of the mob come on.*

LEN (*to* JOYCE *as he comes in*). An' yer reckoned 'e's bin poisoned?

JOYCE. For keeps.

VICTORIA (*goes to meet them*). You can't kill people in heaven. They can only kill themselves.

GRISS. No speeches.

VICTORIA. You're hungry.

LEN. 'Oo says?

VICTORIA. He did. That's why he killed himself.

JOYCE. Do what?

VICTORIA. He told you not to eat each other.

LEN. Right.

VICTORIA. But he knew he was asking something unnatural and impossible. Something quite, quite impossible. And because he loved you – and he only attacked you out of love – he wouldn't ask you to eat yourself, as he did. (LEN *puts his arm behind his back.*) So he died, to let you eat each other in peace.

GRISS. Fact?

LEN. Never.

VICTORIA. His last words were 'Feed them'. (*She gives* ALBERT *the signal.*)

GRISS. Stroll on! (ALBERT *comes in with the hamper.* FLORENCE *comes on with him.*)

GRISS. That grub?

VICTORIA. Yes.

JOYCE. One thing.

JONES. What?

JOYCE. That trial.

GRISS. Yeh.

JOYCE. 'E singed when they put the knife in. I smelt burnin'.

JONES. Thass a fact.

GRISS. Thass what I said.

JOYCE. Never belonged, see.

LEN. Nosh now or later?

VICTORIA. After we've put him in the box. (ALBERT *and*
GEORGE *put* ARTHUR *in the coffin.*) Lid. (LEN *puts the lid
on the coffin.*) Hammer. (FLORENCE *hands her the hammer.*)
Nails. (FLORENCE *drops her hands to her sides.*) I'll use my
teeth. (*She pulls out a tooth and looks at it.*) That'll hold
better. (*She knocks it into the coffin.*) One. (*She pulls out
another tooth and knocks it in.*) Two. Be putting the food
out. (*She pulls out another tooth.*)

LEN. It ain' none a that fancy stuff, ma?

VICTORIA (*knocking*). No.

JOYCE. Shame. I enjoy anythin' exotic. They ain' got the taste
for it.

VICTORIA. One more.

GRISS. Don't pull the lot.

VICTORIA (*knocks*). I've got handy gums.

LEN. She's a girl!

ALBERT (*aside to* VICTORIA). Will it be all right?

VICTORIA (*to* ALBERT). Of course. I pride myself on
my common touch. – Put the nosh on the lid, boys.
(*They lay the food on top of the coffin.* DISRAELI *and
GLADSTONE *come in.*) How nice! We were just talking
about you.

DISRAELI. Ah, ma'am. Having no teeth suits you.

GLADSTONE (*looks at the food*). We timed it nice!

DISRAELI (*to* FLORENCE). I'm sorry about that.

They all sit round the coffin, except FLORENCE. *She sits a bit on one side and faces the audience.*

VICTORIA. Quiet please. For what we are about to receive.
TWO VOICES. Amen. (*All except* FLORENCE *eat.*)
LEN. I'll 'ave that bit.
DISRAELI. Allow me. (*He hands the food to* VICTORIA.)
JOYCE (*to* LEN). Yer already got two bits, guts.

ARTHUR *steps out of the coffin. He stands on the lid. He looks a bit cleaner, but his hair and beard are still dirty and uncombed. He is draped in a long white smock or shawl. Parts of his old clothes are seen underneath. He arranges the smock so that it hangs more comfortably. The others don't see him. They eat and talk.*

GRISS. 'E weren' a bad bloke. Juss couldn't keep 'is-self to 'is-self. Thass a fault – but it don' make yer wicked.
VICTORIA. I'll miss him. But he's better gone. I could never help him, otherwise things would have been different. I'm working out a roster for the order in which we're eaten. Then there'll be no arguments. My name comes first.

ARTHUR *starts to rise in the air. His hands are half raised against his chest. The shawl hangs behind him. His feet are seen.* FLORENCE *doesn't see him. She cries silently.*

VICTORIA. Florence? (*Offers her food.*)
FLORENCE. There's something in my eye.
VICTORIA. Take it out.
JONES. Bit a dirt.
VICTORIA. There's no dirt in heaven. There's only peace and happiness, law and order, consent and co-operation. My life's work has borne fruit. It's settled.
LEN (*to* JOYCE). Pass us that leg.

The Pope's Wedding

THE POPE'S WEDDING was first performed at the Royal Court Theatre on Sunday December 9th 1962 with the following cast:

SCOPEY, twenty-two	Philip Lowrie
BILL, twenty-four	David Ellison
RON, twenty	Michael Standing
LEN*, seventeen	
LORRY, eighteen	Malcolm Patton
JOE, twenty-one	Malcolm Taylor
BYO, twenty	Lawrence Craine
ALEN, seventy-five	Harold Goodwin
PAT, eighteen	Janie Booth
JUNE, sixteen	Adrienne Hill
BOWLER	Julian Chagrin
WICKET KEEPER	George Ogilvie
UMPIRE (heard but not seen)	

Directed by Keith Johnstone

* Excluded from the original production.

BILL and BYO are big-boned and muscular. LEN and SCOPEY are a bit shorter. LORRY is the smallest. JOE is a bit fat. JUNE whitens her face and heavily paints her eyebrows and lashes. She is small and thin. PAT is quite short, but she has heavy shoulders and a very full figure. Her bright country complexion shows through her cosmetics.

In these sixteen scenes the stage is dark and bare to the wings and back. Places are indicated by a few objects and these objects are described in the text. The objects are very real, but there must be no attempt to create the illusion of a 'real scene'. In the later scenes the stage may be lighter and Scene Fifteen may be played in bright light.

Scene One

An open space. An iron railing up stage centre. This is used for leaning against.

SCOPEY, BILL, RON, LEN, LORRY, JOE, BYO.

BILL forces SCOPEY's *head under his left armpit.* SCOPEY *is bent double from the waist.*

SCOPEY. Lego. Lemeegoo!

BILL. 'Ow's that for an arse, boy?

> *He hits* SCOPEY's *arse with his right hand.* SCOPEY *hits him in the kidneys with his right fist.*

Ow! Bastard!

SCOPEY. I 'ope that'll teach yoo a lesson.

BILL. Bastard!

SCOPEY. Next time yoo keep yoor 'ands a yoorself.

BILL. Yoo owd pook – yoo got the money rightnough.

RON. 'Oo's got the time?

LORRY. Gettin on.

BYO. Must be.

JOE. Been fast all day.

BYO. What?

JOE. My watch.

BYO. Put her right.

RON. 'Ow can 'e, 'e ent got the time.

LORRY. Gettin on.

BILL. To me.

BYO. To yoo. (*He kicks a stone.*)

JOE. To me.

BILL. To yoo.

RON. To me.

JOE. To yoo.

BILL. To me. Let's 'ave it.

RON. To yoo. Wake up. (*Kicks the stone to* SCOPEY.)

SCOPEY. Owzat!

JOE. Well stopped.

SCOPEY (*kicks*). Goal!

BILL. 'Oo's settin' the beer up?

    SCOPEY *groans*.

RON. On a Thursday?

LORRY. Syoor turn I reckon, ent it?

BILL. Well lend us the money an' I'll treat the lot on yer.

LORRY. That's a rum owd doo, me lendin' yoo money to pay for my own beer.

BILL. Yoo'll get it back.

LEN. Yoo 'ope.

LORRY. Don't worry, I ent lendin' it. I ent got it.

BILL. No beer? No beer.

    Pause.

BYO. Bleep bleep.

BILL. Yoo got a licence for that, boy?

    Pause.

BILL. Come on, Sco. Fifty p.

SCOPEY. I seen yoo back a Farrin field sarternoon.

BILL. I was 'idin' up from owd man Bullright's woman. Anyone out on the road a see yoo down there, so she 'as t' lay off.

JOE. That's a rum owd doo, ent it, 'avin' the boss's missis come after yer.

BYO. Yoo keep in there, boy. Yoo stan' a doo yoorself a bit a good.

LORRY. I reckon 'e's leadin' 'er on.

BILL. She don't need no leadin', boy. My life!

JOE. 'Er owd man'll cop 'er one day.

LEN. I'd like a see that.

BILL. Shut up.

    Pause.

RON. Light up the vicarage.

BILL. God workin' overtime.

JOE. Yoor mouth.

BILL. Let's goo an' burn a yank.

BYO. Bloody work tmorra.

JOE. Yoo wouldn't know what a doo with yoorself if it wasn't.

BYO. I'd know what a doo with yoo.

BILL. Fifty p. Forty p. Thirty p. A penny with a 'ole in.

SCOPEY. Put it on the slate.

BILL. I tried that yesterday.

JOE. Got a smoke?

BILL. Chriss, I'd sell my sister if I 'ad one.

LORRY. Yoo thirsty?

LEN. If she was anythin' like yoo t'ent likely yoo get much for 'er.

BILL. 'Op it. Oi, I saw that Butty girl bendin' down in 'er yard
    when I come by. Neigh come off my bike.

BYO. Yoo like it fat.

BILL. Soft, mate, soft.

SCOPEY. Where they come from?

BILL. Saw right up 'er arse. Chriss – where's that beer?

SCOPEY. Why she bendin' down?

BYO. That owd stone tore my boot.

BILL. This week I reckon I'll stow a few bottles under that owd
    stairs while I still got the dough.

SCOPEY. That won't be there be Monday.

RON. Lights off up the vicarage.

BILL. Now 'e's showin' 'is missis the second comin'. They're all
    the same in the dark.

SCOPEY. What?

BILL. 'Ow old yoo reckon that Butty girl is?

RON. Seventeen.

BYO. Big ginger crutch.

    Pause.

JOE. I saw.

BILL (*not hearing*). What?

JOE. I saw.

BYO. Not agen?

LORRY. Me?

JOE. I saw it.

LORRY. Yeh?

JOE. I saw all right. Yoo thought I ent lookin'.

LORRY. Me?

JOE. Yoo know.

BILL. No beer?

LORRY. 'Onest a God I never –

JOE. Yoo thought I wasn't lookin', didn't yoo. I was lookin' right
    enough. I saw.

LORRY. 'Oo cares?

JOE. Yoo will, boy.

BYO. Yoo gooin' a make 'im?

JOE. Yeh.

BYO. Goo on then.   .

JOE. What yoo puttin' in for?

BYO. Let's see yoo.

JOE. I was watchin'.

LORRY. My arse.

JOE. I got eyes in my 'ead.

LORRY. Yoo want a use 'em.

JOE. I use 'em all right.

LORRY. Yoo weren't even lookin'.

JOE. No?

LORRY. No.

BILL. Wrap up.

RON. 'Ent yoo gooin' a fight?

BYO. They couldn't 'it a fly on the end a their nose.

JOE. Just let me catch yoo next time an' you'll know it.

LORRY. Yeh?

JOE. Yoo try.

BILL. 'Ent yoo got a few bob. They're drivin' me nuts.

JOE. Little sod.

BILL. Fifty p. an' I'll share me crisps.

RON. I oiled that owd Ferguson this mornin'. Yoo should a seen 'er. My life!

LORRY. They don't know ow t' look after proper gear.

JOE. 'Oo asked yoo?

LORRY. 'Oo asked yoo?

BYO. For Chriss sake fight it out, yes?

LORRY. Eh?

RON. Fight it out, for Chriss sake.

JOE. 'Oo asked yoo what t' doo.?

RON. Well that's – obvious – fight it out.

BYO (*to* JOE). Don't yoo want a 'it 'im?

LORRY. 'E started it.

JOE. I'll 'it 'im anytime. I'll 'it anyone.

BILL. Just carry me down to the Carpenter's Arms.
   Slight pause.

LEN. Five tmorra.
   Pause.

RON. Yoo got a light, boy?

BILL. Yup.

BYO. Ow about a smoke? Ta.

RON. That's three yoo owe me.

BYO. Three? I give yoo two last Wednesday.

RON. Wednesday?

BYO. Wednesday, when yoo come up agen owd Pete's place.

RON. O, long a owd Pete's. That come back now.

BYO. That make one.

RON. That come back now.
   Pause.

BYO. Yoo seen them new shirts they got out?

SCOPEY. Where?

BYO. They got round collars.

RON. That's been out a long time.

BYO. I ent see it. Reckon I'll buy one a them.

BILL. Borrow yoor owd dad's.

BYO. Saucy sod.

> *Hits* BILL *on the ear. They fight.*

BILL. Fix 'im, Sco. Use yoor boot.

BYO. Yoo try.

SCOPEY. Cut it out. (*He parts them.*)

BYO (*to* SCOPEY). That 'urt, boy.

> PAT *and* JUNE *come in down right.*

BILL. Lend us fifty p.

PAT. On a Thursday?

BILL. Yoo broke?

PAT. I was gooin' a ask yoo t' buy me some fags.

BILL. Shouldn't smoke.

PAT. Lot I shouldn't doo by rights.

BILL. No one wants t' see yoo perfect.

PAT. No? (*To* BYO.) 'Ello.

BYO. Comin' 'ome with me?

JUNE. 'Fraid a the dark?

BYO. I like someone t' owd my 'and.

PAT. I bet.

BILL. Didn't yoor owd boy Alen give yoo nothin'?

PAT. You know 'e don't pay me.

BILL. For 'is shoppin'.

PAT. I ent touchin' that.

BILL. Just till tmorra. I'll give yoo back.

PAT. T'ent mine t' lend.

BILL. 'E won't know.

PAT. I ent gooin' a give 'im the chance.

> JOE *laughs.*

JUNE. Yoo takin' somethin' for that?

BILL. Just till tmorra.

PAT. No.

BILL. I'll leave it with yoor gran on my way 'ome from work.

PAT (*to* JUNE). Comin'.

BILL. They'll be closed in 'alf an 'our.

PAT. T'ent worth gooin'.

BILL. Time for a quick one.

JUNE (*to* PAT). Come on.

BYO (*to* BILL). She treat yoo like owd dut, boy. Yoo want a put yoor foot down.

JUNE. On yoo.

BILL. Suppose I kick yoor 'ead in an take yoor purse.

PAT. Wouldn't be worth the bother, boy.

BILL. Forty p.

JOE. Tuppence.

LEN. Brew yoor own.

 JOE *laughs.*

JUNE. 'E's off agen.

PAT. 'Ave a cup of tea. Doo yoo more good.

JOE (*laughing*). 'Er owd mum's beetroot wine!

JUNE. Dial 999.

JOE (*laughing*). That'll rot yoor owd gut.

PAT. What's wrong with 'im?

BILL. Toss yoo forty p.

 SCOPEY *lifts* PAT's *skirt as she passes him.*

SCOPEY. They're white.

PAT (*shrilly amused*). Yoo owd devil! Lemmee goo! Yoo see that? 'E lifted it right up! Yoo wicked owd devil! They're white!

BYO. I reckon that for a pair a top legs.

PAT. Yoo wicked owd sauce! Yoo ent better doo that a Mrs Bullrights. She don't wear none, 'cordin' a owd Bill.

JUNE. What d'ee doo?

PAT. Lucky I 'ad mine on! Cheeky owd devil!

JUNE. What d'ee do?

PAT. 'E saw my (*spells*) n-i-c-k-s! (*Very amused.*) They're white! (*To* BOYS.) Did you see? (*To* BYO.) Did yoo see?

 SCOPEY *snatches her bag.*

Yoo let that be!

He throws it to BYO.

That's new. I just 'ad that.

RON. To me.

    BYO *throws it to him.*

LORRY & JOE. To me.

RON. To yoo. (*Throws it to* LORRY.)

LORRY. To yoo. (*Throws it to* BILL.)

SCOPEY. To me.

PAT. I got that a goo with my new shoes.

JUNE (*to* PAT). Stay there. I'll catch him. (*She goes to* SCOPEY.)

BILL. To yoo. (*Throws it to* BYO.)

LEN. To me.

BYO. To yoo. (*Throws it to* LEN.)

PAT. Yoo sods!

JOE. To me. (*He catches it.*) That's yoors. (*Throws it to* SCOPEY.)

    JUNE *gets one hand on it.*

PAT. 'Old it. (*She runs to* SCOPEY *and tugs at the bag.*) Give me!
(*The strap breaks.*) O!

SCOPEY. Too yoo. (SCOPEY *throws it to* RON.)

JUNE. Yoo broke it.

RON. To yoo. (*Throws it to* LEN.)

PAT. Yoo sods! Yoo sods! Yoo rotten sods!

    LEN *holds it. He is unsure what to do.*

  Yoo rotten stinkin' bastards.

BILL (*to* LEN). Let her 'ave it.

JUNE. Rotten bastards, now look what yoo done.

LEN. Catch. (*Throws it to* PAT.)

PAT. Rotten bastards. That's my new bag.

JUNE. She got that a goo with 'er new shoes. Sods. Is that spoilt,
gal?

PAT. 'Course it's spoilt!

JUNE (*to* SCOPEY). Yoo started that.

PAT. Rotten sod.

JUNE. 'E's the worst one.

PAT. Rotten little sod.

JUNE. Yes.

PAT. Yoo're pay for a new one.

SCOPEY. Don't sod me!

BILL. Well what yoo want a doo that for?

BYO. Twot.

SCOPEY. I was only larkin'.

BILL. Larkin'!

SCOPEY. Yoo 'elped.

BILL. 'Oo started?

JUNE. Yes.

PAT. That's no good a me. June (*She takes handfuls of things from her bag.*) take that. Put that in yoor pocket gal. (*She takes a hanky from the bag and wipes her eyes.*)

JUNE. Sods. Now yoo upset 'er.

PAT. Their great dirty 'ands all over. (*She puts the last of her things in her pocket. She throws the bag to* SCOPEY.) Now yoo buy a new one.

SCOPEY. I ent buyin' nothin'.

PAT. Yoo pay up or I come round yoor 'ouse.

JUNE. An' me.

SCOPEY. Goo where yoo like. Yoo shouldn't a got a cheap owd one in the first place. That won't stand up t' proper 'andlin'.

PAT. I didn't ask for one for yoo t' kick about.

JUNE. Yoo won't think that's cheap when yoo see the bill.

SCOPEY. You know where yoo can stick the bloody bill.

PAT. You'll pay, don't worry. Bastards.

    PAT *and* JUNE *go out left.*

BYO. Don't she get worked up.

BILL. I 'ont gooin' a get no loan off 'er tonight.

BYO. See what yoo *can* get.

    Pause. RON *lights a cigarette and hands one to* BYO.

LEN. Thank God it's nigh on weekend.

BILL. Yoo ought a be in bed.

JOE. Chriss that's close. (*He wipes his neck.*) I been sweatin' like a pig.

SCOPEY. That owd strap pulled off the 'ook, that's all. That ent torn n' nothin'. I can easy fix that. It weren't on right for the first place. She never give much for that, doo they robbed 'er. That could be a pulled off when she were out shoppin', then she'd a been slummocksed. (*Takes a piece of paper from the bag.*) Owd ticket. (*Sniffs it.*) Powder. (*Sniffs.*) Mauve. (*Throws it away.*) Just push the strap back on a nip with the owd pliers. Doo that afore I goo t' bed, easy.

RON. Up in seven hours.

BILL. I'd best goo an' see 'ow she's gettin' on.

BYO. Don't forget a put somethin' on the end a it.

BILL. Thanks for the tip.

LORRY & RON. 'Night.

BILL. See yoo tmorra.

RON. In the saloon, mate.

BILL. Early. 'Night.

SCOPEY & JOE. 'Night.

BYO. 'Night, boy.

> BILL *goes out Left.*
> *Pause.*
> SCOPEY *swings the bag on the strap.*

Scene Two

An apple on the stage.
SCOPEY, BILL, RON, LORRY, JOE.
They each carry a scythe.
RON. Short back and sides.

> JOE *holds* LORRY. BYO *moves the scythe blade over the back of* LORRY's *head.*

BYO. Ha! I got some! (*He pulls some hairs from* LORRY's *head.*)

LORRY. I'll smash yoo, boy!

JOE. Watch out!

BYO. Duck's arse.

LORRY. When I get out!

BILL. Ent yoo mob workin'?

LORRY. First time I 'eard yoo want a work. Ow!

BILL. I ent 'angin' round 'ere all day, mate.

LORRY. Get these bastards off an' we'll start.

They let him go.

Try that agen!

JOE *laughs.*

BYO. Do'n'ee look cross.

LORRY. I'll maim yoo one day.

BILL. One little guzzle an' I'm ready. (*He takes a can of beer from his pocket.*)

SCOPEY. 'Oo yoo pinch that off?

JOE. I got sweat muck all over me.

SCOPEY. Where yoo pinch that?

BILL. I can smell yoo from 'ere. Goo down wind, boy. Move.

BYO. Me an' Bill'll doo under the trees an' yoo lot take the sides atween yer.

SCOPEY. What's Joe dooin'?

BILL. 'Elpin' yoo.

LORRY. Oo's got the fags afore we start?

RON. Where's yoorn?

LORRY. I give mine out this mornin'.

SCOPEY. Not when I was there.

JOE. Yoo what?

LORRY. Don't bother.

JOE. I ent.

BILL (*to* BYO). Yes?

BYO. Ta. (BYO *takes the can. He drinks.*)

RON. Pig.

BYO. Lovely.

LORRY (*to* RON). Ent yoo got no fags?

BILL. Up! (*He swings his scythe in a circle.* LORRY *and* SCOPEY *have to jump.*)

Yoo ent got a leg to stand on as the copper said when the burglar came round on the operatin' table.

SCOPEY. Bloody nut.

JOE. Teach yoo t' jump.

SCOPEY. More 'andy t' duck.

BYO. Finish 'er off. (*He hands the bottle back to* BILL.)

LORRY. Borrow yoor paper? (*Takes paper from* BILL's *jacket.*)
Want t' see what I fancy for this afternoon.

BILL. Oo's layin' ten bob next Saturday?

RON. No thanks.

BILL. Come on, won't bet on yoor own side?

LORRY. I'll believe it when I see it. They thrashed us three times
in the last four year.

RON. We ent got no good bowlers. That's where we fall down.

BILL. We ent never 'ad a battin' side like we got this year afore.
I reckon we could pull it off.

JOE. That's all a question of luck, anyroad.

RON. Cricket ent luck. That's strength and skill and guts.

BILL. Right. (*Sits.*)

SCOPEY. Thought yoo was gooin' a work.

BILL. Must let the beer goo down.

SCOPEY. I knew that wouldn't last.

BILL. Let it settle.

SCOPEY. I never 'ad none.

LORRY. 'Ard luck.

> LORRY, JOE, BYO *and* RON *sit.* BYO *picks up the apple. He eats.*
> *Pause.*

SCOPEY. Up yoo.

> *Pause.*

BYO. Right up.

> *Pause.*

LORRY. They win this year they keep the plack.

BILL. They still got owd man Bullrights. Yoo ent got no one a send
'em down alf fasts 'e doo, 'is time a life –

SCOPEY. No?

BILL. – an' I don't reckon yoo ever will 'ave.

SCOPEY. 'E won't be playin' next year.

BYO. 'E will.

SCOPEY. But I don't reckon 'e'll be captain after this.

BILL. 'E don't even practise. Goo out there year after year an' find perfect length first ball.

LORRY (*wiping scythe blade*). Beautiful owd thing, ent she. 'Ung 'er up in owd apple tree t' take the rust out on 'er.
  (*Sings.*) Betty drop your drawers it's Monday
          No I dropped my drawers on Sunday.

LEN (*sings*). I'm gooin' a pull them off for yoo
          I'll cut yoor tail off if yoo doo.

BILL. Anytime.

BYO. Join the queue.
    Pause.

RON. Owd Tanner Lob's gooin', then.

LORRY. Cancer all over.

SCOPEY. I 'erd it got 'is lungs.

JOE. Up 'is pipe.

RON. Runnin' all over.

BILL. On the brain.

LORRY. 'E won't be 'arvestin' this year.

RON. Ready?

BILL. No.

LORRY. Fair owd day, ent it.

BYO. It got 'im in the groin.

RON. Yoo got it in the groin.

BYO. I got somethin'.

BILL. Doo it grow?

BYO. Only when yoo're around.
    LEN *comes in up left.*

LEN. Mum's chasin' yoo.

BILL. Let 'er.

LEN. She's roarin' for that wringer.

BILL. Yoo fix it for 'er.

LEN. That's yoor job.

BILL. She can wait.

LEN. Yoo ent 'eard 'er roarin'.

BILL. I 'eard 'er all last night on her bloody wringer.

BYO. Ent yoo stand up to 'er yet?

BILL. I just kicked 'er teeth out, kneed 'er in the crutch, set light to 'er 'air, an' she died beggin' me t' forgive 'er.

LORRY. Did yoo?

BILL. No.

LORRY. Got a cigarette?

LEN. No.

BILL. 'E wouldn't give yoo the pickings off 'is arse.

LEN. Yoo comin'?

BILL. No.

JOE. 'E's 'elpin' us. Yoo tell 'er if we don't tidy this place up today we 'ont never get no chance afore the match.

BILL. That's 'er fault anyroad. She 'ont used that wringer right since the day she got it. She wrestle with it.

LORRY (*to* LEN). Yoo smoke?

BILL. 'E's too bloody mean, boy. Oi, gimp howd a that an' make yoorself 'andy. (*He pokes his scythe at* LEN.)

LEN. Yoo ent playin' Saturday.

BILL. No?

LEN. Mum say –

BILL. O yeh? Why?

LEN. Owd man Bullright's been tellin' 'er –

BILL. She can't stop me.

SCOPEY. What's 'e say?

LEN. 'E say if 'e goo off next Saturday 'e'll 'ave t' 'ave someone stayed on the farm.

SCOPEY. That's count a 'is owd red poll.

LORRY. She ent still sick?

BILL. Why me?

LEN. 'E ent got no one for 'andlin' animals barrin' yoo, so 'e say.

BILL. Foxy owd sod.

BYO. Bastard.

BILL. That's rotten play, ent it?

SCOPEY. Can 'e doo it?

BILL. 'E can afford to.

RON. 'E ent takin' no chances this year. That's 'is last year for captain an' 'e's out a keep 'is owd plack.

LORRY. We been playin' for that must be sixty year.

BILL. Bastard.

JOE. Say no.

BILL. With that spiteful owd sod?

SCOPEY. Why not?

BILL. There's plenty waitin' for my job, boy.

JOE. Well that's us finished.

BILL. The sod. (*Twists his scythe.*) I'd like t' 'ave 'is owd 'ead stuck on this.

BYO. Twelfth man in then.

RON. I ent laid that bet.

SCOPEY. I'll doo some trainin'.

BYO. Yoo need to.

JOE. Can't 'e get someone in from outside?

BYO. Don't be bloody daft –

BILL. That's just what 'e don't want a doo, ent it.

    Pause.

    LORRY *practises imaginary off-breaks.*

LORRY. I reckon owd Alen's put 'is curse on us. Owzat! Our owd telly broke down last Wednesday an' the old owd man reckon that's count a 'e cursed us on mum tellin' 'alf the village about Sarah Neat's baby. Owzat!

BILL. Bastard! I'll poison 'is bloody cow. I'll bloody well lay 'is missis for a start. I'll grind 'er, for one. 'E can stick 'is bloody plack but I'll bloody well thread 'is missis.

RON. Supposin' we practise 'ard an' we win the toss or it belts down, we could keep 'em out till it's too late for 'em t' doo much, with a bit a luck.

LORRY. Cricket's a game a skill an' guts an' that.

RON. That ent cricket.

LEN. Owd Sco can howd a catch, anyway.

BILL. Pity 'e can't howd a bat or bowl.

LORRY. Owzat.

BYO. They can't be feelin' too sure a 'emselves, doo they'd never play dirty like that.

RON. That's a fact.

Scene Three

ALEN's *place.*
Across the stage a black and purple corrugated iron wall. A door centre. A couch right. A table down left. Two oil cookers standing on a box down right. Two wooden boxes used as chairs. A stack of newspapers, one foot high, against the wall, right of the door. Three or four smaller stacks of newspapers about the room.

ALEN *alone.*
He stands by the door. He is rigid. He listens. He goes to the table. He goes farther down left. He takes a paper from the floor. He goes to the wall and places the paper on the stack. He goes back down left. Stoops to pick up a paper. Stops. Starts to read. His mouth moves. He slowly withdraws into himself. Wanders aimlessly right. Stops. Listens. Listens more intently. Half turns to the door. Clutches paper. Pause. His attention slowly goes back to the paper. He reads. He goes to the table and spreads the paper on it. He is reading all the time. Stops reading, goes down left, picks up paper, takes it to the wall and places it on the stack. Steps back. Steps forward on to the stack. Pause. Steps down. Wanders aimlessly to the cookers.
Goes back to the table and reads the paper on it. Pause. Scratches chin. Picks up the paper. Goes down left, still reading. Picks up a second paper and goes up right, still reading the first paper. Before he reaches the stack he drops the second paper. Pause. Goes down left and stoops to pick up a third paper, still reading the first paper. Abruptly halts, bent. Listens briefly. Picks up the third paper, still carefully listening. Goes up right. Stops when he reaches the second paper. Looks down at it. Pause. Picks it up. Takes it to the table. Goes up right,

*reading first paper. Places third paper on stack. Steps back. Steps
forward on to stack. With his back to the audience he places his ear
against the wall. He listens. Pause. He steps down. He goes to the
table. He picks up the second paper. He turns and starts to go back to
the wall. Stops. Goes back to the table. Places second paper on table.
Starts to pull table towards wall. Almost immediately a tin falls from
the table on to the floor. Stops. Picks up the tin. Puts it on the table.
Places first paper on a box behind him. Places both palms on the edge
of the table and makes a small effort to raise himself. Gives it up. Sits
on the box. Stands. Takes first paper from box. Sits. Pause. Stands.
Places first paper on box. Goes to the table. Takes second paper from
table and places it on the floor by the table. Stands on second paper
and places both palms on the table as before. Pause. Makes no effort
to raise himself. Steps off second paper. Picks it up. Puts it on the
table. Takes first paper from the box. Reads.
A bang on the door.*

ALEN (*a sigh – gasp.*)

Scene Four

Empty stage.
LORRY *runs in from the right. He is dressed completely in white and
carries a cricket bat. He groans. He follows the high flight of a ball
with his eyes.*

VOICES (*off*). Owzat!

    LORRY *shrugs and walks down right. Clapping. He meets*
    SCOPEY *as he comes on down right.*

LORRY. Whew! 'E's movin' owd Tanner in t' silly mid on.

SCOPEY. Tryin' to get me rattled.

LORRY (*irritated*). Never mind that. Yoo watch out.

SCOPEY. Yoo did all right.

LORRY. I never 'ad no support. Forty t' get. Don't give me a
    chance.

SCOPEY. Yoo knock a couple off, boy.

LORRY. They're comin' down like rockets. I reckon 'e's out t' knacker yer.

SCOPEY. I'll be –

LORRY. Yoo got a get thirty-two. Yoo 'ont never get thirty-two, but owd Joe's good for a dozen. Then that 'ont look like they used us for a mat.

SCOPEY. 'E won't get one if 'e don't come out after 'em –

LORRY. Yoo let 'im play 'is own game. Now don't yoo forget, 'e'll 'it that second ball an yoo run –

SCOPEY. They're waitin'.

LORRY. – like 'ell.

> LORRY *goes out down right.* SCOPEY *takes up his position left centre.* BOWLER *runs in from left and bowls.* SCOPEY *stiffens. Pause.* BOWLER *catches ball as it is fielded back to him. He walks off left. Pause.* BOWLER *runs in from left and bowls.*

SCOPEY. Yes!

> SCOPEY *runs out right.*
> JOE *runs in right and touches into crease.*

SCOPEY (*off*). Yes!

JOE. No! No! CHRISS!

> SCOPEY *runs in from the right.*

JOE. No!

> JOE *dashes out right.* SCOPEY *touches into the crease. Shouts off stage.* SCOPEY *wipes his forehead with a handkerchief. Pause. He looks round at the field. He takes up his position. His heels are three inches apart. His right foot is parallel with the crease. His left foot points to cover. His chest and shoulders are square to point. His knees are relaxed. His weight is evenly balanced. His head is upright and his eyes are level. He alerts. He plays the first ball forward on to the pitch. Pause. Hooks the second ball past deep fine leg.*

JOE (*off*). Yes!

> SCOPEY *runs off right and* JOE *runs in right. He touches into the crease.*

SCOPEY (*off*). Yes!

JOE. No!

SCOPEY *runs in from the right.*

JOE. Bloody fool.

JOE *runs out right.* SCOPEY *touches into crease. He takes up his stance. Suddenly he drives the ball past forward short leg. Applause. Shouts of 'Six!' Pause.* SCOPEY *settles into his stance again. He suddenly cuts to cover. Loud applause. Shouts of 'Four'. Settles into his stance. Moves out and hits a straight drive. Loud applause. Shouts of 'Six!' Pause. Suddenly he tries to glance the ball to leg. Hastily twists to look behind him and touch into his crease. Onlookers groan. Silence. Loud clapping.*

JOE *comes in jerkily from the right.* SCOPEY *goes to meet him.*

JOE. For Chriss sake goo easy!

SCOPEY. What?

JOE. Eighteen in one over! Yoo're takin' chances. Twelve t' win! Yoo 'ont a take them chances, boy, we can't afford it. Goo steady an' let me 'ave a crack. Yoo 'ad yoor turn a luck but that 'ont never last a second time.

JOE *goes out right.* SCOPEY *returns to his crease.* BOWLER *runs in from the left and bowls. He catches the returned ball and spins to face* SCOPEY. SCOPEY *is in his crease.* BOWLER *goes out left, throwing the ball a few feet in the air and catching it.* BOWLER *runs in from left. He bowls. It is a short ball.*

BOWLER AND OTHER VOICES. Owzat!

UMPIRE (*off stage*). No ball.

Murmurs. SCOPEY *looks down at his feet, bending swiftly from the waist.* BOWLER *wipes the back of his neck. He catches the returned ball and goes out left, throwing it and catching the ball with one hand. He runs in from left and bowls. A second passes and the* BOWLER *leaps forward into the air, snatches for the ball, falls forward, his left knee giving way. He lies with his back to the audience. Stands. Tugs at his belt, scoops up the ball – which has landed a few feet in front of him. Goes out left, gripping the ball. Pause. Runs in from left. Bowls. Applause. He catches the returned ball. He goes off left. He runs in. He bowls.*

JOE (*off*). Yes!

SCOPEY. No! No!

> BOWLER *whips up the returned ball. Spins to face* SCOPEY. BOWLER *starts to go left.*

BOWLER (*with a dry spit*). Last 'un.

> BOWLER *goes out left. Runs in. Bowls. Applause.* SCOPEY *runs out right and passes* JOE *as he runs in.* JOE *reaches the crease.*

SCOPEY (*off*). Yes!

JOE. No! Sco!

> SCOPEY *runs in from right.* JOE *runs out right. Applause.* JOE *comes in from right.* SCOPEY *strolls a few steps to meet him.*

JOE. Ten! We could doo that. We got to, Chriss! Doo we'll never 'ear the last on it. Yoo all right? Goo easy. 'Ow yoo doin'?

SCOPEY. All right.

JOE. Chriss, yoo 'ont better try nothin' fancy this time. (*Wipes his forehead.*) Chriss, I'm that 'ot!

SCOPEY. They're ready, Joe.

JOE. 'E's pushed owd Tanner cross t' deep square leg. Goo steady. Chriss, I know somethin'll come a balls it up.

> JOE *goes out right.* SCOPEY *settles into his crease. Pause. He glances the ball elegantly to leg. Shouts of 'Four!' And loud applause. He suddenly flinches. Onlookers groan. Pause, and* SCOPEY *slowly swings his bat from side to side. Stops. Looks round at the field – first and second slips, gully, mid off, forward short leg, deep fine leg, deep backward square leg, cover point and third man. Alerts. Suddenly dashes down the field and smashes the ball past mid on.*

SCOPEY. YES! YES! YES!

> SCOPEY *runs out right.* JOE *runs in right.*

JOE (*running*). God! I can't stand it!

SCOPEY (*off*). YES! YES! YES!

JOE. That voice! (*He drops his bat.*) Aaaaahhhh God!

> SCOPEY *runs in from the right.*

SCOPEY (*running*). YES! YES! YES!

> JOE *whinnies. Snatches up his bat. Dashes right.*

JOE (*running*). FOUR MORE! FOUR MORE!

SCOPEY. YES! YES! YES!

> JOE *runs out right. The onlookers are in an uproar.* SCOPEY *looks patiently down the pitch. Alerts. Leaps forward. Swoops on the ball. The bat cracks. The ball smashes past mid on. Shouts of 'Four!' and uproar.*
>
> (*A wicket-keeper can be used.*)

Scene Five

Up right a patch of light falling from a doorway. Above it the dark outline of the bottom part of an inn sign.

SCOPEY *and* PAT *on the floor down left.*

PAT. Where yoo put that thing?

SCOPEY. Thirty beauties.

PAT (*slight burp*). I like Babycham.

> SCOPEY *stretches.*

Yoo throw that away?

SCOPEY. What?

PAT. Yoo know.

SCOPEY. Why?

PAT. That ent nice for someone a find.

SCOPEY. Things yoo fret 'bout, gal. Oo'd know it was us?

PAT. 'Ave yoo throwed it?

SCOPEY. Yeh.

PAT. O. (*Pause.*) Yoo're a real devil, ent yoo?

SCOPEY. With one 'orn.

PAT (*laughs shrilly*). Not agen?

SCOPEY. Sh!

PAT (*giggling*). They 'ear?

SCOPEY. Oo cares?

PAT. I ent 'avin' a lot a owd talk.

SCOPEY. Ooo cares?

PAT. Yoo're all right.

SCOPEY. Eh?

PAT. Yoo're a boy.

SCOPEY. Sure?

PAT. Cheeky sod.

SCOPEY. I'll tell yoo somethin', gal – yoo make a fair owd lay.

PAT. That's all yoo want.

SCOPEY. What?

PAT. Yoo know.

SCOPEY. Too shy a say it? Eh?

PAT. Stop pullin' my leg.

SCOPEY. The owd crutch piece – what's wrong with that?

PAT. I'll tell my fiancé.

SCOPEY. Sh!

PAT (*after a pause*). What?

SCOPEY. I thought I 'eard 'em.

PAT. Bill'll be mad when 'e find that's gone.

SCOPEY. 'E's too pissed a notice.

PAT. That boy don't miss much.

SCOPEY. We only 'ad a loan on it.

PAT. Yoo did.

SCOPEY. All right. (*Slight pause.*) Wham! Chriss, that shook 'em!

PAT. You look beautiful all in white.

SCOPEY. That second ball on the last over.

PAT. Sounds like a bride.

SCOPEY. I bet that got the wind up yer, ent it?

PAT. What one was that?

SCOPEY. I knew what I was playin' at, though, boy. I weren't takin' no chances.

PAT. O, don't touch the grass.

SCOPEY. No?

PAT. That's wet.

SCOPEY. Yoo're 'and's wet, ent it?

RON *comes in up right. He carries a glass.*

RON. Sco? (*Pause.*) They're drinkin' yoor beer, boy! (*Pause.*) Well 'e ent 'ere?

RON *goes off up right, whistling.*

PAT. I thought 'e'd saw us.

SCOPEY. Oo cares?

PAT. I 'ont 'avin' no talk.

SCOPEY. I'll shut 'em up.

PAT. That's what I'm afraid of.

SCOPEY. Sh a minute.

PAT. What?

SCOPEY. Sh.

PAT. Why? (*Pause.*) Well?

SCOPEY. Nice, ent it?

PAT. What is?

SCOPEY. Lyin' 'ere.

PAT. Why?

SCOPEY. Quiet.

PAT. Yoo pullin' my leg?

SCOPEY. Don't yoo like it?

PAT. It's a bit cold, ent it?

SCOPEY. Yoo cold, gal?

    PAT *giggles.*

    BYO *and* RON *come up right. Pause.* BYO *sighs. Pause.*

RON. That's better.

BYO. Shake it more'n ten times an' yoo're playin' with it.

    They laugh.

RON. Yoo're pissed, boy.

BYO. I'm pissed?

RON. That's right.

BYO. I ent.

RON. Yoo're pissed.

BYO. Yoo're pissed, boy.

RON. Can't even slash straight.

BYO. Yoo wait till I finished 'fore yoo say that, yoo owd devil.

RON. Listen. (*He throws a stone. A splash.*) Yoo can't 'it that owd pond.

BYO. No? (*He throws a stone. A splash.*) Aaah! Oo's pissed? (*He throws a stone. A splash.*) Aaah! Fair owd noise, ent it?

RON. Eh?

BYO. Fair owd noise.

RON. Yoo're pissed.

BYO. Listen. (*He throws a stone. A splash.*) Aaah!

RON. Yoo're pissed, boy, doo yoo 'ont never stand out 'ere throwin' stones. (*He tries to push* BYO.) Pissed!

BYO. That's nice out 'ere. I'd like to stay out 'ere all night. Quiet.

RON. Quiet?

BYO. Eh?

RON. With that pissy row?

BYO. That don't count. That's out the back.

RON. My life, boy. Yoo pissed.

BYO. Next door.

RON. Yoo comin'?

BYO. Quiet.

RON. Yoo'll fall in that pond.

BYO. Quiet!

> *In the pub they start to sing 'He's a Jolly Good Fellow'.* RON *joins in.*

RON (*toasting*). All the best! Where's yoor beer?

BYO. Inside.

RON. Yoo ent likely a see that no more.

BYO. I'd better. (*Turns right.*) What thievin' bastard took my beer?

RON (*following him*). 'E's 'ad too much all ready.

> RON *and* BYO *go off up right.*

PAT. Wait till I tell the gals tmorra. Oi, that damp'll be comin' through.

SCOPEY. Howd still a minute.

PAT. Lazy sod.

SCOPEY. I earnt a rest.

PAT (*giggles*). Yoo should a gone in when they was singin'.

SCOPEY. They'll 'ave t' doo without me.

PAT. I'd like a throw stones in that pond. When yoo gooin' in?

SCOPEY. Ent yoo gooin' a try an' keep me 'ere?

PAT. We're missin' all the drink.

SCOPEY. I'll buy yoo all the drink yoo want anytime.

PAT. Oo's money yoo throwin' away?

SCOPEY. When a gal lays like yoo, mate, she can 'ave anythin'.

PAT. Stop it.

SCOPEY. Come on.

PAT. Fancy yoo askin'.

SCOPEY. Ha!

PAT (*after a pause*). Howd me tight. (*Pause.*) Yoo looked beautiful this afternoon. (*Slight pause.*) I keep seein' yoo standin' there with that bat.

SCOPEY. I felt all right.

PAT. D'yoo like me?

SCOPEY. What yoo think?

PAT. 'Ow many gals yoo been with?

SCOPEY. Enough.

PAT. Yoo can't remember. (*Cross.*) No.

SCOPEY. Come on, yoo like it.

PAT. We ought a goo in.

SCOPEY. Please.

    Pause.

  Fag?

PAT. Now?

SCOPEY. Yeh.

PAT. No.

SCOPEY. First time I 'eard that.

PAT. An' the last.

BILL (*off*). Pat!

PAT. 'E's after 'is sheet.

SCOPEY. Good luck.

PAT. Better put it back.

SCOPEY. Ground's wet.

PAT. 'E'll goo mad.

SCOPEY. Let 'im.

PAT. I told yoo not a take it.

SCOPEY. It's all right.

PAT. Yoo'd better 'ave a good story.

SCOPEY. Sure.

PAT. An' don't bring me into it.

SCOPEY. I won't.

PAT. Well, I 'ont 'avin' no trouble.

SCOPEY. Pat.

VOICE (*off*). Last orders, lads.

PAT. What?

SCOPEY. Let's goo under the trees.

PAT. That's too wet.

SCOPEY. Come on.

VOICE (*off*). Drink up, lads.

PAT. Why?

SCOPEY. It's still early.

PAT. No.

SCOPEY. They're comin' out now.

PAT. Too dark.

SCOPEY. Let me screw yoo agen, Pat. I got to.

PAT. Can we take the sheet?

SCOPEY. Yeh. That'll goo around us, an' over the top.

    PAT *laughs*.

  Howd on a me 'and.

PAT. Yoo ought a goo in once afore it's finished.

SCOPEY. They 'ont see us over there.

PAT. Goo in an' say good night.

SCOPEY. I'd never get out.

PAT. I lost my bag.

SCOPEY. I got it.

PAT. Where's the sheet?

SCOPEY. 'Ere.

PAT. Ooo.

SCOPEY. What's up?

PAT. It's wet.

SCOPEY. Goo steady. That's the pond.

PAT. I'll tell me gran I slept with June.

SCOPEY. I'll find a dry spot we can stay the whole night, gal.

PAT. No.

SCOPEY. Sure.

> PAT *and* SCOPEY *go out up left.*

JOE (*off*). I reckon 'e were dodgin' 'is round.

> LEN *comes up right.*

LEN. Sco should a stayed. That looked bad.

BYO (*off*). I reckon 'e's just wore out.

> BYO *and* JOE *come on after* LEN.

LORRY. I reckon 'e can doo what 'e like.

JOE. Eh?

> LORRY *comes in after the others.*

BILL (*off*). Pat!

LORRY. 's obvious.

JOE. 'Ow?

LORRY. Whatever 'e doo I reckon 'e's great.

JOE. Great?

LORRY. Great!

JOE. My life! That's luck.

BYO. Wrap up, yoo nits.

> BILL *comes in down right.*

BYO. No luck?

BILL. No.

BYO. Should never a left it on that bike in the first place. I told yoo enough.

LORRY. T'ent likely yoo'll see that agen, boy.

BILL. If that's gone, that's gone. Good 'ealth. (*Takes a small bottle of rum from inside his shirt. Drinks.*)

BYO. That's a boy. (*Takes the bottle from* BILL. *Drinks.*) Good owd Billy, then.

LORRY. Yoo'll be sick.

BYO. Over yoo, I 'ope. Taste.

LORRY (*takes the bottle. Drinks*). 'Andsome.

JOE. I'm 'ere.

BYO. We can smell yer.

JOE (*takes bottle. Drinks*). Aaaaaaaaaaaaaaah!

LORRY. Let's goo round Sco's place.

BYO. No.

BILL. Nit.

LORRY. They reckon 'e's been out trainin' on the common early mornin's for months.

BYO. Rum boy.

RON. 'E must a been countin' on gettin' in the team some time.

LORRY. Chriss 'e knocked owd man Bullright all over the place, ent 'e?

JOE. Let's goo an' turn owd Alen's dump over.

BILL. Doo what?

JOE. Smash 'is windows.

BYO. Yeh.

RON. Dirty owd diddy boy.

BILL. 'E ent got no windows.

BYO. Well, smash 'is 'ead in.

JOE. Yeh.

BILL. Nits.

BYO. Eh?

BILL. Nits. I ent runnin' round that owd drain 'ole in the dark.

BYO. Come on, just for a laugh.

BILL. Up t' yoor eyes in cess. Goo on, goo. (*Shakes the bottle against his ear.*) Goo.

JOE. Yoo never want a doo nothin'. Yoo 'ont got no goo, boy.

BYO. Much left?

BILL. Ent nearly started.

BYO. I'll stay 'ere a see yoo get 'ome, boy, doo yoo'll be sleepin' in the ditch.

BILL. Let's sit be the 'edge an 'ave a natter.

BYO (*to* JOE). Get lost.

Scene Six

ALEN's *place.*

PAT *sweeps the floor. She picks up a paper and puts it on the pile by the door. She goes on sweeping.*

PAT. I 'ont got no goo in me today. That'll 'ave t'o doo with just a lick.

   ALEN *takes the paper from the pile and puts it back on the floor.* Why don't yoo put the dut back?

ALEN. That'll get back be itself.

PAT. Yoo'll 'ave t' eat on bread and tatters tmorra. Doo yoo good. Give them owd pipes a rest. (*She sweeps round the table.*) I don't reckon all that owd tin stuff doo anyone's insides no good. Yoo need proper meals. Why yoo don't goo out the back an' dig that little patch, yoo'd 'ave a proper little garden for vegetables out there. Tins. I 'ad a doze dinner time. (*She leans the broom against the wall.*) That look better. Doo till tmorra, anyroad. I'll see if I can't get 'ere early. I ent promisin', mind. (*She puts on her coat.*) I never thought I'd like watchin' that owd cricket. I keep seein' 'im chargin' up an' down in 'is white. (*She picks up her bag and goes towards the door.*)

ALEN. List.

PAT. O yes. Where's my pencil. I 'ad that in the back a my mind but I couldn't think what that was. (*She sits at the table, tears a strip from a paper and starts to write.*) One stew. Three beans. Two large rice. One bread. One fancy. Four ounces boiled. Half tea. That's all, ent it? Yoo got plenty a bread and tatters a see yoo through tmorra. (*She looks in the large bin on the table. She adds to the list.*) Half butter. Then you can fill up in the evenin'. Eggs. (*She takes a folded shopping bag from the table drawer and goes to the door.*) Cheerio.

ALEN. Vaporated.

PAT. I knew I left somethin'.

ALEN. One vaporated.

PAT. I'll remember that.

ALEN. Yoo put that down.

    PAT *goes back to the table and writes on the list.*

Yoo 'ad no right to leave that off in the first place.

PAT. I got other things to remember.

ALEN. One vap. Don't yoo start comin' 'ere 'alf asleep on yoor feet.

PAT. I 'ont takin' my orders from yoo.

ALEN. One vap. Yoo put that down.

PAT. I got it down. (*She goes back to the door.*)

ALEN. An' don't yoo come 'ere forgettin'.

PAT. I'll come 'ow I like.

ALEN. One vap. My milk.

PAT. I 'ope they sold out.

ALEN. Yoo bring that.

PAT. I'll bring your bloody milk.

ALEN. I need my milk same as – listen!

PAT. What?

ALEN. Oo's outside?

PAT. No one.

ALEN. Someone snoopin'.

PAT. Ow d'yoo know?

ALEN. Listen.

PAT. I can't 'ear nothin'. I expect Bill's come t' meet me.

ALEN. 'E whistles an' kicks the stones. Someone's tryin' t' be quiet.

PAT. Leave off, yoo'll give yoorself the creeps.

ALEN. Don't goo through the door.

PAT. Yoo're daft.

ALEN. Don't.

PAT. Cheerio.

ALEN. 'E's one a yoor men.

PAT. Don't be daft, boy.

ALEN. I towed yoo afore I 'ont 'avin' that sort 'angin' round my door.

PAT. What sort?

ALEN. Roughs.

PAT. I'll be in tmorra. (*She starts to open the door.*)

ALEN. Yoo 'ont peeled my tatties.

PAT. Yoo'll 'ave t' peel 'em.

ALEN. That's yoor place t' peel 'em.

PAT. Once 'ont never cripple yoo.

ALEN. Yoo swore t' yoor mum be 'er dyin' bed yoo'll peel my tatties.

PAT. I did not.

ALEN. Liar.

PAT. All I ever said was I'd see yoo kep clean an' swep out.

ALEN. 'E's creepin' be the side.

PAT. After today yoo peel yoor own tatters or bloody well 'ave 'em in their jackets.

ALEN. Yoo swore by yoor dead mum's body.

PAT. I don't give a damn what I swore then, that's what I'm swearin' now.

ALEN. 'E ent moved. 'E must be out the back.

PAT. Yoo been 'ere too long. I said it'd turn yoor 'ead, boy.

ALEN. Dirty owd diddies scratchin' be me door, no decent vittels, no milk, an' all me own cookin' a cope with an' I 'ont 'ardly got the grip in me 'ands a gimp howd on a knife count a me cripplin'.

PAT. That'll learn yoo not a row.

ALEN. Yoor mum's turnin' in 'er grave.

PAT. For Chriss' sake don't keep on about 'er.

ALEN. I ent long for this world. I can't draw me breath today.

PAT. That's a lot a owd tommy rot. All yoo need's a dose a fresh air an' a good scrubbin'.

ALEN. Then why yoo swep all that dut flyin' up?

PAT. Yoo should a let me open that door.

ALEN. All me mates is gone.

PAT. Yoo're sure I got all the shoppin' down.

ALEN. T'ent no use, yoo'll forget 'alf on it, anyroad.

PAT. Then I'm off. I'm late.

ALEN. One a these days yoo'll get tired a comin', I can see it. I'll
die a starvin' or be killed up on the road tryin' a reach the 'ouses.

PAT. Ta-ta.

ALEN. I can throw out my messages in them little bottles agen,
gal. Yoo howd yoor tongue doo I –

PAT. No yoo don't, my boy. I 'ont 'avin' that agen. Yoo come the
owd acid with me an' yoo goo straight back on yoor rations:
salt beef an' one 'alf cup a water per day.

ALEN. No.

PAT. I'll turn off the mains on the road an' I don't see yoo gooin'
down there t' turn it back.

ALEN. Wicked!

PAT. Yoo count your blessin's an' close yoor mouth.

ALEN. Turnin' in 'er grave.

PAT. I 'ope the exercise doo 'er good.

> PAT *goes out through the door* – ALEN *gestures to stop her and
> groans. He bolts the door and turns the key. He bends down and
> puts his ear to the door. He straightens and tilts his head back a
> little, still with his ear to the door. Pause. He turns uncertainly
> back to the room. He turns back to the door and listens. Suddenly
> he scurries down left and stands behind the table. He is shaken
> with convulsions. His throat rattles. He panics. Pause. He gains
> a little control.*

SCOPEY (*off*). Pat.

> ALEN *starts to shake again. He tries to muffle the rattle in his
> throat.*

SCOPEY (*off*). Pat there?

> ALEN *scurries up to the bed and crouches behind it with his back
> to the wall. He starts to pull the bed towards him. It squeaks. He
> stops.*

SCOPEY (*off*). Oi!

> ALEN *pulls the bed again. It squeaks. He stops.*

SCOPEY (*off*). Yoo can 'ear. (*Pause.*) What yoo doo all day?
> *Longer pause.*
> ALEN *rises from behind the bed and strains towards the wall.*

What yoor 'obbies?

    ALEN *ducks behind the bed again. Pause.*

PAT? (*Pause.*) She must a gone. (*Pause. Farther away.*) – Sorry, mate.

    Silence.

Scene Seven

The open.
A bench down left.
JUNE and PAT sit on the bench. They eat sandwiches.

PAT. Nice?

JUNE. No.

PAT. Chriss.

JUNE. I'll 'ave t' try gettin' up early and dooin' me own.

PAT. Yoo ought a ask 'er t' get somethin' nice in. Tell 'er. They 'ont use no imagination.

JUNE. I say anythin' an' she say what yoo expect for eight pound.

PAT. Got a fag?

JUNE. No.

PAT. You ent looked.

JUNE. I know I 'ont got none. I smoke my last tea break.

PAT. I left four in the clock. Gran'll swipe them.

JUNE. Yoo'll 'ave t' goo without.

PAT. Sco'll 'ave some.

JUNE (*opening a magazine*). If 'e get 'ere.

PAT. Yoo should a brought the cards.

JUNE. Yoo owe me forty-two p.

PAT. Chriss.

JUNE (*going through the magazine*). Yoo told 'im anything.

PAT. What about?

JUNE. Ent yoo 'ad a talk?

PAT. What for?

JUNE. 'Bout Bill and them.

PAT. No.

JUNE. O. (*Pause.*) Ent 'e said?

PAT. What about?

JUNE. Fellas?

PAT. No.

JUNE. Didn't 'e notice?

PAT. 'E was too pissed a notice.

JUNE. Some people 'ave all the luck.

PAT. I just said 'ow' and 'e said it won't 'urt next time, you'll see.

JUNE. Saucy sod.

PAT. Then 'e wanted a take a chance.

JUNE. Yoo said no.

PAT. I said if yoo don't treat me with respect yoo ent 'avin' it.

JUNE. Yes.

PAT. I could doo with a fag.

JUNE (*reopening the magazine*). I still think yoo should a told 'im.

PAT. That ent nothin' a doo with 'im.

JUNE. Yoo're supposed a start off tellin' everythin' like that.

PAT. 'E can look after 'is business an' I'll look after mine.

JUNE. Yoo're scared, gal.

PAT. What for?

JUNE. It might put 'im off.

PAT. Don't be bloody daft.

JUNE. Fellas can be funny.

PAT. They know when they're on to a good thing.

JUNE. Yoo bein' married in white?

PAT. No money.

JUNE. Where yoo gooin' away?

PAT. If we get howd on a place we'll 'ave the decoratin' a doo. I'd rather see that done first an' goo away for a good week next year.

JUNE. Did I tell yoo that joke?

PAT. No.

JUNE. 'Bout the honeymoon couple.

PAT. No.

JUNE. It's a laugh.

PAT. Well goo on.

JUNE. Well they goo a this 'otel, see, an' they goo upstairs an' the bloke 'e say I'm just gooin' downstairs for a packet a fags, dear.

PAT. I could doo with a fag.

JUNE. Listen. So 'e goo downstairs an' she get undressed an' 'ops into bed on account a bein' shy, see, an' suddenly there's this big bangin' on the door.

PAT. Yes.

JUNE. A big bangin'. An' she shout out 'No need a knock, dear. I ent afraid' an' 'e say 'Yoo would be if yoo knew what I was knockin' on the door with.'

PAT. That's good, ent it.

JUNE. Bang bang.

PAT. Bang bang. 'Oo told yoo that?

JUNE. My mum.

PAT. She know some lovely stories, don't she.

JUNE. There 'e is.

PAT (*waves*). Oi.

JUNE. Suppose Bill or one a 'em say somethin'?

PAT. 'E's been knockin' about with that crowd long afore I went with 'im. If 'e want a know, 'e know by now. (*Calls.*) Fags?

SCOPEY *comes in from the right.*

SCOPEY. I only got a roll.

JUNE. Take the weight off yoor feet.

SCOPEY (*sitting*). An' on t' me arse.

PAT. If it ent corns it's piles.

JUNE. Like a sandwich?

SCOPEY. No.

PAT. Goo on.

SCOPEY. I 'ad mine.

PAT. Busy?

SCOPEY. Usual.

JUNE. Terrible this mornin'.

SCOPEY. Shall I doo yoo a roll?

PAT. I'll doo it.

 SCOPEY *hands her the pouch, papers and roller. She rolls a cigarette.*

SCOPEY. Goo steady with that bacco. That's got a last.

JUNE. Can she roll one for me?

SCOPEY. Sure.

PAT. Trust yoo.

SCOPEY. No, that's all right.

PAT. I 'ad a postcard from Betty Legs.

SCOPEY. O.

PAT. They reckon 'er 'usband's gooin' a be posted over 'ere agen, so she'll be comin' across with 'im. (*She opens her bag.*)

JUNE. Doo she say when?

PAT. No.

 PAT *hands the card to* SCOPEY. *He looks at it and at the same time* JUNE *tries to look at it.*

JUNE. Let's see.

SCOPEY. Don't snatch. What's that?

PAT. Nice, ent it?

SCOPEY. What is it?

PAT. That's where she lives. They call it a city but that ent no bigger than a little town.

JUNE. Nice.

SCOPEY. Yoo can't tell.

JUNE. I like it.

SCOPEY. Yoo need more than that. Yoo'd 'ave t' see more.

JUNE. It's nice.

SCOPEY. Yoo need more.

JUNE. I know what I like – they keep the streets swep'.

SCOPEY. Where yoo seen streets like that?

JUNE. Only count a people drop dirt all the time. People are pigs.

SCOPEY. Nothin's like that. No more yoo ent seen sky like that.

JUNE. Never said I 'ad. I just said I like it.

SCOPEY. Yoo can't tell. Where's the people an' the corners? (*He turns the card over.*)

PAT. Thanks.

SCOPEY (*reads*). 'Ope yoo are keepin' well an yoor family. We are
are well but baby does not like the heat. Hyram say 'e may be
posted 'ome, 'e 'ear rumour. So look forward to seen' yoo soon.
Love to all, Betty, Baby, Hyram. That don't say a word what's
on the front.

JUNE. She ent got that much room, 'ave she.

PAT. Let's 'ave it. (*She puts the card back in her bag.*)

SCOPEY (*sniffs*). I'd like a stick postcards all over the room.

PAT. Give me a light.

> JUNE *hands her matches. She lights her cigarette.*

SCOPEY. On the floor an' the ceilin'.

PAT. Talk about somethin' else.

JUNE. Cheap wall paper.

PAT. We'll 'ave t' get a wall first.

JUNE. I know what 'e's after. Dirty owd man.

SCOPEY. What?

PAT. Arse an' tit.

SCOPEY. I never said that.

JUNE. Well what?

SCOPEY. Just pictures.

PAT. Why?

SCOPEY. Why? That's what I'd like.

PAT. Not in my place.

JUNE. Yoo said she could doo me a roll.

SCOPEY. Sure.

PAT. Can I borrow it?

SCOPEY. All right.

PAT. Yoo can 'ave it back tonight.

SCOPEY. Okay.

JUNE. Ta.

Scene Eight

ALEN's.

ALEN *alone. He stands at the table. He is opening a tin. He puts the tin opener in his overcoat pocket. He drinks the juice from the tin. He starts to put the tin back on the table. A knock. He snatches his hand away from the tin and half turns right – there are no other reactions. Pause. A knock – not as loud as the first.*

SCOPEY (*off*). Oi. (*A knock.*) She left 'er bag. (*Pause.*) Yoo got 'er bag.

ALEN. She's gone.

SCOPEY. Open this. (*He bangs on the door.*)

ALEN. Yoo'll catch 'er up.

SCOPEY. She'll want that bag when she find she ent got it.

ALEN. She's gone.

SCOPEY (*banging on door*). I'll kick it open.

ALEN. Howd on. (*He goes right, trying to think.*)

SCOPEY. Well?

ALEN. No shoppin' tmorra –

SCOPEY. I want that bag.

ALEN. – that's Tuesday.

SCOPEY. I know yoo got it.

ALEN. That's Tuesday.

SCOPEY. I warned yoo.

ALEN (*angrily*). No!

SCOPEY (*after a pause*). What yoo dooin' now? (*Slight pause.*) I bet yoo get up t' some fancy tricks, boy. In there be yoorself all day (*Pause.*) I could easy get my mates up 'ere. Easy.

ALEN. The police 'ont –

SCOPEY. Police! That's a laugh. They're just waitin' for a chance a get yoo out, boy. They don't reckon yoor sort anywhere. They just moved the gypsies on. I could stop Pat comin 'ere. Anytime.

ALEN (*after a pause*). Wait up on the road. I'll throw it out.

SCOPEY. Open this door!

ALEN. Yoo can't stop 'er comin'.

SCOPEY. What yoo want 'er for? (*Slight pause.*) What yoo two get up to?

ALEN. I'm ill.

SCOPEY. What?

ALEN (*goes to the bed. Slight pause.* SCOPEY *kicks the door violently*). Don't kick my door! I'm ill! I'm ill!

SCOPEY (*kicks the door*). I'm comin', mister!

ALEN. Stop it! (*He goes to the door and opens it.*)

SCOPEY. 'Urry up.

> The door is opened. SCOPEY *steps in. Pause.*

Smoke?

ALEN. Eh.

SCOPEY. Smoke? Fag? Roll? Cheroot, mister.

ALEN. Eh.

SCOPEY. Shame. I'm out. (*He looks at the oil cookers.*) She lug that oil all the way up in winter. She's a strong gal, ent she? (*Pause.*) Yoo collect papers.

> ALEN *holds out a purple and brown leatherette bag.*

Stinks. Can't yoo smell it? Coo.

ALEN. Yoo goo.

SCOPEY. Eh?

ALEN. Yoo don't like it. (*He holds out the bag.*)

SCOPEY. I bet the council ent been round 'ere. What's on the turn?

ALEN. I like it.

SCOPEY. This?

ALEN. Eh?

SCOPEY. Puttin' it down?

ALEN. Eh?

SCOPEY. Grub? (*He taps the opened tin of pears.*)

ALEN. No, no.

SCOPEY. Guts.

ALEN. Bag.

SCOPEY. I ent invited?

ALEN. Eh?

SCOPEY. Yoo don't believe in sharin'.

ALEN. Nothin'. Not eatin'.

SCOPEY. Yoo ought a wash yoor 'ands afore yoo get up t' table. (*He goes up to the stack of papers by the wall, picks up a sheaf, glances at them, and whacks them down on the couch.*) What they for?

ALEN. My bloody work!

SCOPEY. What?

ALEN. Yoo cow!

SCOPEY. Do what?

ALEN'*s anger cools and he is afraid.*

Eh? Yoo cow? What's up? (*Pause.*) What work? (*He goes to* ALEN.) Why d'yoo blow yoor top? (*Pause.*)

ALEN. Bag.

SCOPEY. What's the paper for? That yoor work? (*Pause.*) Ha!

ALEN *sits on the bed.*

What's this for? (*Touches a box with his boot.*) What's this? (*He taps the couch with his boot. Pause.*) Yoo ought a keep a dog. Good company. She 'ont kep yoo all that clean. Oi, I'm marryin' 'er. She said? (*Pause. He takes the bag from the bed.*) Didn't recognize it. Looks different out there. (*Pause. Sniffs.*) Coo. (*Slight pause.*) Can yoo lock up all right?

ALEN. Lock?

SCOPEY. She told me yoo was a grippin' owd bastard. I'll leave the bag, I forgot that was Tuesday amorra. Oi, yoo tellin' 'er I been 'ere?

ALEN. What?

SCOPEY. Don't. Don't. All right? Doo it'll get back a me an' I'll want a know why, mate. I 'ont never been out 'ere an' yoo 'ont seen nothin' of me. (*He stands at the door.*) I'll shut it behind me.

SCOPEY *goes out through the door.* ALEN *goes halfway towards the door. He stops. He stoops slightly and stretches his neck with the concentration of listening.*

(*Off.*) 'Night.
> *Pause.* ALEN *goes quietly to the door. He locks it.*

Scene Nine

SCOPEY's *and* PAT's *place.*
*A table left. A portable bed up right. At the moment it has been
put out of the way up right, where it lies against the wall. Two
chairs.*
PAT *and* SCOPEY. *They talk in the clichés of argument, but they
sound friendly.*
Dark.

PAT. Yoo should a kep it by the fuse box.

SCOPEY. That's a fat lot a help.

PAT. Then yoo wouldn't be lookin' for it.

SCOPEY. Why don't yoo keep it by the fuse box?

PAT. That ent my place.
> *Pause.* SCOPEY *looks in the needlework box.*
That ent there. Goo an' borrow next door.

SCOPEY. Where's our'n?

PAT. Yoo won't find that in a month a Sundays.

SCOPEY. It can't walk.

PAT. Perhaps we used it.

SCOPEY. When?

PAT. Don't ask me.

SCOPEY. Well when? We 'ont 'ad no call a use it. If that's gone,
that little Joany twist it up for 'er brooches every time yoo 'ave
'er up 'ere.

PAT. She ent been 'ere often. Yoo can't blame 'er.

SCOPEY. That's where that's gone.

PAT. More like yoo lost it.

SCOPEY. Sure. (*He sits at the table.*)

PAT. Yoo can't see t' finish yoor dinner.

SCOPEY. I know where the 'ole is.

PAT. Ent yoo mendin' that fuse then?

SCOPEY. That'll wait. I'm 'ungry, gal.

PAT. Yoo ent better make a mess a my clean cloth.

SCOPEY. I 'ont make no mess.

PAT (*after a pause*). Finish off that ice cream?

SCOPEY. Yep.

PAT. Nice, ent it.

SCOPEY. Yep.

PAT. That 'ont keep, anyhow. I 'ad another card from Betty.

SCOPEY. Yeh?

PAT. She ent comin'.

SCOPEY. No?

PAT. They posted 'im t' Germany.

SCOPEY. O.

PAT. I suppose she'll be comin' over t' visit.

SCOPEY. They got the money. What's the picture?

PAT. I'll show yoo when we got some light.

SCOPEY. Say anythin'?

PAT. Not much.

SCOPEY (*after a pause*). What she say?

PAT. She ent comin'. (*Pause.*) I can't see t' put the kettle on.

SCOPEY. Open a bottle.

PAT. I ent scaldin' myself t' death just 'cause yoo're too bloody lazy a mend a fuse.

SCOPEY. I can't find the wire.

PAT. Yoo ent looked.

SCOPEY (*after a pause*). I'll get the bed out.

PAT. Yoo can't goo a bed fore yoo fixed that fuse.

SCOPEY. 'Course I can.

PAT. Yoo ent done the washin' up.

SCOPEY. That'll be there in the mornin'. Then I can see what I'm dooin'.

PAT. Suppose there's an emergency.

SCOPEY. There won't be.

PAT. Suppose the 'ouse catch fire?

SCOPEY. Then there'll be plenty a light. (*Eats.*) All the wirin's US in this place.

PAT. That ent this place. That's just that owd fuse blowed.

SCOPEY. They ought a knocked this owd 'eap down afore the war. The first one.

PAT. Yoo shouldn't a lost the wire.

SCOPEY. What?

PAT. Soon's we get enough t' lay down we'll start lookin' round.

SCOPEY. When's that?

PAT. Yoo ought a brighten this place up.

SCOPEY. Why? I 'ont got no interest. I 'ont wastin' my time on somethin' belongs some other bloke.

PAT. Yoo're usin' it.

SCOPEY. I'm payin' for it.

PAT. Pass yoor plate.

SCOPEY (*passes his plate*). I could meet yoo out a work tmorra an' we could goo see that new estate be Dunmow.

PAT. What's the use on it? We 'ont got no deposit.

SCOPEY. It'll give us some ideas.

PAT. Yoo got plenty a them. That's Thursday tmorra – I doo owd Alen's.

SCOPEY. So.

PAT. Be the time I'm clear a that that'll be too late.

SCOPEY. That owd sod gets on my wick.

PAT. That 'ont 'is fault I 'ave t' goo there.

SCOPEY (*annoyed*). 'Oo's is it then? Yoo spend more time up there than yoo doo in my 'ome.

PAT (*annoyed*). Don't be a liar.

SCOPEY (*annoyed*). I 'ont 'avin' yoo galavantin' up there soon's ever I turn my back.

PAT. I don't like gooin'.

SCOPEY. Suppose we moved out.

PAT. How?

SCOPEY. Suppose we moved out.

PAT. Well we ent.

SCOPEY. We will one day.

PAT. Then we'll 'ave t' see.

SCOPEY. I reckon I pass 'is owd sty every time I come 'ome a work. I can easy keep an eye on 'im.

PAT. That ent a case a keep an eye. Yoo 'ave t' keep him swep' an' clean an' that.

SCOPEY. There's nothin' a that – just poke the owd broom round the corners.

PAT. I'll remember that next time I ask yoo t' doo somethin'. 'Oo doo 'is bits a shoppin'?

SCOPEY. Yoo doo that an' I'll drop it in when I goo.

PAT. 'E'd never let yoo in.

SCOPEY. 'E's too fond a 'is owd gut t' starve.

PAT. Yoo ent serious?

SCOPEY. Sure, if it helps.

PAT. Well . . . I ent thought about it. I always gone up there. I'd feel queer without. Chriss knows I've 'ad my share a slavin' for 'im.

SCOPEY. An' all for nothin'.

PAT. Not so much as a thankyoo. Yoo could try it for a bit an' see 'ow that work. That ent no 'arm.

SCOPEY. If it don't work yoo'll just 'ave a goo back.

PAT. Yes.

SCOPEY. Give us a 'and with the bed.

PAT. O yoo're nice when yoo want a be!

SCOPEY. Come on. It was late agen last night. That 'ont give yoo no time.

PAT. Didn't stop yoo.

SCOPEY. That was just arsin' about. What kep yoo, anyway?

PAT. Nosey bugger.

SCOPEY. I'll find out. (*He lifts the bed from the wall.*)

PAT. I ent gooin' a bed yet. That's too early.

SCOPEY. Get the pillows an' shut up.

PAT. Yoo tired?

SCOPEY. No.

PAT. Yoo been over-dooin' it, boy.

SCOPEY. Oo say?

PAT. Sheila at work only doo it twice a week.

SCOPEY. 'Er owd man must be knockin' a bit outside.

PAT. Yoo reckon so?

SCOPEY. Stands to reason.

PAT. She ought a try 'elpin' 'erself, then she'd find out.

    SCOPEY *tests the bed with his hand.*

That's all yoo married me for.

SCOPEY (*making the bed*). It wasn't yoor money.

PAT (*making the bed*). Sorry?

SCOPEY. Not yet.

PAT. Keepin' off the other gals?

SCOPEY. Where was yoo last night?

PAT. Yoo ought a take up a hobby.

SCOPEY. I got one. Tuck it in straight, gal.

    PAT *goes out right.* SCOPEY *gets into bed.* PAT *comes in cleaning*
    her teeth.

PAT. Yoo meant it 'bout the owd boy?

SCOPEY. I said so.

PAT. Did yoo get that glass a beer?

SCOPEY. No pour it out, gal.

    She pours out a glass of beer.

Get your finger out.

    She hands him the glass.

Ta.

    PAT *goes out right. Sound of a basin. Sound of running water.*
    She comes back and starts to undress. SCOPEY *gets out of bed.*

PAT. Where yoo gooin'?

SCOPEY. I forgot t' slash. (*He stands the glass down beside the bed.*)
Don't tread in that. (*Goes out right.*)

PAT. I need some new nylons. These a gone 'ome. (*She gets into*
bed.)

Scene Ten

ALEN's *place*.
ALEN *stands alone in the middle of the room.*
A long pause.

SCOPEY (*off*). Yoo can't howd out much longer, doo yoo'll die. (*Pause.*) Can't yoo get it in yoor thick 'ead: she ent comin' no more. (*Pause.*) Yoo want me t' fetch the police? They'll put yoo in the institution straight away. (*Pause.*) I got stew-steak, chips, peas, rice, tea. (*Pause.*) Look 'ere, yoo let me an' when Pat's up an' about she'll take over like she was before. I'll ask 'er anyroad. That's my word. (*Pause.*) Yoo gooin' a die, then?

ALEN. Fetch that gal.

SCOPEY. For Chriss sake – she's ill!

ALEN. Yoo come with 'er.

SCOPEY. She's ill! An' yoo're lettin' me in on my own rights, not me an' 'er! (*Pause.*) If yoo think yoo'll leave it t' the last chance yoo know what'll 'appen. Yoo'll pass out and yoo'll goo afore yoo come round agen. Die in yoor sleep. Yoo sound groggy all ready a me.

> ALEN *opens the door.* SCOPEY *comes in.* ALEN *chokes.*

Yoo're in a fine mess. Sit down. Goo on. I 'ont gooin' a eat yoo.

> ALEN *stands.*

My wife's sorry she can't come, but the doctor 'ont let 'er out a the 'ouse. An' I'll tell yoo somethin' else, soon's she starts 'avin' babies she 'ont be at yoor beck an' call no more. Yoo can't 'ave everythin', boy.

ALEN. Grub.

SCOPEY. All right. She told me 'ow t' doo. Where's yoor tin opener?

> ALEN *takes the opener from his pocket and puts it on the table.*
> SCOPEY *opens a tin of stewed steak.*

She said yoo weren't a good mixer. Yoo 'ad a lot a rows with 'er,

ent yoo. Eh? I ent much of a dab at cookin' but I don't reckon
yoo're used t' the best. If I 'ad any sense I'd just give yoo a cup
a milk an' make yoo wait till tmorra for the rest.

ALEN. No.

SCOPEY. All right, all right. (*He empties tins into pots. He lifts an
empty pot, turns it upside down and bangs the bottom.*) Grubby,
ent it? Don't reckon yoo'll mind, eh? I'm fussy for bein' clean
myself. What yoo two 'ave t' row on? (*He stands the pots on the
cookers.*) Chriss, yoo got 'ords a little vermin runnin' round 'ere.
(*He swipes at the top with a paper.*) Like Ben bloody Hur. (*Slight
pause. He twists the paper and throws it on the ground.*) They'll
shift when it gets 'ot. (*He lights the wicks.*) Yep. (*He slams the
tops down.*) Put the 'eat up their arse. Where yoo keep the
spoons? (*He goes to the table and takes spoons from the drawer. He
goes back to the pots and stirs the food.*) Get yoo up t' the table,
that 'ont be long. Goo on. Bet yoo'd eat anything now, eh? Yoo
never sent Pat yoor best wishes. Eh? Yoo should a said yoo 'ope
she'd be all right. She ent a bad gal, is she. (*He stirs.*) Likes yoo.

ALEN. Ta.

SCOPEY. Eh?

ALEN. Don't like it 'ot, thank 'e.

SCOPEY. Yoo'll 'ave t' 'ave it a bit 'ot, doo yoor stomack 'ont never
howd it.

ALEN. Don't like it 'ot.

SCOPEY. I told 'er yoo was askin' after 'er, else she'd a been upset.
Yoo don't look well. (*Pause.*) Daft sod, yoo should a 'ad me in
first day. All right a wipe up on this? (*He picks up a cloth from
the side of the burners.*)

ALEN. Eh?

SCOPEY. Can I wipe up on this? Them. (*He shows the spoon.*)

ALEN. Me?

SCOPEY. What d'yoo use?

ALEN. Eh?

SCOPEY (*after a pause*). Smells smashin', don't it?

ALEN. That's done now.

SCOPEY. Nearly.

ALEN. Don't like it 'ot.

SCOPEY (*after a pause*). Yoo ought a 'ave radio 'ere.

> *Silence.*

Want me a buy yoo a radio?

> *Silence.*

Yoo can pick 'em up cheap, good second 'and.

> *Silence.*

Sod! I burnt my finger, ent I.

ALEN. That'll doo me.

SCOPEY (*sucks finger*). Get up t' the table. Comin' over. That's ready now.

> ALEN *sits.*

I'll get a blister there, eh. (*Takes plate from under burner. He looks at it. He wipes it on the cloth.*) Better. (*He puts the plate in front of* ALEN *and empties peas on to it.*)

> ALEN *eats.*

Guts! Wait. (*He quickly fetches the steak from the cooker.*) Howd on! (*He pulls the plate from* ALEN.)

ALEN. Give that 'ere!

SCOPEY. Wait.

ALEN. My plate.

SCOPEY. Yoo'll be sick, gooin' like that. (*He empties the steak on to the plate. He goes back to the cooker and takes the plate with him.*)

> ALEN *stands.*

I 'ont 'avin' yoo 'oggin that down like that. (*He takes the plate back to the table.*) Take yoor time, doo yoo'll be sick. (*He puts the plate in front of* ALEN.) Smells all right. (*Holds* ALEN's *hand back.*) Now yoo chew on that steady. Chew on it.

> ALEN *lifts his knife and fork. He stops.*

Amen.

> *Pause.* ALEN *pulls the plate a few inches towards him. Pause.*

Why'd I want t' kill yoo, eh?

ALEN. 'Ot.

SCOPEY. Let it stand. Blow on it.

Slight pause. ALEN *grunts.*

If that tastes as good as it smells yoo'll be all right. I reckon I could down that myself.

    ALEN *starts to eat, slowly at first.*

Them tins are proper 'andy, ent they. All right? Doo it taste all right mate? Goo steady, then. Whoa! Yoo'll be sick if yoo goo at it like that. (*He pulls the plate away.*)

ALEN. Letsaveit!

SCOPEY. Yoo'll blow yoor stomack up.

ALEN. Giveusere. (*He tries to grab the plate.*)

SCOPEY. Stop it!

ALEN. My plate!

SCOPEY. No! Piggin' like that! (SCOPEY *scoops up a spoonful of food. He holds it in front of* ALEN's *face.*)

    ALEN *opens his mouth.*

Wider! (SCOPEY *puts the food into* ALEN's *mouth.*)

    ALEN *eats.*

Chew. Goo on, give it a real good chew. No, chew it! (*He holds out the second spoonful.*) Yoo ent 'avin' no more after this if yoo can't chew it properly. (*He puts the food into* ALEN's *mouth.*)

    ALEN *eats.*

More than that. Gobblin' like some owd turkey. Pat said yoo're greedy. (*He goes on feeding him.*) Better. What yoo been dooin' since last Thursday? Eh? Chew it. Yoo been washin' yoorself?

ALEN. Howd it straight, boy! Howd on t' it!

SCOPEY. I'll 'ave t' 'ave that coat off an 'ave a good look after. Chew it, goo on. (*He wipes* ALEN's *chin with the cloth.*) No wonder Pat did yoor washin' 'ere. I can't see 'er 'angin' that out our place.

ALEN. What?

SCOPEY. Yoo'll 'ave t' 'elp with yoor own washin' after this.

ALEN. That's good gravy! Don't waste that. That doo yoo a power a good.

SCOPEY. Yoo manage now. (*He gives* ALEN *the spoon.*)

    ALEN *scoops up the gravy.* SCOPEY *rights a toppled box.*

I'd better put a broom round 'ere, doo she'll blow my 'ead off. Where d'yoo keep it?

ALEN. Eh?

SCOPEY. The broom.

> ALEN *nods to the wall.*

I should a wore me owd clothes. These're new, like 'em? (*He tugs at his trouser creases.*) Yoo got an apron, ave yoo?

ALEN. No.

SCOPEY. Patsy must a used one. Where she kep it? (*He takes an old floral apron from the couch and puts it on.*)

ALEN. Don't want sweepin'.

SCOPEY (*he pushes the broom along the floor*). No? What's that then? That floor ent been swep since last Christmas. (*Sweeps. Pause.*) The lads 'd laugh if they saw me. Jazzy, eh? Ent it? (*Spreads apron.*) I'll 'ave t' come round early tmorra an' give yoo a good dooin'.

ALEN. What?

SCOPEY. I look a piece, don't I?

ALEN. Yoo comin' tmorra?

SCOPEY. No bother.

ALEN. Send the gal.

SCOPEY. Want a goo 'ungry?

ALEN. When she comin'?

SCOPEY. When she can. (*Sweeps.*) What yoo get up to all day? Yoo must 'ave plenty a time, yoo ent put a finger t' this place for months. No more ent she, be the looks on it.

ALEN. Can't sleep with the dut blowin'.

SCOPEY. Eh?

ALEN. Too late for sweepin'.

SCOPEY. Where yoo sleep? That it? (*He looks at the couch.*) Looks snug enough. Be all right curled up. That's a bit grubby, though, ent it? (*He sweeps the dirt into a pile by the door.*) Where yoo put it?

ALEN. Eh?

SCOPEY. I'll chuck it out when I goo. (*Slight pause. He takes off the apron.*) Least that got the worst off. (*He sweeps the dirt into a paper bag, and opens the door a little.* ALEN *grunts and nods to show thanks.*) I thought yoo was gooin' a bed.

ALEN. Eh?

SCOPEY. Ent yoo tired?

ALEN. I goo abed early.

SCOPEY. Don't let me stop yoo.

ALEN. Lock up after yoo.

SCOPEY. I thought yoo might fancy a smoke or a chat. (*Slight pause.*) Yoo don't smoke.

ALEN. Eh?

SCOPEY. Yoo don't smoke.

ALEN. Smoke?

SCOPEY. 'Ow long yoo been 'ere?

ALEN. Don't want no trouble.

SCOPEY. I only asked. Must be fifty years an more since yoo come 'ere. My mum weren't born when yoo come 'ere. (*Pause. He hangs the apron on the wall.*) Ta. That look better 'angin' on a nail. Nice 'ere in a way, ent it. No worry. No one t' nag. My wife'll be wonderin' what I been up to. Yoo ent ever married, 'ave yoo. 'Ow'd yoo doo for sex? (*Pause.*) They say yoo run after Pat's mum one time. But even Pat don't know the truth a that. I bet yoo're a crafty owd sod. Shall I put the kettle on?

ALEN. No.

SCOPEY. I wouldn't put it past yoo t' be 'er dad. I could doo with a cup myself but I reckon there'll be one on my place. We could be in the same family. Bed. Yep. Yoo want your bed an' I could doo with mine. Yoo take a 'ot water bottle?

ALEN. No, no.

SCOPEY. I was gooin' a put the kettle on. I'll get rid a these owd tins for yer. Ha, you could be my dad-in-law. (*He puts the tins in the paper bag.*) I reckon I ent done too bad for a starter. I'll learn. (*Pause.*) I'm off. Don't forget a lock up. (*Pause.*) What's yoor first name?

ALEN. Eh?

SCOPEY. I'm Sco.

ALEN. What?

SCOPEY. That's just a name. (*Shrugs slightly, he goes to the door with the paper bag.*) Anythin' special yoo want brought in?

ALEN. No – I –

SCOPEY. Don't worry, I'll see t' the regular order. (*At door.*) See you, then. (*He goes out. Pause. He pokes his head and half his body back into the room.*) Night.

> SCOPEY *goes out. Pause.* ALEN *goes into the middle of the room and listens. He has the plate in his hand. Pause. He bolts the door. He goes to the heap of paper by the wall. He climbs on to it. He spies through a hole in the wall. He steps down. He takes the apron from the nail and puts it back on the bed. He goes to the table. He looks at the empty plate. He picks up the spoon and makes a vague scooping gesture against the plate.*

Scene Eleven

PAT *and* SCOPEY's *place.*

PAT *sits down left at the table.*

SCOPEY *is up right.*

PAT. Yoo workin' late agen t'morra?

SCOPEY. Why?

PAT. If yoo're workin' late I'm gooin' round June's.

SCOPEY. Don't know. Why yoo gooin' round 'er's for?

PAT. Borrow 'er sewin' machine. Can I 'ave a cigarette?

SCOPEY. No.

PAT. Yoo got some.

SCOPEY. Two.

PAT. One each.

SCOPEY. One for me when I goo abed an' one for me when I get up.

PAT. I'm dyin' for a smoke.

SCOPEY. Yoo're always cadgin'.

PAT. Yoo left your rice dinner time.

SCOPEY. So what.

PAT. Weren't that nice, then?

SCOPEY. All right.

PAT. I ent wastin' it. That's got good milk in it. Yoo can 'ave that cold amorra night. (*Turns a page of the evening paper.*) What time yoo comin' 'ome?

SCOPEY. When?

PAT. T'morra night.

SCOPEY. Why?

PAT. Don't yoo want your dinner?

SCOPEY. Leave somethin' under the plate.

PAT. That 'ont gooin' a doo yoo no good.

SCOPEY. That'll doo me.

PAT (*after a pause*). I'll 'ave t' take some blue thread round June's. T'ent likely she'll 'ave that shade. Mais left work t'day. She comes out so much she look she's 'avin' it t'morra. I feel sorry for the silly cow. She'll 'ave t' give it away – like the others. She don't seem t' mind. (*Slight pause.*) I bumped into Bill.

SCOPEY. 'Ow's 'e dooin'?

PAT. Asked about yoo. Said they 'ont seen yoo down the Carpenter's Arms.

SCOPEY. 'Ow's 'e dooin'?

PAT. Fine.

SCOPEY. I ought a look in there some time. I ought a goo amorra if yoo're gooin' visitin'. I could doo with a night on the beer.

PAT. I told yoo, doo yoo good. (*Turns page.*) We ent been out for months. (*Turns page.*) Yoo tired agen tonight?

SCOPEY. Eh?

PAT. Yoo tired?

SCOPEY. Why?

PAT. I'm askin'.

SCOPEY. I can't 'elp workin' late. Yoo makin' my cocoa?

PAT. There ent no milk.

SCOPEY. Where's it all gone?

PAT. In the rice puddin'.

SCOPEY. Yoo can't make cocoa without milk.

PAT. That won't 'urt t' 'ave it 'alf an' 'alf for once.

SCOPEY. Yoo know I like it milky. Yoo should a kep' it.

PAT. If yoo keep gettin' this tiredness yoo ought a take somethin'.

SCOPEY. I 'ont gettin' no tiredness. I 'ave t' work 'ard.

PAT. Yoo ought a take some pills t' give yoo a lift.

SCOPEY. Muck.

PAT. What? (*Pause*.) Might make yoo a bit more company 'stead a droopin' all over the place an' droppin' off t' sleep.

SCOPEY. I got a right a be tired when I work late.

PAT. Yoo never used a work late.

SCOPEY. I can't 'elp it if I work late.

PAT. I know.

SCOPEY. I doo all I can for yoo.

PAT. I know.

SCOPEY. What else yoo want?

PAT. I know. Let's goo abed.

    Silence.

I'm dyin' for a fag.

    Silence.

If yoo're earnin' all that overtime yoo ought a pay me extra. That's only right.

SCOPEY. I'm savin'.

PAT. Where?

SCOPEY. Where?

PAT. Yes.

SCOPEY. That's a daft question.

PAT. Well where?

SCOPEY. I ent tellin' yoo.

PAT. Why?

SCOPEY. That 'ont last long if I tell yoo.

PAT. Other fellas tell their wives.

SCOPEY. They 'ont a married a yoo, mate. Ent yoo puttin' your 'air in curlers t'night?

PAT. I thought yoo'd like me a leave 'em off. Shall I tell Bill yoo'll see 'im?

SCOPEY. When?

PAT. T'morra.

SCOPEY. No.

PAT. Goo out an' get stinkin' drunk, boy. That's what's wrong with yoo.

SCOPEY. No, no. I'll see 'ow it goo.

PAT. If yoo goo yoo'll come in first.

SCOPEY. Why?

PAT. T' change.

SCOPEY. I'll be all right.

PAT. Yoo ent gooin' drinkin' in your owd work clothes.

SCOPEY. Suits me.

PAT. Yoo used a be fussy 'bout your clothes.

SCOPEY. Now what's the matter?

PAT. I ont 'avin' people say I send yoo out any owd 'ow.

SCOPEY. Don't be daft.

PAT. That's 'ow they'll say.

SCOPEY. They can say 'ow they bloody well like, Jack.

PAT. I'm the one 'oo 'as t' listen.

SCOPEY (*Pause. He takes out a cigarette and lights it. He puts the packet back in his jacket pocket, which hangs on the back of a chair*). 'Oo gave owd Alen that watch?

PAT. What watch?

SCOPEY. 'E got an owd watch tucked behind 'is owd coat.

PAT. I never see it.

SCOPEY. What 'e wear under that owd coat?

PAT. Nothin', that wouldn't surprise me.

SCOPEY. Perhaps that clock don't work. That's a rum owd ticker. (*Pause.*) Ent your mum never said why 'e goo shut up like 'e doo?

PAT. I 'ont 'alf a kid when she die. She 'ad me run 'is errands an' say I'd doo 'is cleanin'.

SCOPEY. But why 'e goo like 'e doo in the first place?

PAT. Gone in the 'ead. (*Pause.*) I miss gooin' up there.

SCOPEY. Yoo're well out a it.

PAT. That's only 'abit, gooin' up there regular all this time. I never could take to 'im. Dirty owd swine.

SCOPEY. What time is it?

PAT. Gettin' on.

SCOPEY. I thought yoo was gooin' a make my cocoa.

PAT. Yoo said yoo'd goo without.

SCOPEY. I can't sleep on an empty stomach.

PAT. It'll 'ave t' be 'alf an' 'alf.

SCOPEY. I'll 'ave what's left.

PAT. I'm keepin' a drop for the mornin'.

SCOPEY. I can 'ave some a it, anyroad. (*He stands and goes right.*)

PAT. Where yoo gooin'?

SCOPEY. I'll make it.

PAT. Yoo leave some for the mornin', doo I'll start a row.

> SCOPEY *goes out right.* PAT *takes a cigarette from his jacket pocket and lights it. She puts the empty packet back in his pocket.*

SCOPEY (*off*). Yoo nearly run dry on cocoa. T'ent 'ardly 'nough for one cup.

> PAT *starts to smoke. She goes back to the table, sits, and reads the paper.*

SCOPEY (*coming in from the right*). Yoo run out a cocoa. Yoo'll 'ave t' get some in the mornin'.

PAT. I forgot.

SCOPEY. Don't.

PAT (*after a pause*). I pinched one a yoor fags.

SCOPEY. Why?

PAT. I told yoo, I was dyin' for a smoke.

SCOPEY. Yoo want a keep your 'ands off a other people's property.

PAT. That's only an owd smoke.

SCOPEY. That ent the point.

PAT. Mean owd sod.

SCOPEY. I don't mind yoo takin' fags. I towd yoo afore. Yoo take the whole packet if I got 'em. I was savin' that for the mornin'.

PAT. You smoked 'undreds a mine.

SCOPEY. That ent the point.

PAT. Course not!

SCOPEY. That weren't yoor last fag!

PAT. It's only an owd smoke.

SCOPEY. Yoo said that all ready.

PAT. Take 'alf back.

SCOPEY. Thanks!

PAT (*holding out the cigarette*). Well, take the whole bloody lot an' I'll buy yoo twenty t'morra.

SCOPEY. Don't be bloody saucy.

PAT (*puts the cigarette back in her mouth and draws*). If yoo don't want it I'll –

    SCOPEY *snatches the cigarette from her mouth. Throws it on the floor. Stamps and stamps on it.*

SCOPEY. Next bloody time bloody well don't take, ask!

PAT (*shaken*). Thanks. (*She goes up right.*)

SCOPEY. Where yoo gooin'?

PAT. Make myself a cup of tea. I won't use yoor water.

    PAT *goes out right. Pause.* SCOPEY *takes the empty packet from his jacket pocket. He shakes it. He puts it in his trousers pocket.*

Scene Twelve

ALEN's *place.*

ALEN *lies on the couch.* SCOPEY *sits at the table. He wears the apron. He is writing the shopping list.*

Pause.

ALEN. Only milk I like come out a tins. (*Pause.*) Count a that's got the sweet in it already.

SCOPEY (*after a pause*). I'm gooin' a fix this place.

ALEN. What?

SCOPEY. One day I'm gooin' a bring some paint up. A few tins'll doo this place out nice.

ALEN. Paint only show the dut up.

SCOPEY. Bring the damp out.

ALEN. The smell's bad for the chest.

SCOPEY (*after a pause*). Time yoo been 'ere yoo could a done this place out smashin'.

ALEN. 'Ow owd's yoor dad?

SCOPEY. Eh?

ALEN. What's 'e done? What's 'e got a show?

SCOPEY. I ent got one.

ALEN. Same thing.

SCOPEY (*after a pause*). Yoo ought a burn logs next winter.

ALEN. Logs?

SCOPEY. Save money.

ALEN. I ont 'avin' no owd smelly logs. Can't doo better than para for a good steady 'eat.

SCOPEY. You 'ad ash in that grate afore I shifted it.

ALEN. That's the time I run out a para.

SCOPEY. You can't expect my wife a lug 'eavy owd cans all that way.

ALEN. Yoo said she weren't comin' n' more.

SCOPEY. 'Ow doo yoo know they'll let me goo on dooin' it? (*Pause.*) I was outside last night.

ALEN. I ont 'eard yoo.

SCOPEY. Yoo were asleep.

ALEN. I'd always woke up afore.

SCOPEY. I kep' quiet.

ALEN. Yoo still see owd Mrs Weep's granboys?

SCOPEY. Now'n agen.

ALEN. All that owd crowd?

SCOPEY. Yep.

ALEN. Yoo tell 'em 'bout me?

SCOPEY. No.

ALEN. 'Ave yoo? They know yoo got the key?

SCOPEY. Nope.

ALEN. Yoo ont showed it?

SCOPEY. Yoo don't trust me.

ALEN. I ont never trust Nellie Weep. Shake yoor 'and one minute
    an' cut your throat the next.

    SCOPEY *folds the shopping bag.*

  They 'ere?

SCOPEY. Last night?

ALEN. Yes.

SCOPEY. No.

ALEN. Hm.

SCOPEY. I dug out some owd photographs.

ALEN. Where?

SCOPEY. 'Ere.

ALEN. Yoo been pryin'.

SCOPEY. No.

ALEN. Yoo ont find nothin'.

SCOPEY. 'Oo was she?

ALEN. 'Oo?

SCOPEY. The lady.

ALEN. What lady?

SCOPEY. In the photographs.

ALEN. I ont seen no photographs.

SCOPEY. I found a photograph shaped like an egg, in brown an
    white, an' there's fly-blows round the edge.

ALEN. Where is it?

    SCOPEY *takes a photograph from his inside jacket pocket. He
    sits on the bed with* ALEN. ALEN *looks at the photograph.*

  'Oo's she?

SCOPEY. That's what I arst.

ALEN. Ah.

SCOPEY. Well?

ALEN. That's come back. I know 'er. Know 'oo she is?

SCOPEY. No.

ALEN. That come out a that owd scrap shop.

SCOPEY. 'Oo is she.

ALEN. I bought she out a that owd scrap shop stood on the corner
    a Dunmow. She were stood out on the pavey in a box. They

knocked that owd shop over years back. She were in three or four a they photographs. They 'ad one a 'er up in a carriage an' 'er dog sat up on the seat aside 'er an a big footman boy stood up the front. 'E was grip howd a the 'orse be the 'ead an' 'e were lookin' straight off that way, but she were starin' straight on yer.

SCOPEY. 'Oo?

ALEN. Fancy that comin' back.

SCOPEY. Yoo kep' the rest?

ALEN. Why'd I buy that owd junk? She could a been dead seventy, eighty year. Perhaps she lie down outside the village.

SCOPEY. Where's the rest?

ALEN. Eh?

SCOPEY. Yoo 'ad some more.

ALEN. Burnt.

SCOPEY. When?

ALEN. Lost. I can't rightly recollect. I used a keep interestin' things. Anythin' interestin'. I'd like a see 'em myself if yoo ferret 'em out.

SCOPEY. What's the shop called.

ALEN. Shop?

SCOPEY. What's the name a the shop, where yoo bought 'em?

ALEN. That's gone.

SCOPEY. In Dunmow.

ALEN. Dunmow.

SCOPEY. What end?

ALEN. Can't think.

SCOPEY. Try.

ALEN. Might a been Saffron.

SCOPEY. Ent you ever seen that lady when yoo was a boy?

ALEN. How?

SCOPEY. Walkin'? Shoppin'? Ridin'?

ALEN. When I were a boy.

SCOPEY (after a long pause). Cold now.

ALEN. Years turned.

SCOPEY. I could doo with that primus gooin'.

ALEN. Too early.

SCOPEY. I'll pay.

ALEN. Too early. Once yoo start yoo can't doo without it.

SCOPEY. Yoo're all right in that coat. Let's see you. Take it off.

ALEN. Catch cold.

SCOPEY. Don't yoo take it off a night?

ALEN. Eh?

SCOPEY. I ent never seen yoo outside it.

ALEN. N'more yoo won't.

SCOPEY. Why?

ALEN. Draft round 'ere'll kill yoo. (*He goes to the couch and takes a coat from between the blankets.*)

SCOPEY. Ent killed me.

   ALEN *shows him the coat.*

 Looks warm.

ALEN. Like it?

SCOPEY. What's the use. I ont gettin' it.

ALEN. That's good.

SCOPEY. Where d' yoo get it?

ALEN. Dunmow. I bought that same time I bought mine. Market Walden. They make a pair.

SCOPEY. Yoo 'ad it that long?

ALEN. Try it. That's good owd stuff.

SCOPEY (*putting on the coat*). I'd say.

ALEN. Feel that. Thick, ent it.

SCOPEY. Yep.

ALEN. That's an owd army great coat. That goo back long afore the great war.

SCOPEY. She's 'eavy?

ALEN. That keeps the owd draft out.

SCOPEY (*walking up and down*). That's a bit long.

ALEN. That's 'ow yoo want it 'ere.

SCOPEY. That's right. Ta. Doo it make me look bigger, doo it?

ALEN. Yoo can 'ave that.

SCOPEY. I feel bigger.

ALEN. Eh?

SCOPEY. The pockets 'ent 'ere.

ALEN. That's 'ow I bought it.

SCOPEY. No pockets?

ALEN. They're sewed shut.

SCOPEY. 'Oo did that?

ALEN. T' keep the shape.

SCOPEY. Ent yoo 'ad a look?

ALEN. Why?

SCOPEY. There might be somethin' inside.

ALEN. I don't want nothin'.

SCOPEY. Where's the scissors? Yoo get that from that same shop in Dunmow?

ALEN. No scissors 'ere.

SCOPEY. That'll doo. (*He takes a knife from the table.*) Chriss yoo might 'ave anythin' in 'ere. (*He cuts open the tops of the pockets. There is a knock on the door.*)

PAT (*off*). 'Ello!

> SCOPEY *hides himself behind the couch.* ALEN *stares after him. There is another knock.*

'Ello. It's me!

> ALEN *opens the door.* PAT *comes in.*

'Ow yoo keepin'? Yoo didn't expect me, did yoo?

ALEN. I didn't expect –

PAT. 'Ow yoo keepin'?

ALEN. 'Ow's I keepin'? Mustn't grumble.

PAT. That's right.

ALEN. My leg ent too good.

PAT. O.

ALEN. I still got that owd guts ache an' the pains in my back.

PAT. O.

ALEN. An' me leg.

PAT. What a shame? 'Ow are yoo?

ALEN. Mustn't grumble.

PAT. Yoo look all right.

ALEN. An' me leg.

PAT. I'll get yoo some a my linament rub for that owd back.

ALEN. My back's been playin' me up.

PAT. 'Ow doo I look?

ALEN. An' me leg.

PAT. Yoo still talk t' yoorself, then.

ALEN. What?

PAT. 'Ow yoo gettin' on with Sco?

ALEN. Eh?

PAT. Sco.

ALEN. All right.

PAT. Yoo get on all right, then.

ALEN. O yes.

PAT. 'E don't mess yoo about, doo 'e?

ALEN. No messin'.

PAT. Sure?

ALEN. What?

PAT. Is 'e regular?

ALEN. Sometime.

PAT. 'E say 'e come 'ere every other day. But yoo can't trust 'im.

ALEN. No.

PAT. Can't be trusted. (*Looks around.*) Yoo're nice an' clean, I'll
    say that. 'E say 'e get a lot a overtime, late work.

ALEN. O.

PAT. 'E ent said anythin' t' yoo?

ALEN. No.

PAT. Doo 'e bring someone with 'im?

ALEN. No.

PAT. Nobody wait outside?

ALEN. No.

PAT. No one?

ALEN. Eh?

PAT. 'E ent suited a marriage.

ALEN. Eh?

PAT. Not suited for marriage.

ALEN. O.

PAT. Soon get tired. I don't see what 'e get out a it, tell yoo the truth. Yoo know.

ALEN. Yes.

PAT. Rum owd lad, ent 'e.

ALEN. Eh?

PAT. Yoo eatin'?

ALEN. All right.

PAT. Yoo eat all right?

ALEN. Yep.

PAT. Oo doo the cleanin'?

ALEN. 'E do.

PAT. Sco?

ALEN. Yep.

PAT. Doo 'e. T'ent like 'im. Won't lift a thing in my place.

ALEN. Eh?

PAT. Won't lift a thing for me.

ALEN. O.

PAT. If anyone stood outside yoo'd know.

ALEN. I'd know.

PAT. 'E ent workin' overtime where 'e work. I checked that.

ALEN. Yoo're lookin' nicely.

PAT. I arst 'em. I ent arstin' 'im, I want a find out first.

ALEN. O.

PAT. Yes.

ALEN. Swep an' wipe.

PAT. Yes. I ent stoppin' now.

ALEN. Everythin' –

PAT. I got someone waitin'. 'E get annoyed if I keep 'im standin'.

ALEN. Yoo ent gooin'?

PAT. I'll come in agen soon. Soon. I bought yoo some boil sweets. (*She hands him a small white paper bag.*) They're your favourite, ent they?

ALEN. I like boil.

PAT. I know.

ALEN. My favourite.

PAT. That's right. I'll look in agen soon's I'm down this way.

ALEN. Yes.

PAT. That's a bit out my way, see. Sure yoo got everything?

ALEN. Eh?

PAT. Good. I'm glad 'e keep yoo nice. Well, I did it for a long time, ent I?

ALEN. Long while.

PAT. I don't see why 'e can't 'elp me a bit. Yoo're on 'is way 'ome.

ALEN. Eh?

PAT. I'll 'ave t' rush. I ont tellin' 'im I arst 'bout anythin'. Doo 'e'll say I'm nosin'. I'll just say we 'ad a bit a talk.

ALEN. I –

PAT. So you behave. Yoo might get some more boil sweets.

ALEN (*he shakes the bag of sweets*). Thank yer.

PAT. That's a pleasure.

ALEN. When yoo comin' back?

PAT. Soon.

ALEN. Thank yer.

PAT. Cheerio.

    PAT *goes out through the door.*

ALEN. Thank yer. (*He bolts the door behind her. He goes to the stack of papers by the wall. He climbs on to them. He peers through a chink in the wall.*)

SCOPEY (*stands and looks at* ALEN). I never 'eard yoo talk a yoor-self. Why's she say that? (*Pause.*) That what yoo use them papers for?

ALEN (*he steps down*). She's on a bike.

SCOPEY. O.

ALEN. Peddled off like the devil after 'er. Roads ent safe.

SCOPEY. Yoo was glad a see 'er.

ALEN. She look all right.

SCOPEY. I thought so.

ALEN. Eh?

SCOPEY. Yoo was glad a see 'er.

ALEN. She say she's comin' back regular.

SCOPEY. That's what you want.

ALEN. I like gals.

SCOPEY. Chriss!

ALEN. When she comin' back?

SCOPEY. I got the sack t'day.

ALEN. O.

SCOPEY. That's count a spendin' too much time 'ere when I should a been a work.

ALEN. That ent my fault.

SCOPEY. I never said it was.

ALEN. Yoo ont get no money out a me.

SCOPEY. I never arst for money!

ALEN. I ont got it.

SCOPEY. I don't want it! Stick it!

ALEN. Eh?

SCOPEY. Yoo'll see if she come back! I'll arst 'er!

ALEN. Yoo gooin' a arst 'er?

SCOPEY. She'll laugh 'er 'ead off.

ALEN. She came a see me.

SCOPEY. Snoopin'. That's all she's after. Chriss, yoo don't know anythin'.

ALEN. What?

SCOPEY. In the war they reckon yoo was flashin' secrets a the jerries with a Woolworth's torch. Yoo couldn't even light a cigarette.

ALEN. Tobacco an' drink are Satan's whores.

SCOPEY. Yoo owd nut! I thought yoo 'ad them papers for keepin'. All yoo want 'em for's t' stare outside. Yoo owd fake!

ALEN. No.

SCOPEY. All day!

ALEN. Don't row at me!

SCOPEY. Don't yoo? Yoo're at that crack all day! Starin' out! It all goos on outside an' yoo just watch!

ALEN. I ont said I –

SCOPEY. Yoo're a fake! There's nothin' in this bloody shop!

ALEN. My little jobs –

SCOPEY. Jobs! Starin' out! Talk t' yourself! I 'eard! What for?

ALEN. No.

SCOPEY. What about? What yoo talk about? Nothin'!

ALEN. No. No.

SCOPEY. What about?

ALEN. Not my –

SCOPEY. Let's 'ear yoo! Goo on – talk! Drivel!

ALEN. Stop!

SCOPEY. Talk!

ALEN. She lied to –

SCOPEY. Liar!

ALEN. I sing sometime.

SCOPEY. Sing?

ALEN. Sometime.

SCOPEY. All right –

ALEN. No.

SCOPEY. Sing! What sort a singing? What sort a songs?

ALEN. Hymns.

SCOPEY. Sing a hymn.

ALEN. No.

SCOPEY. Sing it mate! Sing it. By chriss I'll rip this junk shop up if yoo don't sing! (*He puts his boot through the couch.*)

ALEN (*he starts to sing. At first he wavers, but the rhythm controls his terror*).

> Little babe nailed to the tree
> Wash our souls in thy pure blood
> Cleanse each sin and let us be
> Baptized in the purple flood
>
> Bearing thorns and whips and nails
> Wise men kneel before thy bier
> Let the love that never fails
> Conquer vice and death and fear

Child thy hosts now crowd the sky
Thou who found love here alone
Those who nail thee up to die
Hoist thee nearer to thy throne

(*Pause.*) Amen. (*Pause.*) I ent sure a the words. I used a follow the service on my wireless set but on the last war Mr Lowerly started up rumours count I owed 'im five an' six for milk bill an' the police come up an' took my wireless set so's I couldn't 'ear Lord Haw-Haw, so 'e say.

SCOPEY. God, 'alf the junk in 'ere could be burnt. Yoo don't need it. Look. (*Slight pause.*) What yoo 'ere for?

ALEN. I forget.

SCOPEY. Look at it! For chriss sake try t' tell the truth!

ALEN. I forget. My mum an' dad moved all over. We always stopped just outside places. We were the last 'ouse in the village.

SCOPEY. How?

ALEN. Yes.

SCOPEY. *How?*

ALEN. I never stopped gooin' after people. They stopped gooin' after me.

SCOPEY. I don't believe that.

ALEN. That's all I can bring back. (*Pause.*) Yoo arstin' 'er t' come?

SCOPEY (*after a pause*). Pockets're empty.

ALEN. Sew them back.

    SCOPEY *looks down at the hole in the bed.*

That keeps the owd shape, else that don't look nothin'.

    SCOPEY *sits on the bed with the coat.*

Scene Thirteen

An open space. An iron railing up stage centre. This is used for leaning against.

JUNE, JOE *and* RON *come in from the left.* JUNE *and* JOE *hold hands.*

JUNE. Saw telly last night. Pat come round my place agen.

JOE. Good?

JUNE. Boxin'.

JOE. All right?

JUNE. Why ent they allowed a wear white shorts?

JOE. Eh?

JUNE. Why can't they wear white shorts?

JOE. Don't know.

RON. Count a they'd show the blood.

JUNE. I 'eard it's so's yoo can't see what they got underneath when it get all sweaty. (*She giggles.*)

JOE. It's traditional.

RON. Where they two got to? (*He looks off left.*)

JUNE. They're all right. Leave 'em alone.

JOE. No, let 'em catch up.

JUNE. Can't miss nothin', can yoo.

RON. She off t' owd boy Alen's?

JUNE. She don't goo round there.

RON. Why's that?

JUNE. Scopey doo that for 'er.

JOE. 'E say 'e couldn't stand the owd bastard.

JUNE. Well, that's on 'is way 'ome.

JOE. Doo 'e doo the washin' up for 'er?

JOE *and* RON *laugh.*

JOE. Let's goo there one night an' sort the owd sod out.

JUNE. No yoo ent.

RON. Just for a laugh.

JUNE. 'E ent 'urt yoo.

JOE. Yoo can come.

JUNE. What doo I want to come for? Yoo goo givin' shocks to an owd boy that age and yoo might be sorry.

JOE. Don't be daft.

RON. Just for a laugh.

JUNE. Yoo'll land yourself into trouble, boy.

BILL *and* PAT *come in from the left.*

JUNE. Why ent boxers allowed a wear white shorts?

BILL. So's yoo can see when they get 'it low.

JUNE. There was a lot a that last night.

PAT. I felt sorry for that dark fella.

JUNE. Shouldn't come over 'ere.

PAT. Blood everywhere. Must a got splashed if yoo was sittin' close. Waste.

JUNE. What is?

PAT. That blood?

RON. Why?

PAT. They could use that in 'ospitals.

BILL. They got plenty.

JOE. If yoo give it, they never pay.

RON. Somethin' for nothin'.

JOE. They come round the TA once. Lousy tea an' a dog biscuit. I said no.

RON. I smoke 'eavy, so they won't touch mine.

JOE. We're gooin' down the Carpenter's.

BILL. Comin'.

PAT. Yeh, I ent 'ad a drink for a long while.

RON. Sco 'ome?

PAT. Don't know.

JUNE. 'E never know when 'e'll be in.

BILL. Got a fag?

    RON *gives him one.*

  Ta.

JUNE. Most likely still up owd Alen's.

PAT. I don't think I'll come.

BILL. Make up yoor mind, gal.

PAT. No, I won't, thanks.

JUNE. Yoo come, love.

PAT. No.

BILL. Up t' yoo?

RON. Yoo payin' then?

BILL. I'll see yoo 'ome.

PAT. Ta.

JOE. Be in for a quick one later?

BILL. Sure.

RON. I'll 'ave it on the bar waitin'.

BILL. Better be the best.

BILL *and* PAT *go out right.*

Scene Fourteen

ALEN'S *place.*

There are seven or eight tins of food on the table. One of them has been opened. Down left there is a bundle on the floor.

SCOPEY *stands up right on the pile of papers. He wears his greatcoat. He steps down and picks up the broom. He sweeps. The head comes off the broom. He stoops. He picks the head up. He pulls fluff from the bristles. He drops the fluff on the floor. He sits on the edge of the couch. He makes a wedge from paper and stuffs it in the hole in the broom head. He screws in the broom handle. He lays the broom on the couch. He pulls at the covers with one hand. Pause. He looks up – his head is held stiff. He listens. Pause. He drops his head to just below the normal position, pulling his neck into his shoulders, his chin horizontal. He shivers. He takes up the broom. He screws the handle tighter. He stands. He puts the broom back on the bed. He goes to the burners. He takes out a large watch from inside his coat. He looks at it. He shakes it. He puts it to his ear. He goes to the table and takes a knife from the drawer. He leaves the drawer open and goes back to the burners. He tries to open the watch with the knife. He can't. He sits on a box. He shakes the watch.*

VOICES (*off*).

> I love my babee
> I love her real good
> Love her day and night
> Like a lover should.

        I love my babee
        I squeeze her real tight
        Love her all the day
        Till its broad daylight.

RON (*off. Sings*). Drop your drawers, I'm comin' down the chimney.

BYO (*off*). Number two on the Brylcream.

    A stone strikes the wall.

BYO (*off*). Open up, boy.

LORRY (*off*). Kick the bleedin' door in.

VOICES (*off*).

    While shepherds watch their flocks by night
    A whore lay in the grass
    The angel of the Lord came down
    And stuck it up her pass the mustard share the salt.
    The Lord above is kind
    And if yoo thought of something else
    You've got a dirty arse.

LEN (*off*). Open up, yoo owd bastard.

RON (*off*). Let's 'ave a look at yoo.

    A stone strikes the wall.

JUNE (*off*). Oo's got the matches?

BYO (*after a silence*). Oo yoo got in there, boy?

JOE (*off*). We're comin' down the roof.

JUNE (*off*). Oo's been interferin' with little gals?

RON (*off*). What about that little gal at Finchin?

BYO (*off*). An the boys.

RON (*off*). What yoo got a 'ide for?

JUNE (*off*). Shut up!

BYO (*off*). What?

JUNE (*off*). Listen!

RON (*after a pause. Off*). What?

JUNE (*off*). I 'eard 'im.

    Screams. Laughs. The noise of tins being banged.

BYO (*off*). Perhaps 'e's poopin'.

RON (*off*). Do 'e sit on a po?

JUNE (*off*). Got any paper?

Laughs. Shouts. Stones strike the wall.

RON (*off*). Bastard!

BYO (*off*). Lousy bastard!

JOE (*off*). Rotten bastard!

LEN (*off*). Stinkin' bastard!

RON (*off*). Bastard bastard!

JUNE (*off*). Come yoo 'ere and interfere with me!

Shrieks. Laughs.

JOE (*off*). 'E only like 'em young.

JUNE (*off*). Cheeky bastard!

Shrieks. Laughs.

JUNE (*off*). Stop it! (*She screams.*)

BYO (*off*). Put your boy scout 'at on an' come an' save 'er.

RON (*off*). She's bein' raped.

BYO (*off*). Don't shove till yoor 'ead a the queue.

JUNE (*off*). Next please.

JOE (*off*). I'm on t' a good thing 'ere. I reckon I'll put 'er up in the business.

Laughs. Shouts. A shower of stones strike the wall.

BYO (*off*). The owd sod's asleep.

JUNE (*off*). Come an' buy me a drink, lovie.

JOE (*off*). 'E's put 'is curse on yoo!

BYO *makes ghost noises. Noise of tins being struck.* JUNE *shrieks.*

BYO (*off*). 'E'll come an' 'aunt yoo.

JUNE (*off*). I'm off!

Slight silence. A few stones strike the wall.

JUNE (*farther off*). Byo Luke's pissin' on yoor door.

BYO (*off*). Bring out yoor dead!

A solitary can is struck. Slight silence. A stone strikes the wall.
Laughs. Shouts.

RON (*farther off*). We're gooin' a watch yoo, mate.

BYO (*off*). Red!

RON (*farther off*). See if yoo can 'it that door from 'ere.

Slight pause. A stone hits the wall. Distant shouts. Three stones hit the wall. Distant shouts. Pause. One very distant shout. Silence.

SCOPEY *sits.*

Scene Fifteen

SCOPEY *and* PAT's *place.*

BILL *sits at the table.* PAT *is behind him. She straightens her stocking.*

BILL. Chriss I'm stiff.

PAT. Stiff?

BILL. Yep.

PAT. Ent surprisin'.

BILL. Feel more like gooin' a bed than drinkin'.

PAT. Ooo yoo kiddin'?

BILL. Straight.

PAT. You'd live in the owd pub if yoo won the pools.

BILL (*stretches*). They'd a been lost without owd man Bullright.

PAT. Kill 'imself. Gaddin' bout 'is age.

BILL. I know I'm stiff. Yoo'll 'ave t' doo your stuff, gal.

PAT. I'll rub some a my rub on that latter, but that ont doo now doo yoo'll get stain all over yoor cloths.

BILL. That's a deal. Ent yoo ready yet, gal?

PAT. What about Sco?

BILL. Well?

PAT. I ought a howd on a bit longer, b'rights.

BILL. Did 'e say when 'e'd get back?

PAT. Yo know 'e don't.

BILL. That's that then.

> PAT *goes off right.* BILL *lights a cigarette.*

I reckon 'e's got 'imself fixed up with some piece.

PAT (*off*). What?

BILL. I reckon 'e's gettin' it outside.

PAT (*off*). No. (*Pause.*) 'Oo?

BILL. Anyone.

PAT (*off*). No. (*Slight pause.*) That'd soon get back a me.

BILL. Well 'e must be gettin' it some place.

> PAT *comes in from the right.*

PAT. All right?

BILL. Very nice.

PAT (*wiping her hands on a towel*). 'E ent give me my money this week. (*Pause.*) I don't like gooin' in pubs with an empty purse.

BILL. 'Ow much?

PAT. Don't bother. I'll settle up with 'im.

BILL. I 'ont 'angin' round 'ere all day. (*Pause.*) Comin' in a Stor'ford Saturday? I'm puttin' the deposit down on my new car.

PAT. That sounds nice.

BILL. Comin'?

PAT. Sure. (*She looks at him.*) Don't seem like a year since I been married, doo it.

BILL. No.

PAT. I 'ave.

BILL. 'Urry up.

PAT. Don't shout.

> PAT *goes off right. Sound of water running in a basin. Pause.*
> SCOPEY *wheels in his bike from left and crosses the back stage.*
> *He leans his bike against the centre of the back stage wall. He*
> *comes down.*

BILL. 'Ow yoo dooin', boy?

SCOPEY. Fine.

BILL. Nice t' see yoo.

SCOPEY. 'Ow're yoo?

BILL. Usual.

SCOPEY. Busy?

BILL. Yep.

SCOPEY. Ha.

BILL. Where yoo tore yoor pants?

SCOPEY. O.

BILL. By the side.

SCOPEY. That owd bike.

BILL. Yoo can 'ave mine for a fiver. I want a get rid a it.

SCOPEY. No thanks.

BILL. Worth more. That's a good owd bike.

    PAT *comes in from right.*

PAT. We're gooin' down the pub.

BILL. Yoo comin'?

SCOPEY. Yoo ready?

PAT. Yep.

SCOPEY. I need a clean up.

PAT. That 'ont take yoo long.

SCOPEY. I 'eard the result.

BILL. Yoo should a see owd man Bullright. That's 'is last game, yoo know.

SCOPEY. I 'eard tell.

BILL. Official – or 'e say. I don't reckon they'll ever get anyone a send 'em down like 'e did. We could a used yoo. Pity.

SCOPEY. That's ow it goo.

BILL. Yup. The lads arst after yoo.

PAT. We'll 'e'll see 'imself tonight.

BILL. Sure. Nice 'avin' all the crowd t'gether agen.

PAT. I need some money.

SCOPEY. Now?

PAT. Yeh.

SCOPEY. Not now. I got a get cleaned up.

PAT. I'm gooin' a get it settled afore I set foot out a this 'ouse.

SCOPEY. Sure. Well I'll get my jacket. (*He goes up to his bike and takes his jacket from the handlebars.*)

PAT. 'Ow long yoo gooin' a be?

SCOPEY. Don't know, dear.

PAT. Shall we wait?

SCOPEY. Yoo goo on an' I'll join yoo.

PAT. Where yoo been?

SCOPEY. I come's fast I could. (*He comes down with the jacket. He is searching through the pockets.*)

PAT. Look in on the owd boy?

SCOPEY. Yup.

BILL. 'Ow's the job?

SCOPEY. All right.

BILL. When yoo start bringin' it in?

SCOPEY. Anytime, I reckon.

PAT. What's the matter?

SCOPEY (*going through the pockets again*). I can't recollect where I put it.

PAT. I ent touchin' my money. That's for the hp.

SCOPEY. Ooo arst yoo a touch it?

    BILL *stands.*

PAT. Don't be daft, boy. Sit yoo down.

BILL. They're all gettin' a start on us. There won't be none left.

PAT. Well?

SCOPEY (*putting packet on a chair*). I'll sort it out later. I ont dooin' nothin' till I 'ad my wash. I feel all grit.

PAT. Bill, lend me a quid.

BILL (*embarrassed*). All right, all right.

PAT. Now, please.

BILL. What's the matter with yoo?

PAT. I 'ont let both a yoo let me down.

BILL. All right. (*He quickly hands over a pound note. He tries not to let the paper show, but* PAT *flicks it noisily.*)

SCOPEY. Oo's lettin' you down?

PAT. Where yoo been?

SCOPEY. Eh?

PAT. Where yoo been?

SCOPEY. I told yoo. Ta, Bill. I'll pay you back soon's I –

PAT. Yoo never told me. Yoo said yoo –

BILL. We gooin' or ent we?

PAT. All right!

SCOPEY (*after a pause*). I'll buy the owd boy's grub after today.

PAT. Yoo still owe me for the last two weeks. (*She puts cosmetics into her handbag.*) I'll come round there an collect it myself after this. I can't afford a feed 'im. Yoo get 'is grub! If I relied on yoo 'e'd starve.

> PAT *goes out right. Pause.*

SCOPEY. D'yoo 'ave anythin' t' eat?

BILL. Sandwich.

SCOPEY. That enough?

BILL. 'Ave t' leave a hole for the beer.

SCOPEY. Yeh.

BILL. What we gooin' a doo?

SCOPEY. Yoo take 'er an' I'll join yoo soon's I can.

BILL. Sure?

SCOPEY. Yeh.

BILL. Well don't forget, boy. I'll buy yoo a short for owd times.

SCOPEY. Sounds all right.

> PAT *comes in from the right.*

PAT. Ready?

BILL. I been ready 'ours.

PAT. We're off. (*She takes her bag from the table.*)

BILL. See yer.

SCOPEY. Yup.

PAT. Don't be late.

SCOPEY. No.

> PAT *and* BILL *go out right.*
>
> SCOPEY *goes to the table. He stands and cuts a slice of bread. He butters it. He eats. He sits. He takes a second mouthful. He chews it monotonously. He stops. He chews again. He swallows. He stands. He unbuttons the front of his shirt. He pours a cup of tea, after feeling that the teapot is hot. He adds milk. He drinks. He puts the cup back on the table. He unfastens the cuffs of his shirt. He picks up the loaf and butter. He goes out right. Slight pause. The noise of running water. He comes back. He picks up the cup and saucer. He starts to go right. He hesitates. He stops.*

*He stares at the cup and saucer for a long time. Nothing moves.
Slowly he turns. He puts the cup and saucer back on the table.
He wanders a few steps down right. He turns and pushes the chair
under the table. He fastens his cuffs and front. He picks up his
jacket.*

*He goes out right. The running water stops. Noise of water
being thrown away. He comes back. He scoops up some papers
bundled on the floor. He goes up to his bike. He throws his jacket
over the handlebars. He wheels it off left.*

Scene Sixteen

ALEN's *place.*
SCOPEY *sits down stage slightly left on a box. He wears his greatcoat.
There are five hundred tins of food on the table and floor. They are
heaped round* SCOPEY *and the bundle down left. Only five of the
tins have been opened.*
Pause.
The door opens. PAT *comes in. She wears an old white mack. The
cuffs, collar and hem are dirty grey. She wears on her head a dingy
white and red scarf.*

PAT. Hello. (*She comes down towards* SCOPEY.) Where's the owd
    boy? (*She looks at the tins.*) Scopey? (*She sees the bundle on the
    floor and starts to go to it.*)

SCOPEY. I 'oisted the flap a month back. 'Is 'ead's like a fish.

PAT. 'E's dead.

SCOPEY. All silver scales.

PAT. Why 'ent yoo come?

SCOPEY. I took one 'and on 'is throat an one 'eld 'im up be the 'air.

PAT. Why?

SCOPEY. One 'and.

PAT. That's 'is coat.

SCOPEY. I stole it.

PAT. They'll 'ang you.

SCOPEY. One be the 'air.

PAT. Stay there. (*She goes up to the door.*) I 'ont be far. (*She goes out. Off.*) Bill! Bill!

BILL (*far off*). What?

PAT (*off*). 'Elp!

    SCOPEY *sits.*

Appendix

The first Author's Note to *Saved*,
written for the publication of the play in 1966

Saved is almost irresponsibly optimistic. Len, the chief character, is naturally good, in spite of his upbringing and environment, and he remains good in spite of the pressures of the play. But he is not wholly good or easily good because then his goodness would be meaningless, at least for himself. His faults are partly brought home to him by his ambivalence at the death of the baby and his morbid fascination with it afterwards.

It is true that at the end of the play Len does not know what he will do next, but he never has done. On the other hand, he has created the chance of a friendship with the father, and he has been chastened but he has not lost his resilience (he mends the chair). The play ends in a silent social stalemate, but if the spectator thinks this is pessimistic that is because he has not learned to clutch at straws. Clutching at straws is the only realistic thing to do. The alternative, apart from the self-indulgence of pessimism, is a fatuous optimism based on superficiality of both feeling and observation. The gesture of turning the other cheek is often the gesture of refusing to look facts in the face – but this is not true of Len. He lives with people at their worst and most hopeless (that is the point of the final scene) and does not turn away from them. I cannot imagine an optimism more tenacious, disciplined or honest than his.

Curiously, most theatre critics would say that for the play to be optimistic Len should have run away. Fifty years ago when, the same critics would probably say, moral standards

were higher, they would have praised him for the loyalty and
devotion with which he stuck to his post.

By not playing his traditional role in the tragic Oedipus
pattern of the play, Len turns it into what is formally a
comedy. The first scene is built on the young man's sexual
insecurity – he either invents interruptions himself or is
interrupted by the old man. Len has to challenge him, and
get him out of the house, before he can continue. Later he
helps the old man's wife, and this is given a sexual interpretation by the onlookers. Later still the old man finds him
with his wife in a more obviously sexual situation. The Oedipus
outcome should be a row and death. There *is* a row, and
even a struggle with a knife – but Len persists in trying to
help. The next scene starts with him stretched on the floor
with a knife in his hand, and the old man comes in dressed
as a ghost – but neither of them is dead. They talk, and for
once in the play someone apart from Len is as honest and
friendly as it is possible for him to be. The old man can only
give a widow's mite, but in the context it is a victory – and a
shared victory. It is trivial to talk of defeat in this context.
The only sensible object in defeating an enemy is to make him
your friend. That happens in this play, although in fact most
social and personal problems are solved by alienation or killing.

I also shut out Len from the relation between Pam and
Fred because (among other things) this let me explore the
Oedipus atmosphere at other stages. In particular, the murder
of the baby shows the Oedipus, atavistic fury fully unleashed.
The scene is typical of what some people do when they act
without restraint, and is not true just of these particular
people and this particular occasion. Everyone knows of worse
happenings. This sort of fury is what is kept under painful
control by other people in the play, and that partly accounts
for the corruption of their lives.

Clearly the stoning to death of a baby in a London park is a
typical English understatement. Compared to the 'strategic'

bombing of German towns it is a negligible atrocity, compared to the cultural and emotional deprivation of most of our children its consequences are insignificant.

Like most people I am a pessimist by experience, but an optimist by nature, and I have no doubt that I shall go on being true to my nature. Experience is depressing, and it would be a mistake to be willing to learn from it.

I did not write the play only as an Oedipus comedy. Other things in it – such as the social comment – are more important, but I have not described them in detail here because they are more obvious.

There is, however, a final matter. If we are to improve people's behaviour we must first increase their moral understanding, and this means teaching morality to children in a way that they find convincing. Although I suppose that most English people do not consciously disbelieve in the existence of god, not more than a few hundred of them fully believe in his existence. Yet almost all the morality taught to our children is grounded in religion. This in itself makes children morally bewildered – religion has nothing to do with their parents' personal lives, or our economic, industrial and political life, and is contrary to the science and rationalism they are taught at other times. For them religion discredits the morality it is meant to support.

Their problems in studying science and art are those of understanding – but in a religious morality it one of believing. Most children, as they grow older, cannot believe in religion. We no longer believe in it ourselves, and it is therefore foolish to teach children to do so. The result is that they grow up morally illiterate, and cannot understand, because they have not been properly taught, the nature of a moral consideration or the value of disinterested morals at all.

This is not always noticed because we use words that still have moral connotations, but these are being lost and soon we could well be morally bankrupt. The prevalent morality can be described as opportunist prudentialism, and it is usually expressed with a nauseous sentimentality that I have avoided in this play because it sounds like parody.

There will always be some people sophisticated enough to do the mental gymnastics needed to reconcile science and religion. But the mass of people will never be able to do this, and as we live in an industrial society they will be educated in the scientific tradition. This means that in future religion will never be more than the opium of the intellectuals.

For several reasons morals cannot be slapped on superficially as a social lubricant. They must share a common basis with social organisation and be consistent with accepted knowledge. You cannot, that is, 'have the fruit without the root'. Most people, when they think about this, ask only what *they* believe, or perhaps what has been revealed to them. But if they are interested in the welfare of others they should ask 'what is it possible for most people to believe?' And that means teaching, oddly enough, moral scepticism and analysis, and not faith.